RESEARCH METHODS FOR LIBRARY SCIENCE PROFESSIONALS

RESEARCH METHODS FOR LIBRARY SCIENCE PROFESSIONALS

Gurdev Singh
M.A.(Economics); MLISc; Ph.D.(DU)
Librarian, Sri Guru Gobind Singh College of Commerce
University of Delhi, Pitampura, Delhi-34

Ess Ess Publications
New Delhi

RESEARCH METHODS FOR LIBRARY SCIENCE PROFESSIONALS

ISBN: 978-81-936074-3-5

First Published 2018

Published by:
Ess Ess Publications
4831/24, Ansari Road,
Darya Ganj,
New Delhi-110 002.
INDIA
Phones: 23260807, 41563444
Fax: 41563334
E-mail: info@essessreference.com
www.essessreference.com

Cover Design by *Patch Creative Unit*

Printed and bound in India at Yash Printographics.

Contents

Preface		(*vii*)
List of Tables		(*xi*)
1	Research Methodology : An Introduction	1
2	Research Problem	24
3	Research Design	33
4	Sampling	43
5	Methods and Techniques of Data Collection	97
6	Processing and Analysis of Data	174
7	Statistical Analysis and Interpretation of Data	200
8	Hypothesis and Testing the Hypothesis	248
9	Interpretation of Data and Writing Research Report	274
10	Computer Application : Its Role in Research	308
11	Documentation and Compiling Bibliography	317
Bibliography		350
Glossary of the Terms Used		356
Index		368

Preface

Research is the process of arriving at dependable solution to a problem through a systematic collection, analysis and interpretation of data. It is always starts with a question or problem. Its purpose is to find the answer to questions through the application of systematic and scientific methods. Research is the original contribution to the existing stock of knowledge. It needs a hypothesis, collection of data on relevant variables, analyzing and interpreting the results and reaching the conclusion either in the form of solution or certain generalizations.

Some of the objectives of research are to discover new facts, verify and test important facts, find solution to scientific , non scientific and social problems, to overcome or solve the problems occurring in our every day daily life, etc.

Mere chronological narration of facts related to past is not a research. Research is logical and systematic search for new and useful information on a particular topic.

Research methods are the various procedures, schemes algorithms used in research. All the methods used by a researcher during research study are termed as research methods. Research methods helps us to collect samples, data and find a solution to a problem.

Research methodology is a systematic way to solve

a problem. It is a procedure by which researchers go about their work of describing, explaining and predicting phenomenon are called research methodology. The scope of the research methodology is wider than that of research methods.

Research is very important in each and every field of knowledge because it is only through research it is possible to make progress in the field. Research is not a process that is limited to the field of science. Research is important both in scientific and non scientific fields. Precisely, research assists us to understand nature and natural phenomenon. Research is actually an act of studying something carefully and extensively in order to attain deep knowledge in the same. It can, as well cater to people and scholars from artistic, historic or any other field where one is willing to do extensive study to get relevant information. A research problem refers to difficulty which a researcher or a scientific community or an industry or government organization or a society experiences. It may be a theoretical or a practical situation. Research provides basis for many government policies. Only through research invention can be made; for example, process such as superconductivity and cloning have been discovered only through research. Only through research new inventions and discoveries come into life. Imagine how you would have communicated had Graham Bell not come out with the first ever practical telephone! We need to understand that all the luxuries and the amenities that are now available to us are the result of research done by someone and with the world facing more and more crisis each day, we need researchers to find new solutions to tackle them. Research may lead to inventions or discoveries. Research has made important discoveries and development in the field of health, nutrition, medicine etc. The researches in these fields improved the life expectancy and health conditions of human beings in all parts of the world and helped to eradicate diseases like polio, smallpox completely. Applying the outcome of research for the refinement of knowledge in other subject, or in enhancing the quality of human life also becomes a kind of research and development.

Research is done with the help of study, experiments, observation, analysis comparison and reasoning. For example we know that cigarette smoking is injurious to health; cow dung is useful source of biogas.

How did we know all these? We became aware of all these information only through research.

This book is significant in many ways because it describes the various important aspects of Research Methods such as sampling, various methods and techniques of data collection, processing and analysis of data, statistical analysis and interpretation of data, hypothesis and testing the hypothesis, interpretation of data and writing research report, computer application: its role in research etc.

In this book "Research Method for Library Science Professionals" the attempt has been made to fill the gap by bringing together the relevant material on this topic which can be very useful to the Library Science professionals, students of MLib Sc and MPhil courses of various universities. This book form the part of Syllabi of most of the University Department of Library and Information Science at MLibSc and MPhil level. This book has been written with specific objective of guiding the professionals in general and research Scholars in particular to have sufficient knowledge about the various aspects of Research Methods.

This book is divided into 11 chapters. Special care has been taken to explain the matter in a very simple and easy language. It gives a wide range of information on various aspects of Research Methods. A detailed glossary is given at the end to understand the subject without any difficulty.

It is hoped that this book would be very useful for the Library and Information Science professionals in general and for the research scholars in particular. I hope that this book will serve its intended purpose.

I owe a debt of gratitude to various eminent authors and publishers, whose standard work I have consulted and cited .I am also very thankful to my professional colleagues for their valuable suggestions time to time.

Finally, I thank the editorial and production department of Ess Ess Publications for the careful and timely processing of the manuscript.

Reader's views, comments, and shortcomings related to the present work are most welcome.

Delhi **Dr. Gurdev Singh**

List of Tables

1. Difference between basic and applied Research
2. Census vs Sample
3. Probability Sampling and Non probability Sampling
4. Difference between Cluster sampling and stratified sampling
5. Example of Quota Sampling
6. Classification according to class intervals
7. Inclusive method
8. Example of one way table
9. Example of two way table
10. Example of three way table
11. Frequency Distribution table
12. Example of frequency distribution
13. Example of Bar chart
14. Direct Method of calculating Arithmetic Mean
15. Calculating Mean by Shortcut Method
16. Calculation of Mean
17. Calculation of Simple and weighted Arithmetic mean
18. Calculation of Median
19. Calculation of Mode
20. Example of calculation of Mode
21. Calculation of SD from assumed mean

22. Calculation of SD from actual mean
23. Calculation of coefficient of correlation
24. Calculation of coefficient of correlation using rank differences
25. Computation of Rank correlation coefficient
26. Calculation of Regression
27. Calculation of Chi-square value

1
Research Methodology : An Introduction

MEANING OF RESEARCH

The research refers to search for knowledge. It can be defined as a scientific and systematic search for potential information on a specific topic. It is a method of scientific investigation to search for new facts in any branch of knowledge. It is the original contribution to the existing available knowledge. It is a systematic study of finding solution to a problem. Research is, thus an original contribution to the existing stock of knowledge making for its advancement. It is the pursuit of truth with the help of study, observation, comparison and experiment. The systematic approach concerning generalization and a formation of a theory is also a research. It also includes formulating hypotheses, collecting the fact or data, analyzing the facts etc.

Research has been defined by various authors in different ways. It is always starts with a question or problem. Its purpose is to find answer to questions through the application of systematic and scientific methods. Thus, research is the systematic approach towards purposeful investigation. This needs formulating a hypothesis, collection of data on relevant variables, analyzing and interpreting the results and reaching the conclusions either in the form of solution or certain generalizations.

"Actually research is simply the process of arriving at dependable solutions to problems through the planned and systematic collection, analysis, and interpretation of data." According to Mouly: (1964,p.4.)

According to Kerlinger (1986)[42] "Scientific research is systematic, controlled, empirical, and critical investigation of natural phenomena guided by theory and hypotheses about the presumed relations among such phenomena."

From the above definitions we can say that research is:

- An organized and systematic way of finding answers to questions
- Important components of empirical research
- Problem statement, research questions, purposes, benefits
- Theory, assumptions, background literature
- Variables and hypotheses
- Operational definitions and measurement
- Instrumentation, sampling
- Data analysis
- Conclusions, interpretations, recommendations

Thus, research involve discovery of new facts, analysis of facts, systematic investigation involving formulation of a new hypothesis, testing of hypothesis etc. On the other hand chronological history of a library is not a research. Mere chronological narration of facts related to past is not research. Research is a logical and systematic search for new and useful information on a particular topic or subject. It is a search for knowledge, that is, a discovery of hidden truths. Here knowledge means information about matters. The information might be collected from different sources like experience, human beings, books, journals, nature, etc. A research can lead to new contributions to the existing knowledge. Only through research it is possible to make progress in a field. Research is indeed civilization and determines the economic, social and political development of a nation. Research is not confined to science and technology only. There are vast areas of research in other disciplines such as humanities and social sciences.

Applying the outcome of research for the refinement of knowledge in other subjects, or in enhancing the quality of human life also becomes a kind of research and development. Research is done with the help of study, experiment, observation, analysis, comparison and reasoning. Research is in fact ubiquitous. For example, we know that cigarette smoking is injurious to health; heroine is addictive; cow dung is a useful source of biogas; malaria is due to the virus protozoan plasmodium.

How did we know all these?

We became aware of all these information only through research. More precisely, it seeks predictions of events, explanations, relationships and theories for them.

DIFFERENCE BETWEEN INVENTION, DISCOVERY AND RESEARCH

Invention is creation of some new, hitherto unknown device/technique or remedial creation, where as discovery is related to finding of something already existing but hidden. It is an exploration of hidden things or facts. Research in short, may lead to inventions or discoveries. Research is concerned with finding solution to a problem or set of problems. Research is a process of arriving at dependable solution to problem through a systematic collection, analysis and interpretation of data.

OBJECTIVES OF RESEARCH

The main objective of research is to find out answers to the questions through the application of systematic and scientific way. There is specific purpose behind each research study.

The prime objectives of research are to:

1. Discover new facts
2. Verify and test important facts
3. Analyze an event or process or phenomenon to identify the cause and effect relationship
4. Develop new scientific tools, concepts and theories to solve and understand scientific and nonscientific problems.
5. Find solutions to scientific, nonscientific and social problems.
6. Overcome or solve the problems occurring in our everyday life.
7. Obtain familiarity of a phenomenon.

CHARACTERSTICS OF RESEARCH

Some of the characteristics of research are that:

1. It is directed towards the solution of a problem.
2. It is based on observable experience or empirical evidence.
3. It involves gathering new data from primary sources or using existing data for a new purpose.
4. It requires expertise(i.e. skills necessary to carryout investigation).
5. It involves the quest for answers to unsolved problems.

TYPES OF RESEARCH

Research are of the following types:

1. Basic research

Some of the Features of basic Research are that :

a. It also called as the fundamental or the theoretical research.

b. It is basic and original.

c. It can lead to the discovery of a new theory.

d. It can result in the development or refinement of a theory that already exists.

e. It helps in getting knowledge without thinking formally of implementing it in practice based on the honesty, love and integrity of the researcher for discovering the truth.

2. Applied research

Some of the Features of Applied Research are that :

a. It is based on the concept of the pure research.

b. It is problem oriented.

c. It helps in finding results or solutions for real life problems.

d. It provides evidence of usefulness to society.

e. It helps in testing empirical content of a theory.

f. It utilizes and helps in developing the techniques that can be used for basic research.

g. It helps in testing the validity of a theory but under some conditions.

h. It provides data that can lead to the acceleration of the process of generalization.

3. Exploratory research

Some of the Features of exploratory Research are that :

a. It involves exploring a general aspect.

b. It includes studying of a problem, about which nothing or a very little is known.

c. It follows a very formal approach of research.

d. It helps in exploring new ideas.

e. It helps in gathering information to study a specific problem very minutely.

f. It helps in knowing the feasibility in attempting a study.

4. Descriptive research

Some of the features of Descriptive Research are that:

a. It is simplest form of research.

b. It is more specific in nature and working than exploratory research.

c. It involves a mutual effort.

d. It helps in identifying various features of a problem.

e. It is restricted to the problems that are describable and not arguable and the problems in which valid standards can be developed for standards.

f. Existing theories can be easily put under test by empirical observations.

g. Underlines factors that may lead to experimental research.

h. It consumes a lot of time.

i. It is not directed by hypothesis.

5. Diagnostic Research

Some of the features of Diagnostic Research are that:

a. It is quite similar to the descriptive research.

b. It identifies the causes of the problems and then solutions for these problems.

c. It is related to causal relations.

d. It is directed by hypothesis.

e. It can be done only where knowledge is advanced.

6. Action research

Some of the features of Action Research are that:

1. It is a type of evaluation study.
2. It is a concurrent evaluation study.

But research is mainly classified into following four classes:

1. Fundamental or basic research
2. Applied research
3. Quantitative and Qualitative Research
4. Conceptual and Empirical Research

1. Fundamental or Basic Research

Basically a basic research addresses itself to more fundamental questions. This is also sometimes called fundamental research or pure research or basic research. Basic research is conducted to verify the acceptability of a given theory or to know more about certain concepts. Basic research is an investigation on basic principles and reasons for occurrence of a particular event or process or phenomenon. It is also called theoretical research. Study or investigation of some natural phenomenon or relating to pure science is termed as basic research. Basic researches sometimes may not lead to immediate use or application. It is not concerned with solving any practical problems of immediate interest. But it is original or basic in character. It provides a systematic and deep insight into a problem and facilitates extraction of scientific and logical explanation and conclusion on it. It helps to build new frontiers of knowledge. The outcomes of basic research form the basis for many applied research. Researchers working on applied research have to make use of the outcomes of basic research and explore the utility of them. Research on improving a theory or a method is also referred as fundamental research.

For example, suppose a theory is applicable to a

system provided the system satisfies certain specific conditions. Modifying the theory to apply it to a general situation is a basic research.

Basic research attempts to find answers to the following questions:

- Why are materials like that?
- How does a crystal melt?
- Why is sound produced when water is heated?
- Why do we feel difficult when walking on seashore?
- Why are birds arrange them in '>' shape when flying in a group?

Fundamental or basic research leads to a new theory or a new property of matter or even the existence of a new matter, the knowledge of which has not been known or reported earlier. For example, fundamental research on:

1. Astronomy may leads to identification of new planets or stars in our galaxy,
2. Elementary particles results in identification of new particles,
3. Complex functions may leads to new patterns or new properties associated with them,
4. Differential equations results in new types of solutions or new properties of solutions not known so far,
5. Chemical reactions lead to development of new compounds, new properties of chemicals, mechanism of chemicals reactions, etc.
6. Medicinal chemistry leads to an understanding of physiological action of various chemicals and drugs,
7. Structure, contents and functioning of various parts of human body helps us in identify the basis for certain diseases.

2. Applied Research

In an applied research one can solves certain problems employing well known and accepted theories and principles. Applied research involve formulation of hypothesis, collection of data, analyzing and interpretation of data etc. Applied research is conducted when a decision must be made about a specific real life problem. Most of the experimental research, case studies and inter-disciplinary research are essentially applied research. Applied research is helpful for basic research. A research, the outcome of which has immediate application is also termed as applied research.

Such a research is of practical use to current activity. For example, research on social problems have immediate use. Applied research is concerned with actual life research such as research on increasing efficiency of a machine, increasing gain factor of production of a material, pollution control, preparing vaccination for a disease, etc. Obviously, they have immediate potential applications.

Difference between basic research and applied research

Some of the differences between basic and applied research are summarized in table below. The central aim of applied research is to find a solution for a practical problem which warrants solution for immediate use, whereas basic research is directed towards finding information that has broad base of applications and thus add new information to the already existing scientific knowledge. Research can either is applied research or fundamental (or basic) research. Pure research is concerned with understanding and applied research is concern with getting things done. Pure research leads to practical applications. Applied research as a byproduct ultimately leads to better understanding. Much of the research in Library Science is applied research.

Table I. Differences between basic and applied research

Basic research	Applied research
1. Seeks generalization	1. Studies individual or specific cases without the objective to generalize
2. Aims at basic processes	2. Aims at any variable which makes the desired difference
3. Attempts to explain why things happen	3. Tries to say how things can be changed
4. Tries to get all the facts	4. Tries to correct the facts which are problematic
5. Reports in technical language of the topic	5. Reports in common language

Basic and applied researches are generally of two kinds: normal research and revolutionary research.

Normal and Revolutionary Researches

In any particular field, normal research is performed in accordance with a set of rules, concepts and procedures called a paradigm, which is well accepted by the scientists working in that field. Normal research is something like puzzle-solving: interesting, even beautiful, solutions are found but the rules are remaining same. In this normal research sometimes unexpected novel results and discoveries are realized which are inconsistent with the existing paradigm. Among the scientist, a tense situation then ensues, which increases in intensity until a scientific revolution is reached. This is marked by a paradigm shift and a new paradigm emerges under which normal scientific activity can be resumed.

3. Quantitative and Qualitative Research

1. Quantitative research : The basic and applied researches can be quantitative or qualitative or even both. Quantitative research is based on the measurement of quantity or amount. Here a process is expressed or described in terms of one or more quantities. The result of this research is essentially a number or a set of numbers. Research that is entirely based on the study of quantified facts, for the examination and verification of hypothesis/hypotheses through quantitative investigations and reasoning is necessarily more scientific and precise. The use of quantitative aspect in behavioral sciences research provides the substance of strength to the reasoning process in the validation of a hypothesis. All those approaches of research based on quantity, provide far better and reliable results to the researcher.

Some of the characteristics of quantitative research/ method are:

- It is numerical, non-descriptive, applies statistics or mathematics and uses numbers.
- It is an iterative process whereby evidence is evaluated.
- The results are often presented in tables and graphs.
- It is conclusive.
- It investigates the what, where and when of decision making.

Statistics is the most widely used branch of mathematics in quantitative research. It finds applications not only in physical sciences but also in economics, social sciences and biology.

2. Qualitative research : Quantitative research using statistical methods often begins with the collection of data based on a theory or hypothesis or experiment followed by the application of descriptive or inferential statistical methods. Qualitative research is concerned with qualitative phenomenon involving quality. Quantity orientation in research even though necessary, it is not sufficient. For instance, to evaluate the value of a supervisor's performance it is not only the number of hours of his work, but also with that it is the quality of his work, that provides an effective measures of his performance. Hence research under any substances, cannot forsake qualitative aspects.

Some of the characteristics of qualitative research/ method are:

- It is non-numerical, descriptive, applies reasoning and uses words.
- Its aim is to get the meaning, feeling and describe the situation.
- Qualitative data cannot be graphed.
- It is exploratory.
- It investigates the why and how of decision making.

We measure and weigh things in the study of substance or structure. Can we measure or weigh patterns? We cannot measure or weigh patterns. But to study patterns we must map a configuration of relationships. That is, structures involve quantities whereas patterns involve qualities. If one wishes to investigate why certain data are random then it is a qualitative research. If the aim is to study how random the data is, what is the mean, variance and distribution function then it becomes quantitative. Explaining how digestion of food takes place in our body is a qualitative description. It does not involve any numbers or data and quantities.

The detection of a particular compound is a qualitative analysis. This can be done by carrying out physical or chemical tests. Determination of exact amount of a particular compound present in a volume is essentially quantitative analysis. This can be done by volumetric, gravimetric and colorimetric methods or instrumental methods. Experimental and simulation studies are generally quantitative research.

In fact, qualitative methods can be used to understand the meaning of the numbers obtained by quantitative methods.

4. Conceptual and Empirical Research

Conceptual : Conceptual research is related to some abstract idea or theory. It is generally used by philosophers and thinkers to develop new concepts or to revise the existing one.

Empirical Research : Empirical research based on experience or observation alone. It is data based research, coming up with conclusions which are capable of being verified by observation or experiment. We may also called it as experimental type of research.

Other types of research includes:

1. Action research (fact findings to improve the quality of action in the social world): This is basically applied research as it is based on the launching of a direct action in regard to a problem for the purpose of finding workable solutions and arriving at conclusions.

2. Exploratory research : (searching explanations for events and phenomena, for example finding answer to the question why are the things like what they are?), This is concerned with the discovery of new facts., things focus or ideas. Such discoveries and new findings could help a researcher in providing new explanations and interpretations. Exploratory research would be carried out in business studies; sociology, economics, and other related social sciences on the basis of reliable past data.

3. Descriptive research : (getting more information on a topic): For an exhaustive and detailed investigative study of the various aspects of a problem , a researcher who is on a fact finding mission has to provide appropriate descriptive answer to the questions such as: What is the problem? How does it arise? Etc. Descriptive research can be survey research, comparative research etc. Descriptive research is hypothesis testing. A field survey is the process of finding informative details from the respondents on the basis of the questionnaire and interview.

4. Analytical research : This type of research is based on the analysis of the available facts and figures with regards to a problem of research. Scientific and systematic procedures are adopted for critical interpretations.

5. Historical research : This type of research is of much relevance in social and behavioral sciences. The methodology emphasizes on the past happenings, events, thoughts and actions of eminent historical personalities, for the study of present problems in a situation. This methods has to be adopted with due Care and considerations because the past may not provide reliable basis, mainly because the changing environment of technology.

SIGNIFICANCE AND IMPORTANCE OF RESEARCH

Research is important both in scientific and nonscientific fields. In our life new problems, events, phenomena and processes occur every day. Practically, implementable solutions and suggestions are required for tackling new problems that arise. Scientists have to undertake research on them and find their causes, solutions, explanations and applications. Precisely, research assists us to understand nature and natural phenomena. Research is actually an act of studying something carefully and extensively in order to attain deep knowledge in the same. For being successful, research should be systematic, arranged, summarized and recorded properly. Research is not only a process that is limited to the field of science. It can, as well, cater to people and scholars from artistic, historic or any other field where an individual is willing to do extensive study to get relevant information. Research can be creative, exploring or just reassuring in nature. Each one of us does some or the other research in our lifetime for sure. Research can affect a subject both positively and negatively and can be constructive or destructive in nature. Some people believe that research is mostly destructive in nature. However, we need to understand that it's not the results from a research that determine its use; it's the people who handle the results.

Some important avenues of research are:

1. A research problem refers to a difficulty which a researcher or a scientific community or an industry or a government organization or a society experiences. It may be a theoretical or a practical situation. It calls for a thorough understanding and possible solution.
2. Research on existing theories and concepts help us identify the range and applications of them.
3. It is the fountain of knowledge and provides guidelines for solving problems.
4. Research provides basis for many government policies. For example, research on the needs and desires of the people and on the availability of revenues to meet the needs and helps a government to prepare a budget.
5. It is important in industry and business for higher gain and productivity and to improve the quality of products.
6. Mathematical and logical research on business and industry optimizes the problems in them.
7. It leads to the identification and characterization of new materials, new living things, new stars, etc.
8. Only through research inventions can be made; for example, new and novel phenomena and processes such as superconductivity and cloning have been discovered only through research.
9. Social research helps find answers to social problems. They explain social phenomena and seek solution to social problems.

10. Research leads to a new style of life and makes it delightful and glorious.

1. To Gather Necessary Information

Research provides you with all necessary information in field of your work, study or operation before you begin working on it. For example, most companies do research before beginning a project in order to get a basic idea about the things they will need to do for the project. Research also helps them get acquainted with the processes and resources involved and reception from the market. This information helps in the successful outcome of the project.

2. To Make Changes

Sometimes, there are in-built problems in a process or a project that is hard to discover. Research helps us find the root cause and associated elements of a process. The end result of such a research invokes a demand for change and sometimes is successful in producing changes as well. For example, many U.N researches have paved way for changes in environmental policies.

3. Improving Standard of Living

Only through research can new inventions and discoveries come into life. It was C.V Raman's research that prompted invention of radio communication. Imagine how you would have communicated had Graham Bell not come out with the first ever practical telephone! Forget telephones, what would have happened if Martin Cooper did not present the world the concept of mobile phones! Addicted as we are to mobile phones, we need to understand that all the luxuries and the amenities that are now available to us are the result of research aone by someone and with the world facing more and more crisis each day, we need researchers to find new solutions to tackle them.

4. For a safer life

Research has made ground breaking discoveries and development in the field of health, nutrition, food technology and medicine. These things have improved the life expectancy and health conditions of human race in all parts of the world and helped to eradicate diseases like polio, smallpox completely. Diseases that were untreatable are now history, as new and new inventions and research in the field of medicine have led to the advent of drugs that not only treat the once-incurable diseases, but also prevent them from recurring.

5. To Know the Truth

It has been proved time and again that many of established facts and known truths are just cover ups or blatant lies or rumors. Research is needed to investigate and expose these and bring out the truth.

6. Explore our History

Research about our planets history and human history has enabled us to learn and understand more about our forefathers and helped us learn from their mistakes and absorb good things from their life. Research about the planet's history and existence has told us a lot about how things will shape up in years to come and how we need to respect our planet and work closely together to stop global warming and other scenarios of destruction.

7. Understanding Arts

Research helps us in understanding the work of artists in literature, paintings, sculptures and everything that can be attributed with artistic touch. If no research is conducted into any of these, we will never be able to understand any of these as per the artist's imagination. Also, a lot of great artistic work is hidden in the shadows of history, which needs to be drawn out.

RESEARCH METHODS AND RESEARCH METHODOLOGY

Research Methods

Research methods are the various procedures, schemes and algorithms used in research. All the methods used by a researcher during a research study are termed as research methods. They are essentially planned, scientific and value-neutral. They include theoretical procedures, experimental studies, numerical schemes, statistical approaches, etc. Research methods help us to collect samples, data and find a solution to a problem. Particularly, scientific research methods call for explanations based on collected facts, measurements and observations and not on reasoning alone. They accept only those explanations which can be verified by experiments.

Research Methodology

Research methodology is a systematic way to solve a problem. It is a science of studying how research is to be carried out. Essentially, the procedures by which researchers go about their work of describing, explaining and predicting phenomena are called research methodology. It is also defined as the study of methods by which knowledge is gained. Its aim is to give the work plan of research. In it we study the various steps that are generally adopted by a researcher in studying his research problem along with the logic behind them. The scope of the research methodology is wider than that of research methods. When we talk of research methodology we not only talk of research methods but also consider the logic behind the methods we use in the context of our research study and explain why we are using a particular method or technique.

VARIOUS STAGES OF A RESEARCH

Whenever a scientific problem is to be solved there are several important steps to follow. The problem must be stated clearly, including any simplifying assumptions. Then develop a mathematical statement of the problem. This process may involve use of one or more mathematical procedures. Frequently, more advanced text books or review articles will be needed to learn about the techniques and procedures. Next, the results have to be interpreted to arrive at a decision. This will require experience and an understanding of the situation in which the problem is embedded.

STEPS AND STAGES OF RESEARCH PROCESS

Steps in research process

Any research process consists of following steps:

1. Defining the research problem and reviewing the literature.
2. Formulation of hypothesis
3. Research design: developing the research plan and implementing the research plan
4. Collection of data
5. Analysing of data
6. Testing hypothesis
7. Preperation of report and preliminary analysis
8. Interpretation and reporting of the findings

Various Stages of Library Research

A general set of sequential components of research process are as follows:

1. Selection of a research topic
2. Definition of a research problem
3. Extensive literature survey and reference collection
4. Assessment of current status of the topic chosen
5. Formulation of hypotheses : A hypothesis is a process of being testing is called a Null hypothesis.

6. Preparing Research design: determining sample design
7. Actual investigation or collecting the data: from a recorded sources, through questionnaire, interview, observation methods
8. Data analysis
9. Hypothesis testing
10. Interpretation of result
11. Preperation of Report or thesis

1. Selection of the research topic : Constitutes the first step in a scientific enquiry. Two steps are involved in selection and formulating the research problem. The best way of understanding the problem is to discuss it with one's own colleagues or with some expertise in the subject field. In the academic institution the researchers can seek the help of guide who is usually an experienced man and have several research problems or topics in mind. The researcher must at the time examine all available literature to get himself acquainted with selected topic or problem. It is called review of literature. The basic outcome of this review will be the knowledge as to what data and other material is available on a given area of study. After this researcher put the problem in specific terms.

2. Extensive literature survey : After the problem is formulated, a brief summary (synopsis) of it should be written down. It is compulsory for a researcher who is doing research degree like Ph.D. to write a synopsis of the topic and submit to the research committee for the approval. At this stage a researcher need extensive literature survey. For this purpose number of search tools are available such as indexing and abstracting journals, bibliographies etc. There are number of primary sources are also available such as journals, seminar papers, research reports etc. One source may lead to another source. The earlier studies, if any which are similar to study in hand should be carefully studied. A good library/ documentation center will be very helpful to the researcher at this stage.

3. Development of working hypothesis : After extensive literature survey, a researcher should state in clear terms the working hypothesis or hypotheses. Working hypothesis is tentative assumption made in order to draw out and test its logical or empirical consequences. Hypothesis should be very specific and limited to the research in hand because it has to be tested. The role of hypothesis is to guide the researcher by delimiting the area of research and keep him on the right track. It also indicates the type of data required and the type of methods of data analysis is to be used.

How the working hypothesis is to developed ?

1. Discussion with colleagues and subject experts about the problem
2. Examination of data and records, if available concerning the problem.
3. Review of similar studies in the subject area.

Thus, working hypothesis arises as a result of examination of available data and reading material. Working hypotheses are more useful when stated in precise and clearly defined terms.

4. Preparing the research design : The researcher will now require to prepare research design. He will have to state the conceptual structure within which the research would be conducted. It would yield maximum information. The function of research design is to provide for the collection of relevant evidence with minimum expenditure of effort, time and money. It depends upon the type of research. A research design should be flexible. There are several research designs , such as experimental and non-experimental hypothesis testing. Experimental design may be formal or informal. Out of which the researcher must select one for his project.

5. Determine the sample design : All the items under consideration in any field of enquiry constitutes a 'universe' or 'population'. A complete enumeration of all the items in the population is known as a census inquiry. It can be presumed that in such an enquiry when all the items are covered no element of chance is left and highest accuracy is obtained. But in practice that may not be true. Even slightest element of bias in such an inquiry may affect the results. The researcher must decide the way of selecting a sample or what is popularly known as sample design. In other words, a sample design is a definite plan determined before any data are actually collected for obtaining a sample from a given population.

This type of enquiry involves a great deal of time, money and energy.

QUALITIES OF GOOD RESEARCH

A good research should have following qualities:

1. Good research is logical : This implies that good research is guided by rules of logical reasoning

2. Good research is systematic : A good research study must have various steps well planned. It means that specified steps to be taken in a specified sequence in accordance with specified rules.

3. Free from personnel biases : A good research should be free from personnel biases.

4. Generalisability : We should be able to have almost the same results by using an identical methodology so that we can apply the result to similar situations.

5. The purpose of the research should be clearly defined and common concept be used.

6. The research procedure used should be described in sufficient detail to permit

7. The procedural design of the research should thoroughly planned.

8. The validity and reliability of the data should be checked.

9. The analysis of data should be sufficiently adequate to reveal its significant.

Thus a good research have qualities like systematic, logical, empirical, creative, use of multiple methods.

2
Research Problem

INTRODUCTION

Defining a research problem is the foundation of any research method and experimental design, from true experiment to case study. The first and foremost step in the research process consists of problem identification. A research problem is one which requires a researcher to find out the best solution for the given problem. The researcher will have to state the conceptual structure within which the research would be conducted. The preparation of such a design will provide maximum information. In other words the function of research design is to provide for the collection of relevant evidence with minimum expenditure of effort, time and money. But how these can be achieved depends upon the research purpose. The suitable design will be one that minimizes bias and maximizes the reliability of the data collected and analyzed.

The research purpose can be grouped into four categories:

1. Exploration
2. Description
3. Diagnosis and

4. Experimentation

WHAT IS RESEARCH PROBLEM?

In a research process the first step happen to be that of selecting the properly defined a research problem. The researcher must find the problem and formulate it. Like a medical doctor, must examine all the symptoms before prescribing medicine. Similarly, a researcher must examine the research problem. A research problem refers to some difficulties during his research project. He wants to obtain the solution for the same. All research projects, on whatever subject, there is a need to define the research problem clearly. The research problem is a general statement of an issue meriting research. Its nature will suggest appropriate forms for its investigation. Here are several forms in which the research problem can be expressed to indicate the method of investigation. The research problem in some social science research projects using the hypothetic-deductive method is expressed in terms of the testing of a particular hypothesis. It is therefore important to know what makes good hypotheses and how they can be formulated. However, it is not appropriate to use the hypothetic-deductive method, or even scientific method, in every research study.

COMPONENTS OF RESEARCH PROBLEM

Some of the components of research problem are:

1. There must be an individual or group which has some difficulty or problem.
2. There must be some objectives to be attained at.
3. There must alternative mean for obtaining the objectives.
4. There must be some environment to which the difficulty pertains.

NEED OF DEFINING THE RESEARCH PROBLEM

If we state the problem clearly the half the problem will be solved. It will help to discriminate relevant data from the irrelevant one. The questions like:

What data are to be collected?

What techniques to be used?

What relations to be explored?

Thus, defining the research problem properly is a prerequisite for any study.

There are four general conceptualizations of a research problem in the social sciences:

1. Casuist Research Problem : This type of problem relates to the determination of right and wrong in questions of conduct or conscience by analyzing moral dilemmas through the application of general rules and the careful distinction of special cases.

2. Difference Research Problem : Typically asks the question, "Is there a difference between two or more groups or treatments?" This type of problem statement is used when the researcher compares or contrasts two or more phenomena.

3. Descriptive Research Problem : Typically asks the question, "what is...?" with the underlying purpose to describe a situation, state, or existence of a specific phenomenon.

4. Relational Research Problem : Suggests a relationship of some sort between two or more variables to be investigated. The underlying purpose is to investigate qualities/characteristics that are connected in some way.

AREAS OF RESEARCH PROBLEM

Based upon the objectives, the research problem could be any of the three areas:

1. Exploratory : For gathering preliminary information that may help in defining the problem and suggest hypothesis. The major emphasis of exploratory research is on the discovery of ideas. The idea is to clarify concepts and subsequently make more extensive research on them.

2. Descriptive : This may describe things in detail about the problem

3. Casual : To test hypothesis about cause and effect relationships.

FACTORS

Factors one should keep in mind regarding selection of research problem:

1. Cost factor
2. Time factor
3. Research material
4. Subject is familiar and feasible
5. Avoid too narrow or too vague

FORMULATING THE PROBLEMS

Formulation of the problem means defining the problem precisely. Defining the problem means half the job done. An appropriate technique can be applied to generate alternative solutions. Choosing the best alternative is the best decision under the given circumstances. Once the problem has been selected, the same has to be understood thoroughly and then the same has to be reframed into meaningful terms from an analytical point of view. Researcher must specify the exact issues being examined and the underlying logic in setting the priorities. The proper formulation of research problem would enable a researcher to go ahead in the right direction.

TECHNIQUE INVOLVE IN DEFINING THE RESEARCH PROBLEM

Defining the research problem involves the task of

laying down boundaries within which a researcher shall study the problem with a predetermined objective in view. Defining a research problem properly and clearly is a crucial part of research study. The research problem should be defined in a systematic manner. The technique for the purpose involves the following steps:

STEPS INVOLVE IN DEFINING A PROBLEM

Some facts involved in defining the research problem:

1. Statement of the problem in general way
2. Understanding the nature of the problem
3. Surveying the available literature
4. Developing the ideas through discussion
5. Technical terms, words and phrases
6. Basic assumptions and postulates
7. Sources of data available
8. Scope of the investigation
9. Limitations of the research problem

1. Statement of the problem in a general way

First of all the problem should be defined in a broad general way. In case of social research, it is advisable to do some field observations. The researcher may take some sort of preliminary survey or what is often called pilot survey. Than the researcher can seek the guidance of a guide or subject expert. He put the problem in general terms. The problem stated in broad general way may contain various ambiguities which must be resolved by rethinking the problem.

2. Understanding the nature of the problem

The next step is to understand the nature and origin of the problem clearly. The best way to understand the problem is to discuss it with a person who first raised the problem. Those who have already done research work in this area, having good knowledge of the problem concerned.

3. Surveying the available literature

All the relevant literature available in different sources must be surveyed and examined before examine the research problem in hand. This means that researcher should be well conversant with literature available in the field. He must devote sufficient time in reviewing of research already undertaken in this area. It will narrow the problem itself. Studies on related problems are useful for indicating the types of difficulties that may be encountered in the present study. At this time such studies may also suggest useful and even new lines of approach to the problem in hand.

4. Developing the ideas through discussion

Discussion related to the research topic often produced useful results. Several new ideas can be developed through discussion with a person having knowledge about the topic. Therefore, the researcher must discuss his problem with a person having sufficient knowledge about the same area of research. People with rich experience are in a position to enlighten the researchers on different aspects of his topic. Discussion with such persons help him to formulation of specific problem, possible solution etc.

5. Rephrasing the research problem

Finally the researcher rephrase the research problem into a working proposition. Through rephrasing, the researcher put the research problem in specific terms as possible so that it may help in the development of working hypothesis.

The following points should be observed while defining the research problem:

1. Technical terms should clearly be defined.

2. Basic assumptions or postulates (if any) related to the research problem should clearly defined.
3. The scope of the research problem or the limits within which the problem is to be studied must mentioned in defining the research problem.

TESTING OF HYPOTHESIS

Hypothesis is a tentative assumption which a researcher wants to test for its logical or empirical consequences.

The following steps involved in testing the hypothesis:

1. Formulation of hypothesis
2. Set up a suitable significance level
3. Choose test criterion
4. Compute the statistics
5. Make decision

1. Formulation of Hypothesis : We make certain assumptions about the parameter to be tested. For example when a new drug to be introduced, it is to be tested on some patients. Based on the response of the patient, a decision has to be made whether the drug should be introduced or not. We make certain assumptions about the parameters to be tested. These assumptions are known as hypothesis.

We starts with null hypothesis: H0:, μ 100.This is a claim or hypothesis about the value e or population parameters. This is tested against Alternate hypothesis, H1: μ,100

The null hypothesis is tested with the available evidence and decision is to be made whether to accept the hypothesis or reject it. If the null hypothesis is rejected, we accept the alternate hypothesis.

2. Setting up suitable significance level : There are two types of errors that can be committed in making decisions regarding accepting or rejecting the null hypothesis.

Type 1 error : an error made in rejecting the null hypothesis, when in fact it is true.

Type 2 error : an error made in accepting the null hypothesis, when in fact it is untrue.

The level of significance signifies the probability of committing type 1 error(á) and generally taken as equal to 5% (á =.05), this means that even after testing the hypothesis when a decision is made, we may still be committing an error in rejecting the null hypothesis.

3. Choose a test criteria : This means selection of a suitable probability distribution that can be used for the available information under consideration.

Some of the distributions are:

1. Normal distribution : Z characteristic, this is most often used, when the samples are more than 30.

2. t-distribution : 't' test is used for small sample only.

3. F test and chi square test.

4. Compute the test statistics : This involve the actual collection and computation of the sample data. We have to find out the sample mean(x) and then compute the calculated 'z'. This calculated value (absolute) is compared with tabulated value obtained from normal distribution table again the decided criterion.

5. Make decision : If the calculated value of the test characteristic is greater than the tabulated value, the null hypothesis is rejected and the alternate hypothesis is accepted.

DEVELOPING THE RESEARCH PLAN

The next step of the research process calls for determining the information needed. Developing a plan for gathering it efficiently and presenting the management of the organization.

First of all research objectives must be translated into specific information need. To meet the management information needs, the researcher can gather secondary data and primary data or both.

Implementing the research plan : The researcher next puts research plan into action. This involves collecting , processing and analyzing the data.

Interpreting and reporting the findings : After collecting, processing and analyzing the data collected, the researcher must now interpret the findings, draw conclusions and reporting them to concern authorities.

3
Research Design

INTRODUCTION

The research design refers to the overall strategy that you choose to integrate the different components of the study in a logical way, thereby, ensuring you will effectively address the research problem. It constitutes the blueprint for the collection, measurement, and analysis of data. The research design is like a blue print which an architect prepares for a building. It is like a route map for a journey. For example as we need a blue print for better construction of the house (map of the house).Similarly we need research design for the better and systematic research.

MEANING

According to Kerlinger[42] "research design is the plan, structure and strategy and strategy of investigation conceived so as to obtain answers to research questions and to control variance."

Research design is in fact the conceptual framework within which the research is conducted. Bernard Philips has described the research design as "blue print for the collection, measurement and analysis of data."

For a scientific research one has to prepare a research design. It should indicate the various approaches to be used in solving the research problem, sources and information related to the problem, time frame and the budget. Essentially, the research design creates the foundation of the entire research work. The design will help to perform the chosen task easily and in a systematic way. Once the research design is completed the actual work can be initiated. The first step in the actual work is to learn the facts pertaining to the problem. Particularly, theoretical methods, numerical techniques, experimental techniques and other relevant data and tools necessary for the present study have to be collected and learnt.

It is not necessary that every theory, technique and information in the topic of research is useful for a particular problem. A researcher has to identify and select materials which are useful to the present work. Further, the validity and utility of the information gathered should be tested before using them. Scientific research is based on certain mathematical, numerical and experimental methods. These sources have to be properly studied and judged before applying them to the problem of interest.

The function of a research design is to ensure that the evidence obtained enables you to effectively address the research problem logically and as unambiguously as possible. With this keeping in mind, a common mistake made by researchers is that they begin their investigations far too early, before they have thought critically about what information is required to address the study's research questions. Without attending to these design issues beforehand, the overall research problem will not be adequately addressed and any conclusions drawn will risk being weak and unconvincing. As a consequence, the overall validity of the study will be undermined.

Any well-developed design will achieve the following:

1. Identify the research problem clearly and justify its selection

2. Review and synthesize previously published literature associated with the problem,
3. Clearly and explicitly specify hypotheses [i.e., research questions] central to the research problem,
4. Effectively describe the data which will be necessary for an adequate testing of the hypotheses and explain how such data will be obtained, and
5. Describe the methods of analysis to be applied to the data in determining whether or not the hypotheses are true or false.

WHAT CONSTITUTES THE RESEARCH DESIGN?

Research design provides answer to various questions, during the research and help in effective as well as efficient working. Decisions regarding what, where, when, how much etc. constitutes the research design.

1. What is the study about?
2. What type of data is required?
3. What will be the sample design?
4. Why is the study being made?
5. What techniques of data collection will be used?
6. How will be the data analyzed?

The research design at least contains:

1. A clear statement of the research problem
2. Procedures and techniques to be used for gathering information
3. The population to be studied
4. Methods to be used in processing and analysis of data

The research design depends upon:

1. Questions which research are expected to answer.
2. Variables involves in the research.
3. Measurement of the variable.

WHY WE NEED RESEARCH DESIGN?

Research design is needed because it helps in yielding maximum information with minimum efforts, expenditure, time and money. Research design is similar to blue print or map of a house prepared by the architect. Similarly we need a research design in advance of data collection and analysis of our research project.

Research design is the advance planning of the methods to be adopted for data collection and analysis.

The research design should be prepared with great care because any error in this stage can upset the entire research project. It is therefore necessary that an efficient and appropriate design must be prepared before starting research process.

For a scientific research one has to prepare a research design. It should indicate the various approaches to be used in solving the research problem, sources and information related to the problem and, time frame and the cost budget. Essentially, the research design creates the foundation of the entire research work. The design will help perform the chosen task easily and in a systematic way. Once the research design is completed the actual work can be initiated. The first step in the actual work is to learn the facts pertaining to the problem. Particularly, theoretical methods, numerical techniques, experimental techniques and other relevant data and tools necessary for the present study have to be collected and learnt.

It is not necessary that every theory, technique and information in the topic of research is useful for a particular problem. A researcher has to identify and select materials which are useful to the present work. Further, the validity and utility of the information gathered should be tested before using them. Scientific research is based on certain mathematical, numerical and experimental methods. These sources have to be properly studied and judged before applying them to the problem of interest.

A research design provides:

1. Design of research
2. Type of data required for information gathering.
3. Measurement and scaling requirement
4. Form of data collection
5. Sampling process and sampling size required
6. Data analysis to be done

ASPECTS OF RESEARCH DESIGN

A research design has following aspects:

1. Sampling:
   - What information to be included?
   - How the data is to be gathered?
   - Which source?
2. Methods of data collection
   - Questionnaire method
   - Interview method
   - Observation method
3. Analytical design

FEATURES OF GOOD RESEARCH DESIGN

A good research design is characterized by following features:

- Flexible
- Appropriate
- Efficient
- Economical
- Reliable etc.

Generally the design which minimize bias and maximize the reliability of data collected and analyzed is considered a good design. The design which gives the smallest experimental error is supposed to be the best design in many investigations.

STEPS IN RESEARCH DESIGN

What are the steps in research design?

Following are the steps in research design:

1. The problem : The first step involves the proper selection and then carefully defining the problem. By this researcher will be enabled to know about what he has to search, but it should be kept in mind that the problems selected should not be unmanageable in nature and also should not be based on the desires.

2. Objective of the study : The objective should be very clear in the mind of the researcher as this will lead to the clarity of the design and proper response from the respondents.

3. Nature of the study : The research design should be very much in relation with the nature of the study, which is to be carried out.

4. Data sources : The various sources of the data or the information should be very clearly stated by the researcher.

5. Techniques of data collection : For the collection of the required information, it sometimes becomes very necessary to use some especial techniques.

6. Social cultural context : Research design based on the social cultural concept is prepared in order to avoid the various study variations.

7. Geographical limit : This step becomes a necessity at this point of time as with the help of this step, research linked to the hypothesis applies only to certain number of social groups.

8. Basis of selection : Selecting a proper sample acts as a very important and critical step and this is done with the help of some mechanics like drawing a random stratified, deliberate, double cluster or quota sample etc.

What are the Possible Approaches to be followed by a researcher?

Being a member of a research institution alone is not sufficient to become a scientist. Every great human achievement is preceded by extended periods of dedicated and concentrated effort. As told by Mahatma Gandhi 'satisfaction lies in the effort and not in the attainment' .Full effort is full victory. A researcher can exercise the following aspects regularly throughout the research carrier. These will keep him in right track and tightly bind him to the research activity.

1. Discussion with the supervisor, experts and colleagues about the research work, particularly, the problem and its origin, objectives and difficulties faced in the execution of the problem.
2. Reading of the latest research papers, relevant theories and possible application to the present problem and to overcome the difficulties faced.
3. Review of the work reported on the similar problems.
4. Theoretical calculations, setting-up of an experimental setup, numerical calculations, computer programs, preparation of graphs, tables and other relevant work related to the research should be done by a new researcher by himself without assistance from others.
5. Have a practice of periodically writing the work done, results obtained and steps followed in a work. This is important because sometime we may think that a particular aspect will be a center piece of the problem under investigation. But once we make a write-up of it, this aspect or part of it may turn out to be only of marginal importance. In fact, writing of the progress of the work will help us better understand our work and form a solid basis for further progress. It also points out the gaps in our work.

6. Participation and presentation of research findings in national and international meetings. These regular practices provide useful information like new ideas and can help the researcher to:
   1. Sharpen and focus attention,
   2. Confining to the formulation and
   3. In the interpretation of the solution obtained.

INDEPENDENT RESEARCH

Absolute honesty, patience, stamina, precision and devotion to the subject matter together with imagination and analytical ability are among the requirements for scientific research. Each and every bit of task related to the research work has to be done by the researcher. A young researcher should not do the entire work in collaboration with others. A young researcher should have the ability to do all by himself. In this connection Beasley and Jones wrote: In reality collaborations are commonplace, often necessary–to get samples, to make all the desired measurements or to perform a complete analysis. But such collaborations generally arise naturally in the course of the research and define and limit themselves naturally. A true sense of camaraderie often develops, and students do not lose that sense of having made major contributions on their own. The researcher is advised to perform all the works starting from identification of the problem to report preparation by himself under the guidance of supervisor. Particularly, collaboration work with experts and senior researcher may be avoided. (However, he can discuss his problems with them).

This is important to acquire:

1. Enough knowledge
2. Confidence and
3. Training

TYPES OF RESEARCH DESIGN

The research deign can be classified into:

1. Exploratory research Design : This type of research provide insight and understanding of the problem. Exploratory research method includes secondary data sources, expert opinion, surveys, case studies and observations. This research is diagnostic in nature. It is generally used for the development of hypothesis regarding potential problems. In most of the times, exploratory research is followed by conclusive research for more precise analysis and conclusion. The aim of its investigation is to find out new hypothesis. Formal design is rare in this type of research. He could conduct a study of secondary sources of information or get views from the experts or resort to case study analysis.

Exploratory research using secondary sources of information : Many companies who regularly conduct market research studies have maintain a record of research findings over the years, the access to which is both quick and economical for a market researcher. Looking for hypothesis, a market researcher could consult basic research findings reported in professional journals. Other fruitful sources of secondary data are public libraries, newspapers, trade journals, general books etc.

Exploratory research using expert opinions/ individuals with ideas : Experts can give valuable insights into a marketing problem because of their experience with the problem at hand. A practical solution is to carryout exploratory research using a mix of cooperative, imaginative persons as well as randomly selected persons. Respondents should be given full freedom to respond to get new ideas. Various techniques called qualitative research techniques have been developed to study the consumer behavior.

These qualitative techniques can further be classified into:

1. Depth interview: one to one interview.
2. Focus group interview.

2. Conclusive research : This type of research is more formal and structured as compared to exploratory research. Conclusive research is used to provide information for the evaluation of alternative course of action.

This type of research is sub classified into:

1. Descriptive research and
2. Casual or experimental research

Conclusive method includes descriptive research with cross sectional or time series or longitudinal or case studies method and casual/experimental research with the design of experiments.

In descriptive research, we can make use of both case study and statistical study.

Descriptive research that aim to collect information:

- Demographic, lifestyle
- Attitude, behavior

Experimental research that aims to measure:

- Concept test
- Product test

3. Project techniques : In this technique of interviewing , the respondents are asked to project themselves into a particular situation.

4. Exploratory research using case analysis : It involves the comprehensive study on one of a few specific situations and particularly the study of complex situations in which inter relations of several individuals are important.

4
Sampling

INTRODUCTION

Sampling is a means of selecting a subset of units from a target population for the purpose of collecting information. This information is used to draw inferences about the population as a whole. The subset of units that are selected is called a sample. The sample design encompasses all aspects of how to group units on the frame, determine the sample size, allocate the sample to the various classifications of frame units, and finally, select the sample. Choices in sample design are influenced by many factors, including the desired level of precision and detail of the information to be produced, the availability of appropriate sampling frames, the availability of suitable auxiliary variables for stratification and sample selection, the estimation methods that will be used and the available budget in terms of time and resources.

SAMPLING MEANING

What is sample?

The word sample means a part of any collection of things (population) that are quantitatively expressed. The part of a population selected for investigation is called sample. Population is also called universe. A sample is a subset or some part of a larger population representative of the entire population. A sample is drawn using either probability or non probability sampling procedure. Non-probability sampling is typically applied in exploratory research. It is used when data needs to be collected speedily with little cost. Sampling unit may be the house, office, organization. It is a unit from where a respondent is selected.

A sample is "a smaller (but hopefully representative) collection of units from a population used to determine truths about that population" .

The entire work (process) of selecting samples from a population is termed as sampling.

SOME IMPORTANT TERMS RELATED TO SAMPLING

Population or Universe : The entire aggregation of items from which samples can be drawn is known as a population. In sampling, the population may refer to the units, from which the sample is drawn. Population or populations of interest are interchangeable terms. The term "unit" is used, as in a business research process, samples are not necessarily people all the time. A population of interest may be the universe of nations or cities. This is one of the first things the analyst needs to define properly while conducting a business research. Therefore, population, contrary to its general notion as a nation's entire population has a much broader meaning in sampling. "N" represents the size of the population.

Census : A complete study of all the elements present in the population is known as a census. It is a time consuming and costly process and is, therefore, seldom a popular with researchers. The general notion that a census generates more accurate data than sampling is not always true. Limitations include failure in generating a complete and accurate list of all the members of the population and refusal of the elements to provide information. The national population census is an example of census survey.

Precision : Precision is a measure of how close an estimate is expected to be, to the true value of a parameter. Precision is a measure of similarity. Precision is usually expressed in terms of imprecision and related to the standard error of the estimate. Less precision is reflected by a larger standard error.

Bias : Bias is the term refers to how far the average statistic lies from the parameter it is estimating, that is, the error, which arises when estimating a quantity. Errors from chance will cancel each other out in the long run, those from bias will not. Bias can take different forms.

SAMPLING VS CENSUS

The researcher must decide whether he should cover all the units or a sample of units. When all the units are studied, such a complete coverage is called a census survey. When only a sample of the population is studied, the study is called a sample survey.

The size of the population : If the population to be studied is relatively small, say 100 users, the investigator may decide to study the entire population. The task is easily manageable and the sample may not required. But if the population is large, sampling is required.

Amount of funds for the study : The decision regarding census or sampling depends upon the budget of the study. When budget is small sample is opted. When budget is large census can be opted.

Facilities : It also depends upon the facilities available such as staff, access to computer facilities to be considered in deciding sample or census. When the availability of these facilities is extensive, census survey may be manageable. Otherwise, sampling is proffered.

Time : The time limit within which the study should

be completed is also an important factor in deciding the question of census or survey. Time factor is a primary reason for using sampling by academics and marketing research.

Table 2. Census vs Sample

Census	Sample
1. Great accuracy	1. saving of time/cost
2. All units analyzed	2. Reasonable accuracy
3. Too much time	3. easy to manage
4. Too expensive	4. projections required
5. Unmanageable	5. caution required

Census is done when:

1. The population is small and does not required too much time and expenditure.
2. The population variance is very high .

Sampling is done:

1. When the population is large and needs heavy expenditure and lots of time
2. When the population variance is not very high and sample can represents this variation
3. When quick results are desired

WHY SAMPLE?

Well selected sampling may reflect fairly accurately the characteristics of the population. A specified value of the population, such as average of variance is named parameter; the corresponding value in the sample is termed a statistic. The main aim of sampling is to make an inference about an unknown parameter from a measurable sample statistic. A second aim of sampling is to test a statistical hypothesis relating to population.

Sample is useful because:

1. Sampling is the process of using a smaller number of items /parts of a larger population to make conclusion about the entire population.

2. Pragmatic Reasons (practical) : Research are carried out to solve problems in business entities and due to availability of limited (budget /time constraints)

3. It provides accurate and reliable results : Samples can provide sufficiently accurate findings and truly reflect the population if they are selected properly.

4. Sampling offers advantages over complete enumeration because of;

— Resources (time, money) and workload

— Gives results with known accuracy that can be calculated mathematically

Three factors that influence sample representativeness

1. Sampling procedure
2. Sample size ; the grater the sampling size greater the cost.
3. Participation (response)

MAIN OBJECTIVE OF SAMPLING

It is during the formulation of the research on the practical grounds, one tends to go through a large number of problems. These problems are generally related to the knowing of the features of the universe or the population on the basis of studying the characteristics of the specific part or some portion, generally called as the sample. A Sampling is a part of the total population. It can be an individual element or a group of elements selected from the population. Although it is a subset, it is representative of the population and suitable for research in terms of cost, convenience, and time. The sample group can be selected based on a probability or a non probability approach. A sample usually consists of various units of the population. The size of the sample is represented by "n" or "N".

Thus, the main objective of sampling is to acquire the maximum information about the population with least amount of time, money and energy.

ADVANTAGE AND DISADVANTAGES OF SAMPLING

ADVANTAGES

The theory of sampling provides guidelines to the selection of sample, which will be the representative of the population. The process of inferring something about a large group of elements by studying only a part of it is called 'sampling'.

Some of the advantages of sampling are:

1. **Sampling saves labour :** Relatively very small staff is required for gathering information, analyzing the same and preparation of the report.. A small staff is required both for field work and for processing and analyzing the data.
2. Sample reduces the time and cost of the research studies. It has now possible to undertake even national or global studies at reasonable cost and time. Such economy in time and cost improves the viability of several field studies such as marketing survey.
3. A researcher can collect more detailed information in much less time which otherwise is not possible for census study. Moreover, we can afford to have a few specialists for collection of specialized type of information which otherwise is not possible for a census study because of cost and non availability of specialists.
4. Very accurate
5. Economical in nature; It reduces the cost
6. Very reliable: In many cases sampling provides adequate information needed for the purpose. Also

the sampling technique make it possible to quantify the magnitude of possible error.

6. Take less time (less time consuming): it reduces the time of research studies.
7. In case when the universe is very large than the sampling method is the only method for collecting data
8. High suitability ratio towards the different surveys.
9. Quality of study is often better with sampling than with a complete coverage. The possibility of better interviewing , more thorough investigation of missing, wrong or suspicious information, better supervision, better processing is greater in sampling than in complete coverage (census).
10. Sampling provides much quicker results than the census.
11. Sampling is the only procedure possible, if the population is infinite.

DISADVANTAGES OF SAMPLING

Some of the disadvantages are:

1. Sampling demands through knowledge of sampling methods and an exercise of greater care, otherwise the results obtained may be incorrect or misleading.
2. A complicated sampling plan may require more labor than a complete coverage
3. It may not be possible to ensure the representativeness of the sample, even by the most perfect sampling procedures.
4. Inadequacy of the sample.
5. Chances for bias.
6. Problems of accuracy.
7. Untrained manpower.
8. Absance of the informants.
9. Chances of committing errors in the sampling.

BASIC PRINCIPLES OF SAMPLING

There are two types of sampling:

1. Non-probability and
2. Probability sampling.

Non-probability sampling uses a subjective method of selecting units from a population, and is generally fast, easy and inexpensive. Therefore, it's sometimes useful to perform things like preliminary studies, focus groups or follow-up studies. However, in order to make inferences about the population, one must make the often false assumption that the sample is representative. Probability sampling is based on three basic principles that make up the statistical framework.

1. It is based on randomization, i.e. the units in the sample are selected at random.
2. Second, all survey population units have a known positive probability of being selected in the sample
3. We can calculate those probabilities, which are then used to calculate estimates along with estimates of the sampling error.

The ability to make reliable inferences about the entire population and to quantify the error in the estimates makes probability sampling the best choice for most statistical programs. The sample design should be as simple as possible. The aim is to produce estimates that are both precise and accurate enough to meet survey requirements. Precision is measured by the variance of an estimator. Lack of accuracy manifests itself through biases which are often introduced via non-sampling factors such as inaccurate reporting, processing, and measurement, as well as errors from non response and incomplete reporting.

Theory of sampling is based on the following laws :

Law of statistical regularity : This law comes from the mathematical theory of probability. According to King

"Law of Statistical Regularity says that a moderately large number of the items chosen at random from the large group are almost sure on the average to possess the features of the large group."

According to this law the units of the sample must be selected at random.

Law of Inertia of Large Numbers : According to this law, the other things being equal – the larger the size of the sample; the more accurate the results are likely to be.

CHARACTERSTICS OF GOOD SAMPLE

A sample should be scientific in nature, reliable and very suitable for carrying out different surveys. Whether the results obtained from a sample survey would be accurate or not depends upon the quality of the sample. Some of the characteristics of good sample are:

A good sample is one which satisfies all or few of the following conditions:

1. Representativeness : Sample should be representative of the population. When sampling method is adopted by the researcher, the basic assumption is that the samples so selected out of the population are the best representative of the population under study. Thus, good samples are those who accurately represent the population. Probability sampling technique yield representative samples.

2. Size : A good sample must be adequate in size in order to be reliable. The sample size should be such that the inferences drawn from the sample are accurate to a given level of confidence to represent the entire population under study. The size should be sufficient so that can give good results.

3. Accuracy : Accuracy is defined as the degree to which bias is absent from the sample. An accurate (unbiased) sample is one which exactly represents the population. It is free from any influence that causes any differences between sample value and population value. On measurement terms, the sample must be valid. The validity of a sample depends upon its accuracy. Biasness of a sample should be absent. The degree to which bias is absent from the sample. An accurate (unbiased) sample is one which exactly represents the population. It is free from any influence.

4. Goal oriented : Sample design should be oriented to the research objectives.

5. Measuerability : The parameters under study should be some way or the other measurable so that accuracy could be known.

6. Usability : The sample should be convenient to collect and analyze.

7. Cost factor : The total cost of the sample design, collection and analysis of data should be minimum.

8. Precision : The sample must yield precise estimate. The precision is measured by the standard error or standard deviation of the sample estimate.

GUIDELINES FOR SAMPLE SELECTION

- **Design :** When determining sample size, take into account the required levels of precision needed for the survey estimates, the type of design (e.g., clustering, stratification) and estimator to be used, the availability of auxiliary and contact information, budgetary constraints, as well as other factors, such as non response, presence of out-of-scope units, attrition in longitudinal surveys, etc.
- It's worth noting that the precision of survey estimates is usually influenced more by the total sample size than by the sampling fraction (ratio of the sample size to the population size).
- It is important to remember that most surveys produce estimates for many different variables, and

optimizing the sample for one particular variable may have detrimental effects on other important variables. Handle this problem by first identifying the most important variables and then using this subset of variables to determine the sampling strategy to be adopted

- Stratification consists of dividing the population into subsets (called strata). Within each stratum, an independent sample is selected. The choice of strata is determined by the objectives of the survey, the availability of variables on the frame, the distribution of the variable of interest, and the desired precision of the estimates. Most surveys produce estimates for various domains of interest (e.g., provinces).
- If feasible, take this into account in the design by stratifying appropriately (e.g., by province). Otherwise, it will be necessary to consider special methods at the estimation stage to produce estimates for these domains (see Imputation). To achieve statistical efficiency, create strata in such a way that each stratum contains units that are as homogeneous as possible with respect to the information collected in the survey. For longitudinal surveys, choose stratification variables that correspond to characteristics that are stable over time.
- Establish an expected response rate using a pre-test or data from previous occasions of the same or similar surveys. This rate can in turn be used in sample size determination.

Methods

- For highly skewed populations, create a stratum of large units to be included in the survey with certainty (the so-called take-all stratum). These large units would normally account for a significant portion of the population totals. In order to reduce respondent burden, the creation of a stratum of very small units to be excluded from the surveyed population is sometimes appropriate.

- Sometimes the information needed to stratify the population is not available on the frame. In such cases, a two-phase (or double) sampling scheme may be used, whereby a large sample is selected in the first phase to obtain the required stratification information. This first sample is then stratified and in the second phase, a subsample is selected from each stratum within the first-phase sample. Consider the cost of sampling at each phase, the availability of the information required at each phase, and the gain in precision obtained by stratifying the first-phase sample.
- In practice, it is sometimes not feasible to directly select and contact the units that will report the requested information, due to either cost or lack of information. In such cases, a two-stage sampling scheme may be used by first selecting clusters (called primary sampling units)of reporting units, and then further sub sampling within each of the selected primary sampling units to obtain a sample of reporting units. Budgetary or other constraints may necessitate more than two stages (a multi-stage design). Determine how many stages of sampling are needed and which sampling units are appropriate at each stage. For each possible type of units, consider the availability of a suitable frame of such units at each stage or the possibility of creating such a frame for the survey, ease of contact and of data collection/measurement, the quality of the data provided by the units, and the cost of collection. Multi-stage designs are by definition clustered sample designs. Clustering reduces data collection cost but may result in increased variances due to intra-cluster correlation.

- If samples are to be selected from two or more frames, care must be taken in dealing with units that belong to more than one frame. It is important that the frame membership of each unit can be determined. The principle that the sample design should be simple is especially important when multiple frames are used. Choose sample designs that will simplify estimation procedures.
- In determining sample allocation and size for stratified samples, account for expected rates of misclassification of units and other deficiencies on the frame. If not properly considered at the sampling stage, survey estimates will not be as precise as planned. Address this problem at the estimation stage.
- For more complex situations, for example, when surveying rare or mobile populations, or when the sampling frame is a list of units that are linked, but don't correspond directly, to the units of the target population, special designs may be necessary. Such techniques as indirect sampling, network sampling or adaptive cluster sampling, to name a few, may need to be considered.

Periodic surveys

- For periodic surveys that use designs in which the sample size grows as the population increases, it is often appropriate to develop a method to keep the sample size and therefore collection costs, stable. One approach is to use a random drop method to maintain a stable sample size over time.
- For periodic surveys, make the design as flexible as possible to deal with future changes, such as increases or decreases in sample size, rest ratification, re-sampling and updating of selection probabilities. If estimates are required for specified domains of interest (e.g., sub provincial estimates),

form the strata by combining small stable units related to the identified domains (e.g., small geographical areas), if possible. Future changes in definitions of the strata will then be easier to accommodate.

- For periodic surveys, if efficient estimates of change are required or if response burden is a concern, use a rotation sampling scheme that replaces part of the sample in each period. The choice of the rotation rate will be a compromise between the precision required for the estimates of change and the response burden on the reporting units. Lowering the rotation rate will increase the precision of the estimates of change but may lower the response rate over time because of increased response burden. A low rotation rate has the additional benefit of reducing costs if the first contact is substantially more expensive than subsequent contacts.
- For periodic surveys, develop procedures to monitor the quality of the sample design over time. Set up an update strategy for the selective redesign of strata that have suffered serious deterioration because of uneven growth.

Longitudinal surveys

- For longitudinal panel surveys, determine the length of the panel (its duration of time in the sample) by balancing the need for duration data with sample attrition and conditioning effects. Use a design with overlapping panels (i.e. with overlapping time span) when there is a need to produce cross-sectional estimates along with the longitudinal ones.
- It is particularly important to choose simple design features (i.e., one single frame) with as few stages or phases as possible as the estimation procedures becomes extremely complex with the number of waves.

- It is recommended that longitudinal surveys should be designed primarily to produce longitudinal estimates. Trying to satisfy both cross-sectional and longitudinal requirements can result in very complex design and estimation procedures. If production of cross-sectional estimates is required, the use of a "top-up" sample to cover births and new immigrants is recommended.

Implementation

- At the implementation stage, compare the size and characteristics of the actual sample to what was expected. Compare the precision of the estimates to the planned objectives. Reassess the assumptions used at the design stage. For example, evaluate non response (non-contacts, refusals, etc.) and calculate design effects.
- Where possible, use generalized sample selection software instead of tailor-made systems. One such system is the Generalized Sampling System (GSAM) developed by Statistics Canada. GSAM is especially useful for managing sample selection and rotation for periodic surveys. By using generalized systems, one can expect fewer programming errors, as well as some reduction in development costs and time.

Documentation

- Write detailed and thorough documentation of all aspects of the sample design: which frames were chosen and why, how units were formed, how they were stratified, how sample size was determined and how sample was allocated, choice of stages and/ or phases, which sampling schemes were used and why, and so on.

SAMPLING PROCESS

Steps in Sampling Process

An operational sampling process can be divided into seven steps as given below:

1. Defining the target population.
2. Specifying the sampling frame.
3. Specifying the sampling unit.
4. Selection of the sampling method.
5. Determination of sample size.
6. Specifying the sampling plan.
7. Selecting the sample.

1. Defining the Target Population

It is usually defined prior to the selection of the sample. The population should be completely defined. Defining the population of interest is the first step in sampling process. In general, target population is defined in terms of element, sampling unit, extent, and time frame. The definition should be in line with the objectives of the research study. For example, if a kitchen appliances firm wants to conduct a survey to ascertain the demand for its micro ovens, it may define the population as 'all women above the age of 20 who cook (assuming that very few men cook)'. However this definition is too broad and will include every household in the country, in the population that is to be covered by the survey. Therefore, the definition can be further refined and defined at the sampling unit level, that, all women above the age 20, who cook and whose monthly household income exceeds Rs.20,000. This reduces the target population size and makes the research more focused. The population definition can be refined further by specifying the area from where the researcher has to draw his sample, that is, households located in Hyderabad.

For defining the population the following terms to be specified: sampling units, extend, time etc. A population can be defined as including all people or items with the characteristic one wish to understand. Because there is very rarely enough time or money to gather information from everyone or everything in a population, the goal becomes finding a representative sample (or subset) of that population. Note also that the population from which the sample is drawn may not be the same as the population about which we actually want information. Often there is large but not complete overlap between these two groups due to frame issues etc. Sometimes they may be entirely separate - for instance, we might study rats in order to get a better understanding of human health, or we might study records from people born in 2015 in order to make predictions about people born in 2016.

A well defined population reduces the probability of including the respondents who do not fit the research objectives of the institution.

2. Specifying the Sampling Frame:

Sampling frame : Once the definition of the population is clear, a researcher should decide on the sampling frame. A sampling frame is the list of elements from which the sample may be drawn. Note also that the population from which the sample is drawn may not be the same as the population about which we actually want information. Often there is large but not complete overlap between these two groups due to frame issues etc. A sampling frame should be so selected which consists of all the sampling units. Popularly known sampling frames are: Census report, electoral registers, list of members of professional bodies etc.

In the most straightforward case, such as the sentencing of a batch of material from production (acceptance sampling by lots), it is possible to identify and measure every single item in the population and to include any one of them in our sample. However, in the more general case this is not possible. There is no way to identify all rats in the set of all rats. Where voting is not compulsory, there is no way to identify which people will actually vote at a forthcoming election (in advance of the election) .As a remedy, we seek a sampling frame which has the property that we can identify every single element and include any in our sample. The sampling frame must be representative of the population.

Continuing with the micro oven example, an ideal sampling frame would be a database that contains all the households that have a monthly income above Rs.20,000. However, in practice it is difficult to get an exhaustive sampling frame that exactly fits the requirements of a particular research. In general, researchers use easily available sampling frames like telephone directories and lists of credit card and mobile phone users. Various private players provide databases developed along various demographic and economic variables. Sometimes, maps and aerial pictures are also used as sampling frames. Whatever may be the case, an ideal sampling frame is one that entire population and lists the names of its elements only once.

A sampling frame error pops up when the sampling frame does not accurately represent the total population or when some elements of the population are missing another drawback in the sampling frame is over – representation. A telephone directory can be over represented by names/household that has two or more connections.

3. Specifying the Sampling Unit

A sampling unit is a basic unit that contains a single element or a group of elements of the population to be sampled. It contains the elements of the target population. In this case, a household becomes a sampling unit and all women above the age of 20 years living in that particular house become the sampling elements. If it is possible to identify the exact target audience of the business research, every individual element would be a sampling unit. This would present a case of primary sampling unit. However, a convenient and better means of sampling would be to select households as the sampling unit and interview all females above 20 years, who cook. This would present a case of secondary sampling unit.

4. Selection of the Sampling Method

The sampling method outlines the way in which the sample units are to be selected. The most important decision in this regard is to determine which of the two probabilities or non probability sample to be chosen. The choice of the sampling method is influenced by the objectives of the business research, availability of financial resources, time constraints, and the nature of the problem to be investigated. All sampling methods can be grouped under two distinct heads, that is, probability and non-probability sampling.

5. Determination of Sample Size

The sample size plays a crucial role in the sampling process. The decision about the number of elements to be chosen i.e. number of observations in each sample (n) of the target population. There are various ways of classifying the techniques used in determining the sample size. A couple those hold primary importance and are worth mentioning are whether the technique deals with fixed or sequential sampling and whether its logic is based on traditional or Bayesian methods. In non-probability sampling procedures, the allocation of budget, thumb rules and number of sub groups to be analyzed, importance of the decision, number of variables, nature of analysis, incidence rates, and completion rates play a major role in sample size determination. In the case of probability sampling, however, formulas are used to calculate the sample size after the levels of acceptable error and level of confidence are specified. The details of the various techniques used to determine the sample size will be explained at the end of the chapter.

6. Specifying the Sampling Plan

In this step, the specifications and decisions regarding the implementation of the research process are outlined. This means that one should indicate how decision made so far are to be implemented. All expected issues in sampling survey must be answered by the sampling plan. Suppose, blocks in a city are the sampling units and the households are the sampling elements. This step outlines the modus operandi of the sampling plan in identifying houses based on specified characteristics. It includes issues like how is the interviewer going to take a systematic sample of the houses. What should the interviewer do when a house is vacant? What is the re contact procedure for respondents who were unavailable? All these and many other questions need to be answered for the smooth functioning of the research process. These are guide lines that would help the researcher in every step of the process. As the interviewers and their co-workers will be on field duty of most of the time, a proper specification of the sampling plans would make their work easy and they would not have to revert to their seniors when faced with operational problems.

7. Selecting the Sample

This is the final step in the sampling process, where the actual selection of the sample elements is carried out. At this stage, it is necessary that the interviewers stick to the rules outlined for the smooth implementation of the business research. This step involves implementing the sampling plan to select the sampling plan to select a sample required for the survey. However it depends mainly upon the sampling plan and the sample size required.

The Sampling Design Process

The sampling design process can be summarized in following steps:

Define the population → Identify the sampling frame → specify sampling unit and sampling methods → determine the sampling size(n) → specify sampling plan and select the sample

TYPES OF IMPORTAT SAMPLING METHODS/TECHNIQUES

There are mainly two types of sampling techniques/ methods:

1. Probability sampling method (random sampling : simple random sampling, cluster sampling, stratified sampling, and systematic sampling)
2. Non probability sampling method (e.g. purposive sampling)

1. Probability Sampling

A probability sampling scheme is one in which every unit in the population has a chance (greater than zero) of being selected in the sample, and this probability can be accurately determined. It is based on the theory of probability. It is also known as random sampling. Selection of the specific units in the sample depends entirely on chance.

When every element in the population does have the same probability of selection, this is known as an 'equal probability of selection' (EPS) design. Such designs are also referred to as 'self-weighting' because all sampled units are given the same weight.

The major sampling methods under the probability sampling methods are:

- Simple Random Sampling,

- Systematic Sampling,
- Stratified Random Sampling,
- Cluster Sampling
- Multistage Sampling.
- Multiphase sampling

Characteristics of Probability Sampling

Some of the characteristics are:

1. In probability sampling every population has a chance of being selected.
2. Such chance is known as probability.
3. Probability sampling yields a representative sample, and hence the findings of the sample survey are generalisable to the population.
4. The closeness of the sample to the population can be determined by estimating sampling bias or error.

2. Non Probability Sampling

Non probability sampling or non random sampling is not based on the theory of probability. This sampling does not provide a chance of selection to each population element. The some of the merits of this sampling are simplicity, convenience and low cost.

Any sampling method where some elements of population have no chance of selection (these are sometimes referred to as 'out of coverage'/'under covered'), or where the probability of selection can't be accurately determined. It involves the selection of elements based on assumptions regarding the population of interest, which forms the criteria for selection. Hence, because the selection of elements is nonrandom, non probability sampling not allows the estimation of sampling errors.

Example: We visit every household in a given street, and interview the first person to answer the door. In any household with more than one occupant, this is a non probability sample, because some people are more likely to answer the door (e.g. an unemployed person who spends most of their time at home is more likely to answer than an employed housemate who might be at work when the interviewer calls) and it's not practical to calculate these probabilities.

Merits

1. It does not ensure a selection chance to each population unit.
2. The selection probability is unknown.
3. A known probability sample may not be representative one.
4. When there is no other feasible alternative due to non availability of a list of population, non availability of some population elements for collection of data etc.
5. Useful when the cost required for probability sampling may be too large, and the benefit expected from it is not commensurate with such cost and
6. When probability sampling requires more time, but the time constraints and the time limit for completing the study do not permit it.

Non probability sampling includes:

1. Accidental sampling,
2. Quota sampling and
3. Purposive sampling

In addition, non response effects may turn any probability design into a non probability design if the characteristics of non response are not well understood, since non response effectively modifies each element's probability of being sampled.

Table 3. Probability Sampling and Non probability Sampling

Probability sampling	Non probability sampling
1. A simple designs • simple random sampling • stratified random sampling • systamatic random sampling 2. Complex design • clusture and area sampling • multistage and sub sampling • multiphase sampling	convenience or accidental sampling judgment sampling Quota sampling

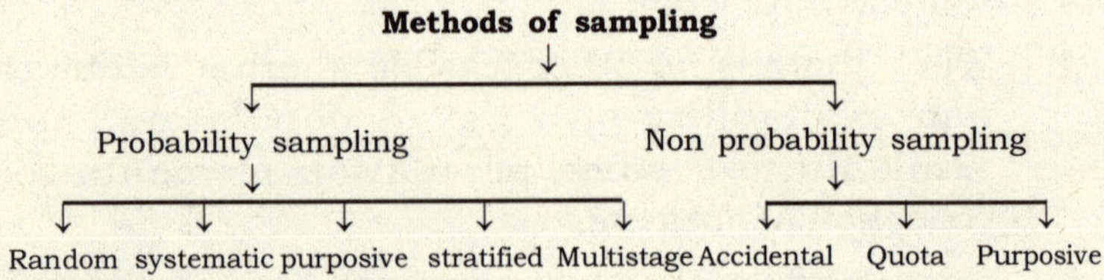

PROBABILITY SAMPLING

1. Simple Random sampling

This sampling technique gives each element an equal and independence chance of being selected .Equal chance means equal probability of selection. In a population of 200, each element has 1/200th chance of being selected. An independent chance means that the drew of one element will not affect the chances of other elements being selected.

A sample that consists of members that are chosen at random from the population is called a random sample and the entire process of selecting members at random from a population is known as random sampling. Simple random sampling is the simplest type of sampling in which we draw a sample of size (n) in such a way that each of the N numbers of the population has the same chance of being included in the sample. A sample selected in this way is called a simple random sample. In this method each unit of the population must have equal probability of being selected. It is best when roaster of the population exists.

Procedure

For example: there is set of N books. We are interested in taking a sample of n books out of N. The procedure involve is: enumeration of all elements in the population; prepare a list of all elements , giving then serial number 1,2,3,....so on and drawing sample number by using 1.Lottery method 2.a computer etc.

Step 1 : assign number serially from 1 to N

Step 2 : select a random number (between 1 and N)

Step 3 : the document which bear this number is to be considered for sampling

Step 4 : replace the number in the bowl or consider the random number again (if selected).

Step 5 : select n random numbers in a similar way, we will get n documents that constitute the sample

A simple random sample is a subset of a statistical population in which each member of the subset has an equal probability of being chosen. A simple random sample is meant to be an unbiased representation of a group.

This method ensure that probability of each member of population in the sample is equal. Each member has the same chance of being selected in the sample. For example If population lists consists of 36000 members and sample of 600 is required, than we can select every sixtieth item of the population. But before doing that it is necessary to select first member by random sampling from the number 1 to 60. For instance if 25 happen to be the number selected at random than it will be first number, 85 will be the second number, 145 will be the third and so on.

Features

- Applicable when population is small, homogeneous and readily available
- All subsets of the frame are given an equal probability. Each element of the frame thus has an equal probability of selection.
- It provides for greatest number of possible samples. This is done by assigning a number to each unit in the sampling frame.
- A table of random number or lottery system is used to determine which units are to be selected
- Estimates are easy to calculate.
- Simple random sampling is always an EPS design, but not all EPS designs are simple random sampling.

Advantages of this method

This method is good method because members of the sample are chosen purely according to the principle of random sampling. That is without and prejudice. Random samples are the best method of selecting your sample from the population of interest. The advantages are that your sample should represent the target population and eliminate sampling bias, but the disadvantage is that it is very difficult to achieve (i.e. time, effort and money)

Some of the advantages are:

- All elements in the population have an equal chance of being selected.
- Estimates are easy to calculate
- Of all probability sampling techniques, simple random sampling is the easiest to apply
- It is the most simple type of probability sampling to understand

- It does not require a prior knowledge of the true composition of the population.
- Simple random sampling is always an EPS design, but not all EPS designs are simple random sampling

This method is considered to be very useful and hence universal applications.

Disadvantages of this method

- It is often impractical, because of non availability of population list, or of difficulty in enumerating the population
- The use of simple random sampling may be wasteful because we fail to use all of the known information about the population.
- If sampling frame large, this method impracticable.
- Minority subgroups of interest in population may not be present in sample in sufficient numbers for study.

Methods of Random sampling

Further, to overcome bias or errors due to human weakness, certain methods of random sampling have been devised. Some of the methods are:

1. Method based on mechanical devices such as lottery drum method
2. Method based on random sampling numbers

1. Lottary drum method : This is the simplest and most familiar procedure of random sampling. In this method members of population are numbered on slips of uniform size and color. These slips are placed in a drum and are drawn at random. This procedure is continued till the cards drawn give the required size of the random sample. If the sample of 20 students to be drawn out of list of 100 students , take 100 slips of equal size number them 1 to 100 each bearing only one number. Roll each slip and put them in a container/drum, and thoroughly mixed them. Take 20 slips from the container one after the other. Each time before drawing the slip , mixed the slips in the container thoroughly. The unit bearing the numbers of slips drawn constitute the random sample. But in case of large sample, these methods are not considered to be useful.

2. Systamatic Sampling : The systematic sampling also employs the principle of random sampling. However in this method of sampling the selection of unit depends upon the selection of a proceeding unit in contrast to simple random sampling where the selection of a unit is independent of each other. Systematic random sampling in this sense is called quasi random sampling. In this sampling, we systematically spread the sample through the population. In this method complete population lists are available. The method consists of selecting at random the first member and thereafter the other members in a systematic way.

Systematic random sampling or fixed interval method

This method of sampling is an alternative to random sampling. It consists of taking every k^{th} item in the population after a random start with an item from 1 to k. For example suppose it is desired to select a sample of 20 students , from a list of 300 students , divide the population total of 300 by 20, the quotient is 15.(if there is any fraction in the quotient ignore the fraction and take the whole number)Select a number at random between 1 and 15, using lottery method etc. Suppose the selected number is 9 The students numbered 9, 24(9+15), 39(24+15), 54(39+15), 69, 84.... are selected as sample. As the interval between sample unit is fixed , this method is also known as fixed interval method.

Systematic random sampling is done through some ordered criteria by choosing elements from a randomly arranged sampling frame. In both the simple random sampling and the systematic sampling you will be required to generate a list from the sampling frame. It also requires that the elements within the sampling frame be homogeneous, which means the same. A systematic sampling is selected by including every i^{th} item. Item may be document or user. From the population, the selection is drawn by pulling out the actual sampling units. For example if the population list comprises 56000 members and a sample of 7000 is required, than we can select every 8th item of the population. But before doing that it is necessary to select the first member by random sampling, from number 1 to 80.For instance if 25 happen to be the number selected at random then it will be the first number, 105 will be the second number, 130 will be the third number so on.

This method is simple, easy to understand, and hence very useful and has universal applications.

1. Systematic sampling relies on arranging the target population according to some ordering scheme and then selecting elements at regular intervals through that ordered list.
   - Systematic sampling involves a random start and then proceeds with the selection of every k th element from then onwards. In this case, k= (population size/sample size).
   - It is important that the starting point is not automatically the first in the list, but is instead randomly chosen from within the first to the k th element in the list.

A simple example would be to select every 10th name from the telephone directory (an 'every 10th' sample, also referred to as 'sampling with a skip of 10').

As described above, systematic sampling is an EPS method, because all elements have the same probability of selection (in the example given, one in ten). It is not 'simple random sampling' because different subsets of the same size have different selection probabilities - e.g.

the set {4,14,24,...,994} has a one-in-ten probability of selection, but the set {4,13,24,34,...} has zero probability of selection.

Systematic sampling in practice

Systematic selection can be applied to various populations such as students in a class, telephone directory, etc. Strictly speaking this method of sampling is not a probability sampling. Hence sometimes called 'pseudo-random' sampling.

Step 1 : find simple fraction: K = N/x or N/n

Where N= population size, x= sample size

50000/500= 100 in this case

Step 2 : select the number between 1 and 100, at random say it is 19.

Step 3 : then the sample comprises of nos. 119, 219, 319, 419 .... 99918.

If we have 50000 books in a population and if we want to take a sample of 500 books, the sampling interval is 50000/500= 100, that is every 100 the book from the sampling start. Suppose we select the random number 19, than the other sample units are: 119,219,319,419 .... 99918.

Advantages of Systematic Sampling

The main advantage of using systematic sampling over simple random sampling is its simplicity. It is quick and easy method. The precision of an estimate from a systematic sample is, most often quite good. But sometime may leads to a wrong conclusion especially when the distribution in the population is highly skewed.

Another advantage of systematic random sampling over simple random sampling is the assurance that the population will be evenly sampled.

- Sample easy to select

- Suitable sampling frame can be identified easily
- Sample evenly spread over entire reference population

Limitations of Systematic Sampling

The systematic method assumes that the size of the population is available. For instance, suppose a researcher wants to study the size of rats in a given area. If he doesn't have any idea how many rats there are, he cannot systematically select a starting point or interval size. A population needs to exhibit a natural degree of randomness along the chosen metric. If the population has a type of standardized pattern, the risk of accidentally choosing very common cases is more apparent.

For a simple hypothetical situation, consider a list of favorite dog breeds where (intentionally or by accident) every evenly numbered dog on the list was small and every odd dog was large. If the systematic sampler began with the fourth dog and chose an interval of six, the survey skips the large dogs.

There is a greater risk of data manipulation with systematic sampling because researchers might be able to construct their systems to increase the likelihood of achieving a targeted outcome rather than letting the random data produce a representative answer.

Disadvantages of Systematic Sampling

- Sample may be biased if hidden periodicity in population coincides with that of selection.
- Difficult to assess precision of estimate from one survey.

Sometimes, however, the standard error in a systematic sample is sufficiently large and thus it may lead us to a wrong conclusion especially when the distribution in the population is highly skewed.

4. Stratified Random Sampling

The word stratified means division into strata or separate groups. Stratified sampling refers to a type of sampling method. With stratified sampling, the researcher divides the population into separate groups, called strata. Then, a probability sample (often a simple random sample) is drawn from each group .It simply means division into strata or separate groups. In the singular, a group is called a stratum. A population is usually far from homogeneous. Stratified sampling techniques are generally used when the population is heterogeneous. When population is divided into a certain number of strata then number of members to be selected from a particular stratum by random sampling is proportional to the size of the stratum. Therefore, the process of such a sample selection is termed stratified sampling. For example: If we would like to take sample of 100 books. We may take a few books from management collection, a few from auditing collection, etc. Here stratum is obtained by subject. Similarly, if we have user population, we may consider the strata by their status – students, faculty member, researcher etc.

Need of Stratification

The stratification is necessary for:

1. Increasing a sample's statistical efficiency.
2. Providing adequate data for analyzing the various sub populations and
3. Applying different methods to different strata.

Stratification is essential when the researcher want to study the characteristics of population sub-groups such as male and female users of the library. Stratification is also useful when different methods of data collection etc. are used for different part of the population.

Suitability : The stratified random sampling is appropriate for a large homogeneous population.

Advantages

The chief merit of this method, apart from stratification, is that the manner of picking up items from each stratum is purely according to random sampling principles. When we compared with systematic and random sampling methods, stratified sampling prominently stands out as the better choice. This is because it overcomes the chief hurdle of random sampling by giving unequal representation. It means that certain part of population may be better represented than others in the sample. The chief merit of this method, apart from stratification, is that the manner of picking up items from each stratum is purely according to random sampling principles.

The major advantages of systematic sampling are:

- It is much simpler than random sampling and is easy to use.
- This method may require less time. A researcher operating on a limited time schedule will prefer this method.
- This method is cheaper than random sampling.
- Every unit in a stratum has same chance of being selected.
    - Using same sampling fraction for all strata ensures proportionate representation in the sample.
    - Adequate representation of minority subgroups of interest can be ensured by stratification and varying sampling fraction between strata as required.
    - Finally, since each stratum is treated as an independent population, different sampling approaches can be applied to different strata.

Disadvantages

Some of the disadvantages are:

- This method ignores all elements between two 'k' th elements selected. Further, except the first element, other selected elements are not chosen at random. Hence, this sampling cannot be considered to be a probability sampling in the strict sense.
- As each element does not have an equal chance of being selected, the resulting sample is not a random one.
- This method may sometimes give a biased sample. If by chance, several 'k' the element chosen represents a particular group, that group would be over representative in the sample.
  - First, sampling frame of entire population has to be prepared separately for each stratum
  - Second, when examining multiple criteria, stratifying variables may be related to some, but not to others, further complicating the design, and potentially reducing the utility of the strata.
  - Finally, in some cases (such as designs with a large number of strata, or those with a specified minimum sample size per group), stratified sampling can potentially require a larger sample than would other methods.

Stratification process

This involves three major discussions:

1. The stratification base to be use used should be decided. The ideal base would be the principal variable under study.
2. **The number of strata :** what should be the number of strata? Larger the number of strata, greater may be the degree of representativeness of the sample.

3. **Srata sample size :** There are two alternatives, first, the strata sample size may be proportionate to strata's share in the local population. Second, they may be disappropriate to strata's share

5. Cluster Sampling

When the population elements scattered over a wider area and a list of population elements is not readily available, the use of simple or stratified random sampling method would be too expensive and time consuming. In such case clustered sampling is usually adopted.

What is cluster sampling?

Cluster sampling means random selection of sampling units consisting of population elements. Each such sampling unit is a cluster of population element. Then for each selected sampling unit, a sample of population elements is drawn by either simple random selection or stratified random selection.

Suppose a researcher wants to select a random sample of 2000 households out of 50,000 estimated households in the city for a survey. A direct sample of individual households would be difficult to select, because list of households does not exists and would be too costly to prepare. Instead, he can select a random sample of a few blocks/wards. The number of blocks to be selected depending upon the average number of estimated households per block. Suppose average number of household per block is 200, than 10 blocks comprise the sample.

Cluster vs stratified sampling

The main difference between cluster sampling and stratified sampling is that in cluster sampling the cluster is treated as the sampling unit so analysis is done on a population of clusters.

Table 4. Difference between cluster sampling and Stratified sampling

Cluster sampling	Stratified sampling
1. The sampling unit is a cluster or a group consisting of Population elements.	The population element itself is the sampling unit
2. The population is divided into many cluster or Sub groups, each with a few elements	The population is divided into a few sub groups or strata
3. Cluster is done on the basis of geographical areas (district, taluka)	Stratification is done on the basis of variables under study e.g. organizational unit (department ,section)
4. We make a random selection of sub-group or cluster	We make a random selection elements from each sub group
5. The resulting sample may give a lower degree of representativeness for a given sample size	It yield a higher degree of representative sample for the same sample size
6. The sampling error may be great	The sampling error may be less
7. The cost per element is lower	The cost per element is higher

Determine the number of stages

Shall we use single stage or multistage cluster? It depends upon the geographical area of study , scale of the study, the size of the population and considerations of the costs.

There are two types of cluster sampling methods:

1. Single-stage sampling : Select cluster on random basis and study all elements in each of the sample cluster. All of the elements within selected clusters are included in the sample.

2. Two-stage sampling : Select cluster and then select elements for each selected cluster. A subset of elements within selected clusters are randomly selected for inclusion in the sample.

3. Multi-stage sampling : Extend the above method to more stages.

Application: The application of the cluster sampling in social science research are extensive, particularly in socio-economic surveys, demographic studies etc.

CLUSTER SAMPLING.......

	Freq	c f	cluster
I	2000	2000	1
II	3000	5000	2
III	1500	6500	
IV	4000	10500	3
V	5000	15500	4, 5
VI	2500	18000	6
VII	2000	20000	7
VIII	3000	23000	8
IX	3500	26500	9
X	4500	31000	10
XI	4000	35000	11, 12
XII	4000	39000	13
XIII	3500	44000	14,15
XIV	2000	46000	
XV	3000	49000	16
XVI	3500	52500	17
XVII	4000	56500	18,19
XVIII	4500	61000	20
XIX	4000	65000	21, 22
XX	4000	69000	23
XXI	2000	71000	24
XXII	2000	73000	
XXIII	3000	76000	25
XXIV	3000	79000	26

- XXV 5000 84000 27, 28
- XXVI 2000 86000 29
- XXVII 1000 87000
- XXVIII 1000 88000
- XXIX 1000 89000 30
- XXX 1000 90000
- 90000/30 = 3000 sampling interval

Difference between Strata and Clusters

Although strata and clusters are both non-overlapping subsets of the population, they differ in several ways.

- All strata are represented in the sample; but only a subset of clusters is in the sample.
- With stratified sampling, the best survey results occur when elements within strata are internally homogenous. However, with cluster sampling, the best results occur when elements within clusters are internally heterogeneous.
- It is an example of 'two-stage sampling' .
- First stage a sample of areas is chosen;
- Second stage a sample of respondents within those areas is selected.
- Population divided into clusters of homogeneous units, usually based on geographical contiguity.
- Sampling units are groups rather than individuals.
- A sample of such clusters is then selected.
- All units from the selected clusters are studied.

Advantages of clustered sampling

- This method is much easier and convenient to apply when large population are studied or large geographical area are covered. A researcher can simply draw a random sample of geographical sections and adopt single or multistage sampling depending upon the area to be covered in the study.

- The cost of this method is much less as compared with other sampling methods
- Sampling in this method does not require more time.
- This method is flexible. Where it involves multistage sampling , it is possible to employ different types of sampling in successive stages.
  - Cuts down on the cost of preparing a sampling frame.
  - This can reduce travel and other administrative costs.

Disadvantages

Some of the disadvantages of this method are:

- The cluster size may vary and this variation could increase the basis of the resulting sample. There would be certain bias resulting from the large coverage of big families.
- Sampling error is higher for a simple random sample of same size. Thus, this method is statistically less efficient than other probability sampling methods.
- Often used to evaluate vaccination coverage in EPI

Identification of clusters

- List all cities, towns, villages and wards of cities with their population falling in target area under study.
- Calculate cumulative population and divide by 30, this gives sampling interval.
- Select a random no. less than or equal to sampling interval having same no. of digits. This forms 1st cluster.
- Random no + sampling interval = population of 2nd cluster.

- Second cluster + sampling interval = 4th cluster.
- Last or 30th cluster = 29th cluster + sampling interval

POST STRATIFICATION

- Stratification is sometimes introduced after the sampling phase in a process called "post stratification".
- This approach is typically implemented due to a lack of prior knowledge of an appropriate stratifying variable or when the experimenter lacks the necessary information to create a stratifying variable during the sampling phase. Although the method is susceptible to the pitfalls of post hoc approaches, it can provide several benefits in the right situation. Implementation usually follows a simple random sample. In addition to allowing for stratification on an ancillary variable, post stratification can be used to implement weighting, which can improve the precision of a sample's estimates.

In a stratified sampling, we try to increase the efficiency of sampling by dividing a heterogeneous population in such a way that:

1. There is as great homogeneity as possible within each stratum.
2. There is a great difference between the strata.

How to do it?

1. Devide the population into homogeneous sub groups.
2. Select a random sample from within each sub group.

It is useful when

1. Population can be broken down into homogeneous sub groups.
2. Varience within each sub group is lower than across group.

Advantages and Disadvantages

Stratified sampling is usually of great importance when the population distribution is highly skewed. Further it yields separate estimate for each strata apart from an estimate for the parameters of the population. However, precision of an estimate in a stratified sampling is not always better than that of the precision of an estimate in other sampling methods.

6. Multistage Sampling

In this method, sampling is carried out in two or more stages. The population is regarded as being composed of a number of first stage sampling units. Each of them is made up of a number of second stage units and so forth. That is , at each stage , a sampling unit is a cluster of the sampling unit of the subsequent stage.

First, a sample of the first stage sampling unit is drawn, than from each of the selected first stage sampling unit, a sample of second stage sampling unit is drawn and so on. Appropriate random sampling method is adopted in each stage.

In this method selection of units is done in more than one stage. The number of stages in a multistage sampling is based on convenience and the availability of suitable sampling frames at different stages.

Stages

- Complex form of cluster sampling in which two or more levels of units are embedded one in the other First stage, random number of districts chosen in all states.
- Followed by random number of talukas, villages.
- Then third stage units will be houses.
- All ultimate units (houses, for instance) selected at last step are surveyed.
- This technique is essentially the process of taking

random samples of preceding random samples.

- Not as effective as true random sampling, but probably solves more of the problems inherent to random sampling.
- An effective strategy because it banks on multiple randomizations. As such, extremely useful.
- Multistage sampling used frequently when a complete list of all members of the population not exists and is inappropriate.

Moreover, by avoiding the use of all sample units in all selected clusters, multistage sampling avoids the large, and perhaps unnecessary, costs associated with traditional cluster sampling.

For example in national survey:

1. First stage : districts
2. Second stage : cities
3. Thirth stage : wards localities
4. Fourth stage : hose holds

Usage

Multi stage sampling is appropriate where the population is scattered over a wider geographical area and no list is available for sampling. It is also useful when a survey has to be made within a limited time and cost budget.

Advantages

This method is best method to use when large scale nationwide surveys are to be undertaken. In this method the entire sampling is undertaken in a certain number of stages depending upon the nature of the survey. The main merit of this method is that it is less expensive and more practicable.

Some of the advantages of multistage sampling are:

1. It result in concentration of fieldwork in compact

small area and consequently in a saving of time, labor and money.

2. It is more convenient, efficient and flexible than single stage sampling.

Disadvantages

The major disadvantage of the multistage sampling is that the procedure of estimating sampling error and cost advantage is complicated. It is difficult for a non statisticians to follow this estimation procedure.

Sampling may be undertaken as follows:

The process of selecting a few districts in the state by random sampling constitutes the first stage; selecting a few town by random sampling a few towns and cities from these selected districts constitutes the second stage; selecting by random sampling few words and localities from these selected towns and cities constitutes the third. finally selecting by random sampling, individuals from these selected blocks and localities constitutes final stage.

7. Multi Phase Sampling

When this procedure is extended to more than two phases of selection, it is than called multiphase sampling. This is also known as sequential sampling, as sub sampling is done from a main sample in phases.

- Part of the information collected from whole sample and part from subsample.
- In Tb survey MT in all cases – Phase I
- X –Ray chest in MT +ve cases – Phase II
- Sputum examination in X – Ray +ve cases - Phase III

Survey by such procedure is less costly, less laborious and more purposeful

Usage

Multi phase sampling is a compromise solution for

dilemma posed by undesirable extremes. In multi phase sampling, the general sample should be larger enough to yield adequate subsample or for detailed investigation. Multiphase sampling can result in considerable economies and reduce the burden on the respondent. Moreover, the information collected from the full sample can be used for stratification purpose in the selection of the sub sample or for estimating the effect of non response in the sub sample.

Multi-phase Vs Multi-stage sampling

Multiphase sampling is different from the multistage sampling. In multiphase sampling, the different phases of observation relate to sample unit of the same type while in multi stage sampling, the sampling units are of different types at different stages.

II. NON PROBABILITY SAMPLING METHODS

The non probability sampling does not adopt the theory of probability and it does not give a representative sample of the population.

The primary methods of non probability sampling are:

1. Accidental sampling or convenience sampling
2. Quota Sampling
3. Purposive or judgment sampling

In addition, non response effects may turn any probability design into a non probability design if the characteristics of non response are not well understood, since non response effectively modifies each element's probability of being sampled.

1. Accidental Sampling or Convenience Sampling

It means selecting sample unit in just 'hit and miss' fashion. This method is also known as accidental sampling because the respondents whom the researcher meets accidentally are included in the sample.

The selection of the sample is left to the researcher who is to select the sample. The researcher normally interviews the users in a groups at the place (library) and interview the person who happen to be there .This type of sampling therefore is also called 'accidental sampling' as the respondent in the sample are included merely because of their presence on the spot. The data collection and sample cost is minimum in this case. However the method suffers greatly from the quality, i.e. accuracy point of view which is no way can be determined. However this type of sampling is more suitable in 'exploratory' Research' where the focus is on getting new ideas/insights into a given problem.

Usefulness

Though convenience sampling has no status, it may be used for simple purpose such as testing ideas or gaining ideas or rough impression about a subject of interest. It lays a ground work for a subsequent probability sampling. Sometimes it may have to be necessarily used. For example when the population can not be defined or a list population is not available, there is no other alternative than to use convenience sampling.

Advantages

1. Convenience sampling is the cheapest and simplest.
2. It does not require a list of population.
3. It does not require any statistical expertise.

Disadvantages

1. Convenience sampling is highly biased, because of the researchers' subjectivity, and so it does not yield representative sample.
2. It is least reliable sampling method. There is no way of estimating the representativeness of the sample.
3. The findings cannot be generalized.

2. Quota Sampling

This is a form of convenient sampling involving selection of quota groups of accessible sampling units by traits such as sex, age etc. when the population is known to consists of various categories by age sex etc. in specific proportions.

Quota sampling is a method of stratified sampling in which selection within strata is non random. It is this non random that constitutes its greatest weakness. Quotas are stratified by such variables as age, sex, etc. It is easy to classify the accessible respondents under sex, age and religion, but it is difficult to classify them into social categories, since social class usually involves a combination of factors such as occupation, income and caste and interviewer's subjective judgment and bias play some role in the social class classification of respondents.

The quota sampling is the most frequently used non probability sampling method. This method consists of: establishment of quotas (sample size) for each stratum. Sample size, called quotas are established for each stratum. Example: We have three categories of population and are in the ratio of 20%, 40% and 60% respectively. Using quota sampling, determining the number of representatives for each category in a sample size of 100.

Table 5. Quota Sampling

Category 1 (BCom.) students	= 20% of 100 =20
Category 2 (BSc) students	= 40% of 100= 40
Category 3 (B.A Eco.(H))students	= 60% of 100 =60
Total	100

Application : Quota sampling is used in studies like marketing surveys, opinion polls and leadership surveys which do not aim at precision, but to get quickly some crude results.

Advantages

Some of the advantages of quota sampling are:

1. It is economical as travelling cost is reduced
2. It is easy to administered
3. When field work is to be done quickly, this method provides the biggest advantage.
4. No sampling frame is required
5. It takes less time
6. Field work can easily be organized. Strict supervision need not be required.

Disadvantages

Some of the disadvantages of quota sampling are:

1. It is not possible to know the accuracy being achieved because this method is not based in random selection.
2. The sample may not be a representative sample.
3. The quality may suffer if skilled interviewers are not employed.
4. Strict control of field work is difficult.
5. It is difficult for sampling on more than three variable dimensions.

The population is first segmented into mutually exclusive sub-groups, just as in stratified sampling.

Then judgment used to select subjects or units from each segment based on a specified proportion.

For example, an interviewer may be told to sample 200 females and 300 males between the age of 45 and 60.

It is this second step which makes the technique one of non-probability sampling.

In quota sampling the selection of the sample is non- random. For example interviewers might be tempted to interview those who look most helpful. The problem is that these samples may be biased because not everyone gets a chance of selection. This random element is its greatest weakness and quota versus probability has been a matter of controversy for many years.

4. Purposive Sampling or Judgement Sampling

This method means deliberate selection of sample units that conform to some predetermined criteria. This is also known as judgment sampling. This involves selection of cases which we judge as the most appropriate one for the given study. It is based on the judgment of the researcher.

The main objective of this method is to serve a particular purpose. Purposive sampling, also known as judgmental, selective or subjective sampling, is a type of non-probability sampling technique. In judgment sampling the judgement or opinion of same expert forms the basis of the sampling method. It is expected that we could have better samples as the experts are supposed to have known the population. As the individual members of the sample are chosen in accordance with a certain principle, the method of such a selection is called purposive sampling. This method has its limitations and is used mainly for situations requiring extremely small size of samples i.e. use of rare events etc.

Non-probability sampling focuses on sampling techniques where the units that are investigated are based on the judgment. The nature of this sample technique is such that the members of the population have unequal probabilities of inclusion in the sample. Which means that some members have a high probability of inclusion over others. For instance while undertaking an opinion survey, only the personnel judgment of a particular group of persons may be taken into consideration. It is due to the purposive nature of the survey.

In many real life situations, the use of clustered sampling method and that of convenience sampling is being made mainly because the cost per observation is much economical as compared to other methods.

Applications : The method is appropriate when what is important is the typicality and specific relevance of the sampling units to the study and not their overall representativeness to the population.

Advantages

1. It is less costly and more convenient.
2. It guarantees inclusion of relevant elements in the sample. Probability sampling plans cannot gives such guarantee.

Disadvantages

Some of the disadvantages are:

1. This does not ensure the representativeness of the sample.
2. This is less efficient for generalizing when compared with random sampling.
3. This method requires more prior extensive information about the population one studies. Without such information , it is not possible to judge the suitability of the sample items to be selected.

Criteria for selecting sampling techniques

Let us now examine the criteria for selecting an appropriate sampling plan for a given study.

Following are the criteria for governing the choice of the sampling techniques:

1. Purpose of the survey : What is the purpose of the survey by the researcher. If he intends to generalize the findings based on sample survey to the population, than an appropriate probability sampling method to be selected. The choice of the particular type of probability sampling depends upon the geographical area of the survey, size and nature of the population under study.

2. Measurability : The application of statistical inference theory requires computation of the sampling error from the sample itself. Probability sampling only allow such computation. Hence, where the research objective requires statistical inference, the sample should be drawn by applying simple random sampling method or stratified random sampling method, depending on whether the population is homogeneous or heterogeneous.

3. Degree of precision : Should the result of the survey be very precise, or even rough results could serve the purpose? The desired level of precession is one of the criteria of sampling method selection.

4. Information about the population : How much information is available about the population to be studied? Where no list of population and no information about its nature are available, it is difficult to apply a probability method.

5. Nature of the population : In terms of the variables to be studied, is the population homogeneous or heterogeneous? In case of homogeneous population, even a simple random sampling will give a representative sample. If the population is heterogeneous, stratified random sampling is appropriate. Systematic sampling would however be preffered in those cases where the list of units of population is available or easily obtainable and where there is no periodic variation or trend present in the population.

6. Geographical area of the study and the size of the population : If the area covered by a survey is very large (e.g. country or state) and the size of the population is quite large, multistage cluster sampling would be appropriate. But if the area and the size of the population is small, single stage probability method could be used.

7. Financial resources : Is the available finance is a limiting factor or not? If the available finance is limited, it may become necessary to choose a less costly sampling plan like multistage cluster sampling or even quota sampling as a compromise. Where finance is not constrained, a researcher can choose the most appropriate method of sampling that fits the research objective and the nature of the population.

8. Time limitations : The time limit within which the research project should be completed restrict the choice of a sample method. Then, as a compromise, it may become necessary to choose less time consuming method like simple random sampling instead of stratified sampling with probability proportional to size; multistage cluster sampling instead of single stage sampling of elements.

CALCULATION OF SAMPLE SIZE

There are some misconceptions about the required size of a sample. One misconception is that large the sample size, greater may be the accuracy of the sample results. Although an increase in sample size will increase the precision of the sample results, a large sample size does not guarantee the accuracy of the result.

The sample size can be statistically estimated by deciding the required level of accuracy.

(As given by Toro Yamane)

Sample size n= N/1+Ne

Where N= total population

e = error(confidence level) such as 5% or 10% that is 0.05 or 0.010

Suppose N= 10000

e= 0.05, than

n= 10000/1+10000(0.05)2 =10000/1+25 = 384.615= 385 approximately

A random sample of size 385 would represents a population of 10000 at 5% level (error).

SAMPLING AND NON-SAMPLING ERRORS

The basic objective of a sample is to draw inferences about the population from which the sample is drawn. Therefore, it is necessary that the sampling technique be a reliable one. A sample taken from a population is likely to possess almost the same characteristics as in case of population.

A survey aim at estimating or inferring selected population characteristics or parameters by studying either the entire population or a sample of the population. The research results may differ from the true values of the parameters under study. Such differences are known as errors and biases.

1. Random sampling error : The difference between the sample result and the result of a census conducted using identical procedures.

2. Non-sampling error : Results from some imperfect aspect of the research design due to response error or from a mistake in execution of research.

In the total process of data collections to inferring results, errors are bound to be erupt in.

These errors are classified into two groups:

1. Sampling error
2. Non-sampling errors

1. Sampling errors : Sampling errors are those which arises due to drawing faculty inferences about the population based on the results obtained from the samples. In other words it is difference between the results which would have obtained if the entire population was taken for such a study and the results obtained from the samples drawn from it. The sampling errors would be smallest if the sample size is large relation to the population and vise-versa. The errors which arise because of studying only a part of the total population are called sampling errors. These may arise due to non representativeness of the samples and the inadequacy of sample size. When several samples are drawn from a population, their results would not be identical. The degree of variations of sample result is measured by standard deviation and it is known as the standard error of the concern statistics. As sample size increases the magnitude of the error decreases. As sample size increases the magnitude of the error decreases. Sample size and sampling errors are thus are negatively correlated.

2. Non sampling errors : Non sampling errors are introduced due to technically faulty observations or calculations during the processing of the data. These errors which arise from the sources other than sampling. They include error of observation, error of measurement and errors of responses. Data are collected through the method of observation or interviewing. Measurement error consist of error in processing and analyzing. Errors of response include incorrect responses of the respondents, mistakes in noting their responses etc.

Some errors are:

1. Incomplete coverage of the population
2. Inaccurate information provided by the participants
3. Errors occurring during editing, tabulation and mathematical manipulation of data.

Both the sampling as well as non sampling errors must be reduced to a minimum in order to get as representative sample of population as possible.

Total error

In sampling theory, a popular model combines sampling and non sampling errors and biases into the total error. This total error is the square root of the sums of squares of variables errors and squares of bias.

It is often called the Root Means Square Error (RMSE)

Total= “VE+Bias^2

The variable errors are caused only by sampling errors, and VE equals the standard error of sampling. Bias is mostly caused by measurement biases (i.e. non sampling errors).

The total error depends upon the length of both of the legs. The sampling error/standard error leg can be shortened by improving the sampling design and by increasing the sample size. The length of the biases leg may be reduced by improving the tool of data collection, the precision of methods of data collection, field work, coding, processing and analysis.

The measurement of sampling errors does not pose much problem but the measurement of non sampling error requires special procedures and it is a costly effect. Hence, the reduction of non sampling error is a challenge to the researchers.

CONCLUSION

Among the various sample designs, we can say that one should resort to simple random sampling because sampling error can be eliminated. But purposive sampling is considered more appropriate when universe happen to be small. In a situation when random sampling is not possible, than we have to use sampling design other than random sampling. Several methods may be used in same study.

5

Methods and Techniques of Data Collection

INTRODUCTION

Once the researcher has decided the 'research design' the next job is of data collection. The search for answers to search question is called collection of data. Data are facts and other relevant information. Statistical investigation requires systematic collection of data so that all groups are represented in data. The quality of data will generally affects the conclusions and hence, utmost importance must be given to this process and every possible precaution should be taken to ensure accuracy while gathering and collecting data.

Data

Data are numerical facts. They are figures collected in a systematic manner for a predetermine purpose.

The data may be : (a) pertaining to human being (b) Data relating to organization and c. data petaing to territorial areas. The personnel data or data relating to human being consists of :

1. Demographic : Such as age, sex, religion, education etc.

2. Behavioral variables : Such as attitude, opinions, awareness etc.

3. Territorial data : These type of data are related to geographical characteristics population, village, cities etc., etc.

4. Organisational data : This type of data consists of data relating to organization such as ownership, resources, functions etc.

Importance of data

The data serve as the raw material for analysis. Without an analysis of factual data, no specific inferences can be drawn on the questions under study. Inferences on the basis of imagination or guess work can not provide the correct answer to research questions. The relevance and reliability of data determines the quality of the findings of a study. Data forms the basis for testing the hypotheses formulation in the study. Data also provide the facts and figures required for constructing measurement scales and tables, which are analyzed with statistical techniques. Thus, the scientific process of measurements, analysis, testing and inferences depends upon the availability of the relevant data and their accuracy.

The data can be classified into two categories.

1. Primary data and
2. Secondary data.

1. Primary data : The primary data are original in character. Primary data is that data which is collected by the investigator himself for the purpose of specific study. Such data is collected by surveys by the individuals or institutions and is original in character.

2. Secondary data : Secondary data are those data which have collected by some other person. When the investigator used the data which has already been collected by others, such data is called secondary data.

SOURCES OF DATA

The sources of data can be classified into :

1. Primary sources and
2. Secondary sources

1. Primary sources : Primary sources are original sources from which the researcher directly collected data that have not been previously collected. Primary data are first hand information collected through various methods such as observation, interviewing, mailing etc.

2. Secondary sources : Secondary sources consists of already compiled statistical statements and reports whose data may be used by researchers for their studies. For example census report, annual report, reports of trade associations, etc. Secondary sources consists of not only published records and reports but also unpublished records.

The sources of secondary data may be internal or external. Internal sources of data represents the data that already available with research organization. The information available with outside the organization are external. There are varieties of published sources from which one can get information for his research work. The secondary data can be obtained from the secondary sources such as journals, publications of research professional and research organizations, official publications of central, state, and local governments. Official publications of foreign governments and international bodies such as UNO and its subordinate bodies, reports submitted by research scholars, scientists etc. Secondary data are in the shape of a finished product.

Features of secondary sources

Some of the features of secondary sources are:

1. They are ready made and readily available and do not require the trouble of constructing tools and administering them.

2. They consists of data over which a researcher has no original control over collection and classification. Both the forms and contents of secondary sources are shaped by others.
3. Secodry sources are not limited in space and time.

USE OF SECONDRY DATA

The secondary data may be used in three ways by the researchers :

1. Some specific information from secondary sources may be used for reference purpose.
2. Secondry data may be used as bench marks against which the findings of a research may be tested. For example the findings of a local or regional survey may be compared with national average.
3. The secondary data may be used as the sole source of information for a research project. For example year books, statistical reports of government departments etc. serve as major data sources for such research studies.

ADVANTAGES AND DISADVANTAGES OF SECONDARY DATA

Advantages

Some of the advantages of secondary data are:

1. Secondry data can be secured cheaply and quickly. Once their source of documents and reports are located, collection of data is just a desk work.
2. Wider geographical area and longer reference period may be covered without much cost.
3. The use of secondary data broaden the data base from which the scientific generalization can be made.
4. The use of secondary data enables a researcher to verify the findings based on primary data. The researcher need not await the time when additional

primary data can be collected.

5. Faster
6. Less Expensive
7. Less activities (Field trip, Survey etc.)

Disadvantages/Limitations

Some of the disadvantages of secondary data are:

1. The available data may not meet our specific needs. The units of measures may not match, time period may also be different.
2. The available data may not be accurate as desired. To assess their accuracy we need to know how the data were collected.
3. The secondary data are not up to date and become obsolete when they appear in print, because of time lag in producing them.
4. Not easily available
5. Not adequate
6. May not meet the needs of researcher
7. Outdated information
8. Variation in definition

PURPOSE OF SECONDARY DATA

- Extracting the relevant information from other sources, previous studies.
- Fact findings: Descriptive information to support research.
- Model Building: specifying relationship between two or more variables.
- Data mining : Exploring data through computer . Using computer technology to go through volumes of data to discover trends about an organization's sales customers and products.
- Identifying the relevant sources to avoid plagiarism

Primary data collection procedure

Various steps involved in primary data collection are:

1. Planning the study
2. Modes of data collection
3. Sample selection
4. Editing the primary data

Planning the study : Since the quality of results gained from statistical data depends upon the quality of information collected. It is to be ensured that the data is highly representative and unbiased. This requires a high degree of skill.

METHODS OF COLLECTING PRIMARY DATA

Primary data are directly collected by the researcher from their original sources. But the collection of primary data is costly and time consuming. Yet for several types of social science research required data are not available from secondary sources and they have to directly gathered from primary sources. In such cases where available data are inappropriate, inadequate or obsolete, primary data have to be gathered. They include socioeconomic surveys, opinion polls, marketing research etc.

There are various methods of data collection. A method is different from tool. While a method refers to the way or mode of gathering data, a tool is a an instrument used for the method. The important methods are:

1. Survey method (Questionnaire; mail survey)
2. Observation
3. Experimentation
4. Interviewing

THE CHOICE OF METHOD OF DATA COLLECTION

The choice of the or methods depends upon the following factors:

1. The nature of the study of the subject matter : If it is a study of opinions/preferences of persons, interviewing or mailing may be appropriate depending upon the educational level of the respondents.

2. The unit of enquiry : The unit of enquiry may be an individual, household, institution or community. To collect data from the household interviewing is proffered. Data from the institution can be collected from mail survey and studies on communities calls for observation method.

3. The size and the spread of the sample : If the sample is small and the area covered is compact, interviewing may be preffered, but a large sample scattered over a wider area may requiring mailing.

4. The educational level of respondents : For a simple survey among educated persons concerned with the subject matter of the study, a mail survey is appropriate. But for the survey of less educated /illiterate persons like rural people, interview is the only suitable method.

5. The type and depth of information to be collected : For collection of general, simple, factual and non emotional data, interviewing or mailing is appropriate.

The most common methods are:

1. Survey method that includes questionnaire and interview method.
2. Observation method.
3. Secondary analysis method.

Observation method as name indicates is based on observation. Observation is keen and scientific study of a problem. For example in the study of user behavior in the library the investigator instead of asking the user, may himself observe and watch.

1. Survey Method

A survey is conducted through a questionnaire or interview to find out opinion about the library services and sources. In both these methods involve questioning techniques. This method offers the user an opportunity to express their opinion about the library sources and services. Users express their opinions by answering the questions related to library sources and services. With these methods verbal or expressed behavior of the users can be analyzed. In both these methods involve questioning techniques.

Uses of Questionnaires and Surveys and their Value

There are two warnings on surveys:

1. Firstly, don't expect anywhere near 100%, in fact estimate relatively low responses.
2. Secondly, it takes a while to work through the responses. You may try to implement some of the things that come out of the survey quickly, but other suggestions or ideas may take a while to be acted upon.

Surveys are a good idea as they often tell you things that you had no idea about people thought about the library and suggestions for services.

Narrow the Survey Focus

Developing the right questions to ask in a survey is one of the most important steps in eliciting community input. A single questionnaire, however, should not try to answer every issue confronting a library. The scope of the questions must be narrowed to encourage community members to complete the entire survey while gathering the most valuable information needed for library decision making.

Select a Target Audience

Once the library has decided on a set of relevant

issues for the survey, the work begins on crafting a short survey for the target audience. Depending on the target audience, the survey may be distributed at the library, mailed to community members, or created for patrons accessing the library's web pages.

Write Survey Questions

No matter who the audience is, it is important that participants take the time to answer every question. For this reason, most library surveys are short, asking between ten and fifteen clearly written multiple-choice questions. The following pages contain a compilation of library survey questions. Pick and choose the questions for your library survey based on the specific information you want to gather from your community. You can use a selection of the following questions to create your own survey, or you can use the following questions as a guide for creating a custom survey specific for the library's community. When planning the survey distribution strategy, it is important to note that many libraries find it useful to gather information from community members who do not regularly use the library.

When constructing the survey, experts recommend that the personal information in the survey be left to the end in order to keep the participant interested and to avoid suspicion created by personal questions.

Test the Survey

Finally, it will be important to test the survey on a small audience in order to confirm questions are clearly written and correctly interpreted by the target audience.

COLLECTION OF DATA THROUGH QUESTIONNAIRE METHOD

According to Krishan Kumar (1992)[47] a questionnaire is a written document listing a series of questions pertaining to the problem under study, to which the investigator requires the answers." It is given, sent or mailed to respondents. Questionnaire is a written list of questions, the answer to which are recorded by the respondents. The researchers most commonly use this method for collecting data. The main dependence for gathering of data was on questionnaire method as it provides a cost efficient coverage for quantitative research with available resources.

This method of data collection is very popular method. This method is very important method of collecting primary data. This method is being adopted by various organizations, institutions, research workers, government departments etc. A questionnaire is a set of questions pertaining to a particular problem under study. It is either self-completed by the respondent or completed by an interviewer who read out the questions and record the response. In this method questionnaire is either sent by post or completed by the interviewer himself. Questionnaire method is the main instrument for data collection. A Questionnaire consists of a set of written questions for respondents to answer. These answers become primary data for investigation.

For designing the questionnaire, care should be taken keeping in view the does and does not.

After preparing the questionnaire it should be pre-tested by getting the questionnaire filled by some representatives users from the population under study. Final form of questionnaire can be designed on the basis of the results from this questionnaire. The questionnaire should be accompanied by covering letter stating the objectives of the study. Assurance should be given to the respondents that information provided should be kept confidential.

DIFFERENCE BETWEEN QUESTIONNAIRE AND SCHEDULE

Schedule method : Schedule is performa containing a set of questions. This method of data collection is similar to questionnaire method. The little difference is that schedule are being filled by the enumerator who have specially appointed for the purpose. These enumerators along with the schedule go to respondent, put to them the questions from the performa in the order the questions are listed and record the response.

Both questionnaire and schedule are popular method of data collection in research survey. The questinnare is generally sent through mail to the informants.

Collecting the data through questionnaire is relatively cheep and economical because no field staff is required. Collect the data through the schedule is expensive since considerable amount of money required for appointing enumerators.

Non response is high in case of questionnaire method as many people do not response. It is very low in case of schedule because it is filled by the enumerator.

The questionnaire method is likely to be very slow since many respondent do not return the questionnaire in time despite several reminders.

Questinnare method can be used only when respondents are literate and cooperative, but in case of schedule the information can be gathered when the respondents happen to be illiterate.

Risk of collecting incomplete and wrong information is relatively more under the questionnaire method but in case of schedule the information collected is generally complete and accurate.

The success of the questionnaire method depends upon the quality of questionnaire itself, but in case of schedule much depends upon the honesty and competence of the enumerator.

Before using this method, it is always advisable to

conduct pilot study or pilot survey for testing the questionnaire. Pilot survey is the same as the original one (replica).

1. General form of questionnaire

The questionnaire are of two types –structured and unstructured. Structure questionnaires are those questionnaires in which there are definite, concrete and predetermined questions. The questions are presented with exactly the same wordings and in the same order to all respondents. A structured questionnaire is used for the survey conducted by questionnaire method. This questionnaire is generally given to the user to fill and return back to the person concerned. Unstructured questionnaire is used to conduct the interview. The questions in the questionnaire can be categorized as general, close end, open ended on the basis of the purpose of the study etc. The form of questions is either closed (i.e. 'yes' or 'no') or open (i.e. inviting free response). A highly structured questionnaire is one in which all questions and answers are specified and the comments in the respondent's own words are held to minimum. When these characteristics are not present in a questionnaire, it can be termed as unstructured or non structured questionnaire.

Structured questionnaires are simple to administered and inexpensive to analyze.

2. Questions sequence

In order to get the good results, a researcher should pay the attention to the sequence of the questions in preparing the questionnaire. The questions sequence must be clear and logical. The first few questions are important because they are likely to influence the attitude of the respondent. The following types of questions should be avoided.

1. Questions of personal character.
2. Questions that put too much strain on the memory of the respondent.
3. Questions related to personnel wealth etc.

The relatively difficult questions must be put towards the end so that even if the respondent decides not to answer such questions, considerable information would have already been obtained. The question sequence should usually go from the general to more specific

Features of Good Questionnaire

A good questionnaire should have following features:

1. The questionnaire should be short and simple.
2. Questions should be presented in logical sequence.
3. Personel questions should be avoided.
4. Questions should be dichotomous(yes or no), multiple choice type.
5. Technical terms should be avoided.
6. Questions affecting the sentiments of the respondents should be avoided.
7. Sufficient space for answers should be provided.
8. Questinnare should be attractive, specially the mail surveys.
9. Questions should be simple and easy to understand.
10. Questions should be framed keeping in view the objectives and purpose of the study.
11. Questions of confidential nature should be avoided.
12. Number of questions should be restricted.
13. Sufficient space should be provided for giving suggestions etc.

3. Questions formulation and the wordings

Each question should be very clear and understandable. The questions should be impartial and unbiased. Questions should be easily understood, should be simple,

There are generally two types of questions. 1.Multiple choice questions (only two possible answers 'yes or 'no') also known as close ended and 2. Open ended questions (answer in his own words).

There are some advantages and disadvantages of each possible form of questions. The close questions or multiple questions have the advantages of simple to answer, quick and relatively inexpensive to analyze.

But main drawback of such types of questions is that they may force a statement of opinion on an issue about which the respondent does not infect having any opinion. Getting the replies in respondents own words is, thus the major advantage of open ended questions. Open ended questions permits a free response from the respondents. But from analytical point of view, open ended questions are more difficult to handle, raising problem of interpretation, comparability and interviewer biased. The researcher should pay the attention to the wordings of the questions. The words are likely to affect the response. Only the simple words which are familiar to the respondents should be employed. Words with ambiguous meaning should be avoided.

The success of the questionnaire method depends upon a great deal on the drafting skills of the researcher and willingness on the part of the respondent. Questionnaire is considered as the heart of survey operation.

It is perhaps the most familiar tool used in getting responses. Questionnaires are cheap, relatively flexible and can be used to reach a very large number of people. The questions are all present in a consistent format and style and there is little scope for bias to be introduced by different researchers. Linked to this is the fact that the survey is impersonal and avoids some of the problems that can develop during the interaction between an interviewer and a respondent. The questionnaire can also be completed at the respondents' own place, and the respondents can, if so desired, look through the whole questionnaire before committing themselves to anything. One disadvantage of the questionnaire is that, it is a one-way communication that generally does not allow respondents to clarify answers. The techniques of distributing questionnaires are also varied. Questionnaires can be handed out personally, mailed out to respondents, or made available to users at their department.

Questionnaire Design

A good questionnaire is one that is easy for the respondent to complete and easy to analyze. The layout of the questionnaire is, therefore, very important.

The following guidelines was outlined by Kawatra[50] to be kept in view:

- be consistent,
- make clear where and how the responses is to be recorded,
- leave adequate space for responses,
- use the smallest number of different types faces possible, but distinguish questions and instructions,
- number all questions in a continuous sequence and only use letters to identify subparts of question, and
- do not split questions or responses categories between pages.

The format of the questionnaire is based upon open-ended questions and close-ended questions to measure the intensity of views of respondents to the questionnaires. These structured questions are multiple-choice items from which respondents were asked to choose. A few open questions can be included in the questionnaire so as to get the views of the respondents in their own words.

CONSTRUCTION OF QUESTIONNAIRE

When information to be collected by asking questions of people who may have the desired data, the standardized form called questionnaire is prepared.

Steps for the construction of questionnaire

1. Decide the type of questionnaire to be used (mail, personnel distribution).
2. Decide the contents of individual questions.
3. Decide on wording of questionnaire.
4. Decide on question sequence.
5. Decide on types of questions (open, multiple choice) to use.
6. Determine forms, layout and method of reproduction of questionnaire.
7. Make preliminary draft and present it.
8. Revise and prepare the final questionnaire.

Basically questionnaire serves two purposes. It must translate research objectives into specific questions and it must motivate the respondents to cooperate with the survey and to furnish the information correctly.

1. Determine the type of questionnaire to be used : The questionnaire can be used by mail, by personel distribution, by telephone, e-mail, etc. The choice depends upon the type of information to be obtained and the type of respondent to whom it is to be obtained.

2. Determine the contents of individual questions : A first problem is to decide what to include in the individual questions. Ones the specific information needed is known and method of communication is decided, the researcher is ready to being formulating his questionnaire. The following questions to be checked:

1. Is the question necessary?
2. Are several questions needed instead of one?

3. Can the respondent remember the information?

3. Describe the wording of the questionnaire : It should be easily understood, simple, close ended questions should be selected, questions should arranged in a systematic way.

4. Determine the types of question to be use : Once the content of individual question is decided, the researcher is ready to began forming the actual questions. He must decide on the types of questions to be used. There are three main types from which he may choose: 1. Open 2. Multiple choice and 3. Dichotomous.

5. Multiple choice questions : To overcome some of the disadvantages of open questions, open questions are subject to interviewer bias in the recording of answer. This is not mearly as important with multiple choice questions where answers are in once or more to the stated alternatives.

Thus, the multiple choice questions are faster and less subject to bias in the field.

The multiple choice questions simplifies the tabulating process. Multiple choice questions give a list of alternative answers.

6. Dichotomous questions : The dichotomous, or two way questions is an extremes of the multiple choice questions. The idea is to offer only two choices yes or no. Such questions are most widely used of three basic types.

Some of the examples are:

1. Do you visit the library daily? yes/no
2. Timing of library is suitable? yes/no

7. Decide on question sequence : Once the wording of the individual questions has been determined it is necessary to set them up in some order. The order chosen can change the results obtained. There are generally three sections in the questionnaire:

1. ***Basic information*** : Sought from the body of the questionnaire.
2. ***Classification information*** : age, sex, education, institution etc.
3. ***Identification information*** : name, address of the respondent.

8. Decide on layout and reproduction : The physical layout and reproduction of a questionnaire can influenced its success. Three main points to be considered in planning the layout and reproduction of the questionnaire.

1. Making it easy to handle the questionnaires
2. Securing acceptance to the questionnaire by respondent

9. Pretesting of questionnaire : Before the distribution of the questionnaire, it is to be pretested on some respondents. Pretest are better done by personnel interview. After any pertinent changes in the questionnaire have been made, another pretest can be run by mail or telephone.

10. Revision and final draft : After the revision of the questionnaire, the researcher is ready to print the actual questionnaire to be used for the survey.

11. Selection of a sample : Selection of sample on which observation can be made or from which the statistical information can be ascertained according to well defined procedure.

After collection of data, it is to be processed by computers, than it must be coded and converted into computer language. This coding job should be done while editing the data.

ITEMS TO BE INCLUDED IN THE QUESTINNAIRE

The following items are mandatory for the questionnaire:

1. The name of the organization collecting the data should be appear at the top of front page. The address to which they are to be sent must be clearly specified.
2. The title of the study should appear in the large print next to the name of the organization on the first page.
3. The confidentialness of the data should be made clear.
4. A serial number to each questionnaire should be assigned.
5. **Pre coding :** All the items in the questionnaire should be pre coded so as to facilitate the transcription of the data. For example items in section 1 may be numbered as 1.1, 1.2, 1.3. and so on. Sufficient space should be left for coding the responses to the open ended questions.
6. **Sectionalisation :** There should be separate section for each topical area. Each section should be given serial number : 1,2,3,.. and soon.
7. **Spacing :** For each open ended question, adequate space should be provided for answer. Even short answer question should be spaced, so that the interviewers/respondent will not easily confuse the line, from which he is reading.

In case of mailed questionnaire in the end sheet space may be provided under 'general remarks' with a note: "please furnish any other information relevant to the study".

Paper and printing : the paper and printing should be of good quality.

Margin : One inch margin on the left side of the sheet and one half inch margin on other sides may be provided.

Indentation : This is required for 'yes' or 'no' question. If the respondent's answer is 'yes' then a series of questions is offered. If the answer is 'no' a different series of questions is offered. For example : if your answer is yes than answer the following questions.

Note of thanks : A final note of thanks for the cooperation of the respondent should be included at the end of the questionnaire.

METHODS

The following are the methods of collecting data for questionnaire techniques:

1. By mailing questionnaire(mailing survey)
2. By personnel interview
3. Telephone enquiries
4. By e-mail

MAIL SURVEY METHOD

This method involves sending questionnaire to the respondents with a request to complete them and send back by post. This method can be used in case of educated respondents only. The mailed questionnaire should be simple so that the respondents can easily understand the questions and answer them. The questionnaire should preferably contain mostly close end and multi choice questions so that it could be completed within few minutes.

The distinct feature of the mail survey is that the questionnaire is self administered by the respondents themselves and the responses are recorded by them, and not by the investigator as in case of personnel interview method.

Procedure

The researcher should prepare a mailing list of selected respondents by collecting the addresses by the directory of the association or organization to which they belong.

A copy of the questionnaire with covering letter should be mail to the respondent. It must explain to the respondent the purpose of study.

Specimen of the covering letter

SRI GURU GOBIND SINGH COLLEGE OF COMMERCE
UNIVERSIT OF DELHI, PITAMPURA, DELHI

Dr. Gurdev Singh

Associate Prof.

Dear Respondent,

May we ask you a favor that takes only a few minutes of your time?

We are conducting a study on "use of e-resources in management institutions in Delhi" with a few to knowing the use of e-sources and services in management institutions in Delhi.

We solicit your cooperation in completing the enclosed questionnaire. We assure you that your reply will be kept confidential and the results of the study will be shown tabular and statistical form only.

At your earliest convenience , please return the complete questionnaire in the enclosed self addressed stamped envelop.

We thank you for your cooperation.

Sincerely yours
Dr. Gurdev Singh

Improving the Response Rate

The response rate in mail survey is generally very low. In order to increase the response rate , certain techniques have to be adopted. Some of these techniques are:

1. Quality Printing : The questionnaire should be neatly printed in very good quality paper so as to attract the attention of the respondent.

2. Covering letter : The covering letter should be couched in a pleasant style so as to attract the attention of the respondent.

3. Advance Information : Advance information can be provided to potential user by a telephone call or by letter.

4. Incentive : Money, stamps for collection and other incentives are also used to induce respondents to complete and return mail questionnaire.

5. Large sample : A large sample may be drawn than the estimated sample size. For example if required sample size is 2000 , a sample of 3000 may be drawn.

ADVANTAGES AND DISADVANTAGES OF MAIL SURVEY

Advantages

Some of the advantages are:

1. They are less costly than personnel interview, the cost of mailing is the same thought the country, irrespective of the distance.
2. They can cover extensive geographical areas.
3. The respondent can complete the questionnaire at their convenience.
4. Mail questionnaires are totally free from the interviewers biased, as there is no personnel contact between the respondents and the investigator.

Each of these methods has its own advantages and disadvantages. By telephone interviewing method is best method of gathering quick data. It has an advantage over mail questionnaire. In this method interviewer can talk to one or more persons and clarify his questions if they are not understood. Response rate is also better than mail questionnaire. Drawback is that only person having telephone connection can be interview.

Contents of the Questionnaire

(eg. to judge the information seeking behavior) (Questionnaire sample No. 2).

The questionnaire can be divided into three sections:

Section A: Demographic Profile

The respondents were required to state their major, semester and year of study. A question on gender was also included. Altogether there are only three questions to be answered by the respondents in this section.

Section B: Information needs and Information Seeking Behavior

The respondents were asked on their present academic assignment and for what paper / course and the need of the information. They have to indicate the words or keyword used when searching for the information in the database. The respondent was asked on how long and how often they have been using the electronic resources. The rest of the questions comprised of questions regarding the students' expectation, approach, experience, exposure, evaluation, and understanding of their searching through electronic resources. The last question on this section was to get the feedback from students whether the library have adequate facilities of electronic resources. Altogether there are 17 questions from this section.

C. Suggestions

The questionnaire are of two types–structured and unstructured. A structured questionnaire is used for the survey conducted by questionnaire method. This questionnaire is generally given to the user to fill and return back to the person concerned. Unstructured questionnaire is used to conduct the interview. The questions in the questionnaire can be categorized as general, close end, open ended on the basis of the purpose etc. The success of the questionnaire method depends upon a great deal on the drafting skill of the researcher and willingness on the part of the respondent.

TYPES OF QUESTIONNAIRE

Following four types of questionnaires are generally used by the researchers all over the world for their research.

1. Structured Direct Questionnaire
2. Structured Indirect Questionnaire
3. Unstructured Direct Questionnaire
4. Unstructured Indirect Questionnaire

1. Structured Direct Questionnaire

This is the most commonly used type of questionnaire that is used in social science and management research .Here the questions are direct. This type of questionnaire is generally used when some personality characteristic is attached. Data collected by means of this type of questionnaire have the advantage of being relatively easy to record, tabulate and analyse.

2. Structured Indirect Questionnaire

In the process of research there is the possibility that the researcher often comes across such respondents who do not like to answer direct questions .In this process the researcher motivate them and tends to ask the pre-decided questions indirectly. In this type, the questionnaires are going to be structured but are collected indirectly.

3. Unstructured Direct Questionnaire

In this type of questionnaire the researcher frames general questions based on the purpose of research. The researcher has complete freedom of arranging the questions in any sequential order in the questionnaire. The question may be asked in any order as per the researcher's direction.

4. Unstructured Indirect Questionnaire

In this type of questionnaire no formal method is followed to get the desired answer from the respondents. The patterns of the questions are also no direct. In this case of questionnaire collection complete freedom is allowed to the researcher to put any of the question in any order. The only condition is that the researcher should keep on questioning on the purpose of the study without any diversification from the objective. This method is rarely used in practical life and there is every possibility that the conversation may turn out to be a mere causal link.

For designing the questionnaire, care should be taken keeping in view the does and does not.

- Questions should be simple and easy to understand.
- Questions should be framed keeping in view the objectives and purpose of study.
- Questions of confidential nature should be avoided.
- Number of questions should be restricted.
- Sufficient space should be provided for giving suggestions etc.

After preparing the questionnaire it should be pre-tested by getting the questionnaire filled by some representative users from the population under study. Final form of questionnaire can be designed on the basis of the results from this questionnaire. The questionnaire should be accompanied by covering letter stating the objectives of the study. Assurance should be given to the respondents that information provided should be kept confidential.

Advantages of Questionnaire Method

Some of the advantages of questionnaire method are :

Majority of the investigators follow the questionnaire methods because of the following reasons:

1. It is a simple and convenient method of data collection.
2. This method is useful especially in case the population is large and scattered geographically.
3. Less expensive and quick.
4. Relatively flexible and can be used to reach a large number of people.
5. Easy to prepare and distribute.
6. Questionnaire method is most convenient and inexpensive way to get information from a large and representative group of people.
7. Questionnaire is familiar for all the user. The questionnaire can also be completed at the respondents' own pace, and the respondents can, if so desired, look through the whole questionnaire before committing themselves to anything.
8. The responses are gathered in a standardized way, so questionnaires are more objective, certainly more so than interviews.
9. It is relatively quick to collect information using a questionnaire.
10. Information can be collected from large groups. If the questionnaire is delivered to the respondent in the class, the result will be batter.
11. Easy tabulation of answer and distribute in questionnaire method.
12. The anonymity of the respondent is safeguard.

Disadvantages of Questionnaire Method

1. One major disadvantage of written questionnaires is the possibility of low response rates.
2. Another disadvantage of questionnaires is the inability to probe responses.
3. Respondents may answer superficially if the questionnaire takes a long time to complete. The common mistake of asking too many questions.
4. Questionnaires like many evaluation methods occur after the event, so participants may forget important issues.
5. Questionnaires are standardized so it is not possible to explain any points in the questions that participants might misinterpret take a long time to process and analyses.
6. Respondent may not be willing to answer the questions.
7. People may read differently into each question and therefore reply based on their own interpretation of the question –i.e. what is a 'good' to someone may be 'poor' to someone else, therefore there is a level of subjectivity that is not acknowledged.
8. It is a one-way communication that generally does not allow respondents to clarify answers.
9. Inappropriate questions, incorrect ordering of questions, incorrect scaling, or bad questionnaire format can make the survey valueless.
10. It is generally low level of response. On an average approximately 55 % of mailed questionnaires will return. It is difficult to get adequate response. This may affect the findings of the study.
11. Some questions may lead to ambiguous answers.
12. Sometimes user may not able to answer the questions due to poorly phrased questions.

13. The information provided by the respondents may not be correct, it is difficult to verify.

Despite of the above disadvantages of questionnaire method this method is still very popular method of data collection.

SPECIMEN QUESTIONNAIRES

Some of the Sample questionnaires are given below:

I. QUESTIONNAIRE

Topic : *"Use of E-resources and Services by Students and Faculty Members in Selected Libraries of Management Institutions in Delhi and NCR"*

The Questionnaire is designed to seek information about different aspects of electronic resources in your library and your viewpoint regarding these attributes of development. The information received through the Questionnaire shall be kept confidential and shall be used for the research work only.

PERSONEL DATA

1. Name ....
2. Gender : Male ☐ Female ☐
3. Are You Student ☐ Faculty Member ☐
4. Age Group (Please tick mark the appropriate box)

   18-22 ☐ 23-27 ☐ 28-32 ☐

   33-37 ☐ 38-42 ☐ 43-47 ☐

   48-Above ☐
5. Name of Institution : ....
6. E- Mail Address : ....
7. If You are Student, Please indicate your Course of Study ?

   BBA ☐ MBA ☐ PGDIM ☐
8. If you are Faculty, Please indicate your academic rank

   Assistant Prof. ☐ Associate Prof. ☐ Professor ☐

   Any other please specify ....
9. Academic Qualifications : ....
10. Professional Qualifications : ....

11. Experience : ....

....

12. Which is your field /area of Specialization / Research, Please specify ....

....

USE OF E-RESOURCES

13. Which form of Library resources you generally use for getting information?

Print ☐ Electronic ☐ Both ☐

14. Do You use Electronic -Resources ?

Yes ☐ No ☐

If no Please state the reason of dissatisfaction on available e-resources. Please tick mark (✓)

* Lack of access to computers ☐
* Lack of searching skill ☐
* Not aware of ☐
* Poor connectivity ☐
* Infrastructure is not proper ☐
* E-resources are not as per need ☐
* Library time is not suitable ☐
* Library staff are not co-operative ☐

Any other reason please Specify ....

....

15. Ease of access of e-resources

Yes ☐ No ☐

16. From which place do you mostly access required information/ electronic resources?

Computer center	☐	Library	☐
Home	☐	On-Campus Location	☐
Off-campus location	☐	Hostel	☐
Department	☐	Cyber cafe	☐
Search engines	☐	At Other Place	☐

FREQUENCY OF USING E-RESOURCES

17. Please tick mark (✓)indicating your awareness, frequency of use and also rank the following e-resources in the order of used for your academic work (most used resources be ranked 1 and next 2 and so on)

S. No.	*Name of E-Resources*	*Awareness*		*Use of E-Resources*			*Rank*
		Yes	*No*	*Freq-uently*	*Some time*	*Never*	*(Pref-erence)*
1.	Internet website						
2.	E-Journals (Back Volumes)						
3.	E-Journals (current)						
4.	E-Books						
5.	E-Data Archives						
6.	E-Manuscripts						
7.	E-Maps						
8.	E-Thesis/ Dissertations						
9.	E-Magazines						
10.	WWW						
11.	E-Newspaper						
12.	E-Mail						
13.	E-Research Reports						
14.	CD-ROM /DVD –ROM						
15.	Indexes /abstract						
16.	Online Database						
17.	Online Public Access catalogue						
18.	Reference sources (in electronic form)						
19.	Statistical Sources						
20.	Sound Recordings						
21.	Video cassettes						
22.	Search engines						
23.	E-articles						
24.	Journal articles (full text)						
25.	Journal articles (abstract)						

18. How often do you use e-resources providing by your library?

Daily	☐	Once in a week	☐
2 times a week	☐	Once in a fortnight	☐
Once in a month	☐	Occasionally	☐

TIME SPENT IN THE USE OF E-RESOURCES

19. On an average, how many hours you spend in a week to use the e-resources ? Please tick mark (✓)

* 0 to 1 hours/week ☐
* 2 to 4 hours/week ☐
* 5 to 6 hours/week ☐
* 7 to 9 hours/week ☐
* 10 to 20 hours/week ☐
* Over 20hours/week ☐

REASONS FOR USING E-RESOURCE

20. Why do you prefer to use E-Resources? Please tick mark (✓)

Less time in searching (Time saving) ☐

Availability of Journals much before the print copy ☐

Simultaneous usages ☐

Easy accessibility ☐

Downloading Facility ☐

Author can be contacted Directly through e-mail ☐

Archival facility ☐

Easy to use ☐

More informative ☐

More useful ☐

Less expensive ☐

Any Other, Please specify ....

PURPOSE OF USE OF E-RESOURCES

21. For what purpose you are using e-resources?

S. No	*Purpose*	*Using*		*Rank order of priority*
		Yes	*No*	
1.	For doing Homework			
2.	For writing projects			
3.	For preparing notes			
4.	To update the subject knowledge			
5.	To update the general knowledge			
6.	To gain current and general information			
7.	For Assignment work			
8.	To support academic work			
9.	For doing Research work			
10.	For Seminar/ workshop presentation			
11.	For writing books			
12.	For publishing article			
13.	For preparing Lectures			
14.	For finding relevant Information in the area of specialization			
15.	For supporting academic work			
16	For Discussion			
17.	For teaching Purpose			
18.	To read newspaper/ magazines (online)			
19.	For Any Other purpose, please specify			

22. Requirement for e-resources for study, teaching and research. Please indicate the requirement :

Requirement	*For study*	*Teaching*	*Research*
Most required Required Less Required Not required			

23. From where do you Learn about e-resources? Please tick mark (✓)

- Library Bulletins ☐
- Library/ Institute Web Pages ☐
- Personally from library staff ☐
- Library Training Sessions ☐
- From friends/colleagues ☐
- E-mail ☐
- Institute Newsletter ☐
- Library Notice /circular ☐
- From Instruction /workshops /seminars ☐
- Course offered by the Institute ☐
- Guidance from the library ☐
- External Courses (courses offered by other Institution) ☐
- Guidance from computer staff ☐
- Office Circular ☐
- Other, Please specify ☐

USE OF INTERNET

24. Do you use/browse Internet?

Yes ☐ No ☐

25. Have you ever visited library website?

Yes ☐ No ☐

26. There are several electronic journals/portals that list electronic journals available freely/free access. Are you aware of such electronic journal/portals?

Yes ☐ No ☐

If yes please name a few

1.

2.

27. Whenever you use internet/website /electronic resources you prefer to :

- Download the information and copy to CD / floppy ☐
- Takes print out ☐
- Only reading ☐
- Any other Please specify ....

28. How do you rate the quality of information you acquire from internet on World Wide Web (WWW)?

Poor ☐ Good ☐ High Quality ☐

29. How much it is important to use the internet for getting information related to you subject / profession?

Less important ☐ More Important ☐

Most Important ☐ Not at all ☐

30. Purpose for using/browsing internet : Please tick mark (✓)

I mostly use internet for:

- Email /Chatting ☐
- Finding Relevant Information ☐
- Career development ☐
- Entertainment ☐
- Study /Research work ☐
- Read Newspaper/magazine (online) ☐
- Search /find article and information ☐
- Chat online with friends ☐
- Any other please specify ....

31. How often do you use Internet ?

- Daily ☐
- Once in a week ☐
- Once in a month ☐
- Occasionally ☐
- As and when required ☐

TRAINING OF USE OF E-RESOURCES AND SERVICES

32. Do you need training on the access of e-resources

    Yes ☐ No ☐

    If yes what mode of training do you need in connection with the effective use of e-resources. Please tick mark (✓)

    - Lecture ☐
    - workshops/seminars ☐
    - Online tutorials ☐
    - Guidance from library staff/Librarian ☐
    - Demonstration ☐
    - Guidance from computer staff ☐

    Any other please specify ....

Guidance from computer staff

- Through short term courses/ training offered by your institution. ☐
- Through short term courses/training offered by other institution/departments ☐
- Any other, Please specify ....

33. Is your library providing adequate training on how to use electronic resources?

    Yes ☐ No ☐

34. Do you feel training is important to make maximum use of library Electronic resources and services?

    Yes ☐ No ☐

35. Do you feel computer literacy is important to use electronic resources?

    Yes ☐ No ☐

36. Do you feel training can improved your ability to access and use E-Resources ?

    Yes –a lot ☐ Yes –a little ☐

    Not at all ☐

IMPACT OF E-RESOURCES / SERVICES ON YOUR ACADEMIC WORK

37. If trained how has it impact on your Academic work : Please tick mark (✓)

Access to current and up- to -date information ☐

Easier access ☐

Faster access of information ☐

Access to wider range of information ☐

Improvement in information access & retrieval ☐

Improved referencing skills ☐

Increased quality in research output ☐

Save the time ☐

Get right information at right time ☐

Any other please specify

ASSISTANCE FROM LIBRARY STAFF

38. If you are getting any assistance from library staff in the use of e-resource/ services

Yes ☐ No ☐

If Yes than what type of assistance do you get from the library staff?

- Assistance in usage of e-resources ☐
- Assistance in locating the e-resources ☐
- Assistance in downloading the e-resources ☐
- Any other assistance , please specify ☐

BARRIERS /PROBLEMS FACED WHILE USE OF E-RESOURCES

39. Which of the following Barrier/Problems do you face in context with the use of e- resources.

S. No	*Barriers/Problems*	*Yes*	*No*
1.	The material is difficult to use		
2.	Difficulty to read from the screen		
3.	Technical Problems		
4.	Host website is slow		
5.	Facility for Copying is not Sufficient		
6.	Searching Information is Complicated		
7.	Library staff are unwilling for service/help		
8.	Incomplete information materials		
9.	Do not know how to use the catalogue		
10.	Lack of IT knowledge in using the Library e-resource/ services		
11.	Information is too vast		
12.	Lack of Training facilities		
13.	Time consuming		
14.	Too much information is retrieved		
15.	Limited access to computer		
16.	Lack of information on electronic resources		
17.	Cannot find what to look for		
18.	Not easy to use		
19.	E-resources are not as per need		
20.	Library time is not suitable		
21.	Searching instruction is complicated		
22.	Any other problem, please specify		

LIBRARY SERVICES

40. Access of online database services please tick (✓) mark

    1. Access Yourself Yes/No
    2. Through staff Yes/No
    3. Through Friends Yes/No
    4. Others Yes/No

41. Are You satisfied with existing IT infrastructure ?

    Yes ☐ No ☐

42. Are You Satisfied with exiting Library Services : Please tick mark (✓)

    Very Satisfied ☐ Satisfied ☐

    Partial Satisfied ☐ Not Satisfied ☐

43. Please name some databases useful to your work ?

    ....

44. Which of the following services provided by your library have you used for your academic work ?

S. No.	*Services*	*Use*		
		Frequently	*Sometime*	*Never*
1.	E-mail			
2.	online Enquiry			
3.	Chat based Reference			
4.	Virtual Reference			
5.	E-book directory			
6.	Inter-Library Loan			
7.	Xerox / Printing Service			
8.	CAS/SDI service			
9.	Bulletin Board Service			
10.	File Transfer Protocol (FTP)			
11.	Remote Login (TELNET)			
12.	Browsing the World Wide Web			
13.	Automated Web Search (Search Engines)			
14.	Audio and video Communication			
15.	Internet Service			
16.	Online searching and retrieval service			
17.	CD-ROM database Services			
18.	Online Public Access catalogue /Web OPAC			
19.	Online download service			
20.	Indexing /Abstracting service			
21.	Reference Service			
22.	Database search/ browsing service			
23.	Display Board Services			
24	Any Other Please specify :-			

Any Suggestions would you like to give for the improvement and effective use of e-resources services in your institution library?

....

....

Thanks for giving your precious time in completing this Questionnaire

2. TOPIC: INFORMATION NEEDS AND PATTERNS OF INFORMATION SEEKING BY JOURNALISTS

QUESIONNAIRE

PART 1

Personal Data

1. Name ....

2. Name of Institution/Origination in which you are working. .

....

3. Designation /Status ....

4. Age Group

1. Under 30 Years	☐	2. 31 to 35 Years	☐
3. 36 to 40 Years	☐	4. 41 to 45 Years	☐
5. 46 to 50 Years	☐	6. 51 to 55 Years	☐
7. 56 to 70 Years	☐	8. Over 60 Years	☐

5. Gender Male ☐ Female ☐

6. Academic Qualification

(Please tick mark (✓) the appropriate place)

1. Undergraduate .... 2. Graduate ....

3.Postgraduate .... 4. M.Phil./Ph.D. ....

7. Professional Qualification, please specify ....

8. Years of Experience

1. As a journalist ....

2. Prior to being a journalist ....

9. Specific area of journalist

10. Name(s) of professional/learned association (s), of which you are a member ....

....

11. Whether writing for

1. Newspaper ....
2. Journal ....
3. News Magazine ....
4. Any other, Please specify ....

12. Published Work :

1. No of items (articles, editorials ,news items etc. published
....
2. No. of other publication(s), please specify ....
....

PART II : LIBRARY USED

13. Give names of libraries/information centers/ documentations centers used by you, please tick mark (✓) the appropriate ones.

S.N.	*Libraries*	*Used*
1.	Your own institutional library	
2.	Your own personal library collection	
3.	American Center library, New Delhi	
4.	Parliament library, New Delhi	
5.	British Council Library, New Delhi	
6.	Any other library, please specify	

14. Frequency of visit to the Library used by you please tick mark the appropriate ones. (✓)

1. Daily ....
2. 2 times a week..
3. Once in a week ....
4. Once in a fortnight ....
5. Once in a month..
6. Occasionally ....
7. Never ....

15. Time Spent in The Library

How much time do you generally spend in the library each time you visit it ?

(Please tick mark (✓) at appropriate box).

1. Less than 15 minutes ( )
2. 15-30 minutes ( )
3. 30 minutes to 1 hour ( )
4. 1 to 2 hours ( )

16. Purpose of visit to The library

S.N.	*Purpose*	*Rank (order of priority)*
1.	Verification of facts	
2.	Background information	
3.	Supplement information	
4.	Information for preparing specific article	
5	General information	
6.	Reading of books	
7.	Browsing new periodicals	
8.	Locating photograph	
9.	Any other, please specify	

Please indicate the purpose of visit to the library .Mark as 1 to 10 indicating order of priority

17. Information Needs

What is your specific area of information needs ? Marks 1 to 12 indicating order of priority 1 stands for first priority ,2 stands for second priority etc.

S.N.	*Area*	*Rank (Order of Priority)*
1.	Political activities	
2.	Govt. affairs	
3.	Social activities	
4.	Economic activities/development	
5.	Religious activities	
6.	Hobbies and recreational activities	
7.	Writing on sports	
8.	Educational activities	
9.	Health	
10.	Personalities	
11.	Business/finance	
12.	Any other, Please specific	

18. Purpose of Information Search

Indicate the purpose for which the information obtained from the library is used .Mark as 1 to 12 indicating order of priority .1 stands for first priority 2 stands for second priority etc.

S.N.	*Purpose*	*Rank (Order of Priority)*
1.	Writing a feature article	
2.	Writing a news item	
3.	Writing an article	
4.	Writing a personality profile	
5.	Writing a column	
6.	Writing an editorial	
7.	Editing a news item	
8.	Writing stories	
9.	General knowledge	
10.	Writing on sports	
11.	Any other, Please specify	

19. Information Sources

Please tick mark the following sources of information indicating purpose and frequency of use.

Sources	*Purpose of use of Information*			*Frequency of Use*		
	For specific in formation	*For keeping update*	*For background information*	*frequ- ently*	*Some- times*	*Never*
1	*2*	*3*	*4*	*5*	*6*	*7*
Formal sources						
Journals/ Periodicals						
Books other than reference						
News magazines						
Current issues of newspapers						

Sources	*Purpose of use of Information*			*Frequency of Use*		
	For specific in formation	*For keeping update*	*For background information*	*frequ- ently*	*Some- times*	*Never*
1	*2*	*3*	*4*	*5*	*6*	*7*
Back issues of newspapers						
Newspaper clipping files						
Book reviews						
Photographs						
Newspapers in microforms						
Encyclopedias						
Dictionaries						
Handbooks						
Indexes						
Maps/atlases						
Informal Sources						
TV/Radio						
Parliamentary databases						
Conferences						
Conversation with professional colleagues						
Interview with political leaders						
Press agency messages						
Information from other media houses						
Eye witness accounts						
Trade fairs						
Any other, Please specificy						

Are the reference books in the library used by you adequate ? Please tick mark (✓)

20. If not adequate, what reference books would you suggest for the library, give below the titles :

1. .... 2. ....

3. .... 4. ....

5. .... 6. ....

21. Do you find the press clipping in the library used by you useful for your work ? Please tick mark (✓) Yes/No

22. How often do you use the files of press clippings in the library used by you ?

1. Daily ....
2. 2 times a week ....
3. Once in a week ....
4. Once in a fortnight ....
5. Once in a month ....
6. Occasionally ....
7. Never ....

USE OF JOURNAL /NEWSPAPERS/MAGAZINES

23. Which journals including newspapers and magazines do you scan regularly for your work ? Please enlist them in order of priority.

Title of periodicals/ Newspapers / News magazine	*Kind of Access*					
	Indian	*Foreign*	*Personal copy by subs-cription*	*Personal copy through member-ship*	*From a collea-gue*	*From the library of my institution*
1.						
2.						
3.						
4.						
5.						
6.						
7.						
8						
9.						
10.						

24. Library Services

The following are some of the services provided by the library to its readers. Please indicate (i) whether or not you are aware of these and (ii) the degree of use for your work.

Services	*Awareness*		*Usage*		
	Yes	*No*	*Frequently*	*Sometime*	*Never*
Reference service					
Referral service					
Xerox service					
Newspaper clipping					
Microfilming service					
Translation service					
Computerized database service					
Any other, please specify					

25. Assistance Provided by the Library staff

What do you think about the assistance provided by the library staff ? Please indicate the frequency of assistance please tick mark (✓) at the appropriate place.

Assistance	*Frequency of Assistance*		
	Frequently	*Sometime*	*Never*
Checking facts			
Helping in locating reference material			
Conducting database search			
Providing background information			
Helping in identifying the best of library material			
Identifying and selecting photographs			
Helping in locating clippings			
Providing photocopying facilities			
Any other assistance, please specify			

RESPONSE TIME

26. Whether you disclose your deadline to your library staff to meet required information? Please tick mark (✓) Yes/No

1. Less than 15 minutes ....
2. 15 to 30 minutes ....
3. 30 to 1 hour ....
4. More than 1- hour ....

27. On an average per week how many queries do you refer to the library staff ?

....

28. Of these, how many are answered on an average ? ....

....

29. Information Barriers

What Are the difficulties you usually face in seeking required information ? Please tick mark (✓) against the appropriate column.

Kind of Difficulty	*Level of Difficulty*			
	No difficulty	*Very little difficulty*	*Considerable difficulty*	*Extreme difficulty*
Lack of time to look for or read information				
Inadequate library resources				
Information scattered in many sources				
Library staff is not qualified enough to locate information				
Information not readily available				
Inadequate library services				
Lack of Xerox				

Kind of Difficulty	*Level of Difficulty*			
	No difficulty	*Very little difficulty*	*Considerable difficulty*	*Extreme difficulty*
facilities				
Not aware of the availability of library material				
The library materials are disorganized				
Lack of finance				
Bureaucracy				
Language				
Professional risks while carrying out officials duties				
Any other difficulty please specify				

30. Library Collection

Do you find collection in your field of interest in libraries you use adequate enough to meet your demands ? Please tick mark (✓) in the appropriate column.

Name of the Library	*Excellent*	*Adequacy of Collection*			
		Very Adequate	*Adequate*	*Inadequate*	*Poor*
Your institutional Library					
Other libraries					

PART III : SUGGESTIONS

What are the suggestions you would like to make for the improvement of the various services of the libraries used by you ? List these in the order of your priority along with the name of the concerned library. Please also comment on problems faced by you in seeking information.

Name of the library	*Suggestions*	*Comments*

PILOT STUDY AND PRE TESTING

Meaning : A pilot study is a small scale replica of the main study. It is the rehearsal of the main study. It covers the outline of the entire process of research.

Why we need pilot study?

It is difficult to plan a major study or project without adequate knowledge of subject matter, the population is to cover, their level of knowledge and understanding etc. In order to get such a pre knowledge of subject matter of an extensive study a preliminary investigation is conducted. This is called pilot study.

Functions of pilot study

Some of the functions are:

1. It provides a better knowledge of the problem under study.
2. It assists in discovering the nature of relationship

between variables and in formulating hypothesis.

3. A pilot study shows whether the available sampling frame from which sampling is to be drawn is adequate, complete, accurate, up to date etc.
4. It shows the adequacy of the tool for data collection.
5. It also help in discovering mechanical problems relating to interviews/mailing.
6. It helps the researcher to develop an appropriate plan of analysis.
7. It helps the researcher to identify field problems to be encountered and suggested remedial approach.

Pre-testing

Pre testing is a trial test of a specific aspect of the study such as method of data collection or data collection instruments-interview schedule, mailed questionnaire etc.

Need for pre testing

An instrument of data collection is designed with reference to the data requirements of the study. Pre testing means trial administration of the instrument to a sample of respondent before finalizing it.

Pre testing has several purposes.

Some of these are:

1. To test whether the contents of the instrument is relevant and adequate
2. To test whether wording of the question is clear and understandable to the respondent.
3. To test the other qualitative aspects of the instrument like question structure and question sequence.

Pre testing procedure

The first testing of a draft instrument can be done

among one's colleagues in order to find out the short comings. After that it should be revised and tested in the field. The instrument may be administered to 15 to 20 sample respondents drawn from the universe relating to planned survey. The pre test responses should be carefully examined and analyzed in order to identify the weaknesses of the instrument. Necessary corrections, deletions, additions and changes in question wording and sequences should be made to eliminate the imperfections discovered.

2. INTERVIEW METHOD

Kahn and Cannell (1957) describe interviewing as "a conversation" with a purpose. The participant's views are valuable and useful. Interview method is also very popular and prominent method of data collection. It is two way systematic conversations between an investigator and the informant. In this method there is verbal interaction between the researcher and the respondent. Interview method is a direct method of collection of data. Interviewing requires face to face contact or contact over telephone. Through this method we know the views and ideas of other persons. It is a method of social integration. Interview can be conducted through personnel, telephone etc. It is a process of personal interaction between the researcher and the respondents. It can be conducted face to face or through telephone or through e-mail, online chat etc. It may be through personnel interview and , if possible through telephone interviews.

This method requires a person known as interviewer asking questions generally face to face contact to other person.

Personnel Interview

The interview can be conducted in two ways. It can be done by pre-designing questionnaire or it can be done by some sort of verbal dialogue between the respondent and the investigator. There is no fixed order of questions. The investigator may not use the pre-designed questionnaire. When person-to-person interaction between two or more individuals with a specific purpose is called interview

According to Kumar[47] "interviewing is a process of personal interaction between a researcher and a respondent". In case the personal interaction is used , then the technique available for questioning is an interview .The face-to-face conversation between the researcher (or his agent) (who hopefully knows what he wants from the respondent) and the respondent (who has the desired information in his mind or possession) is called an interview.

According to Kvale,[49] the qualitative research interview seeks to describe and the meanings of central themes in the life world of the subjects. The main task in interviewing is to understand the meaning of what the interviewees say.

Conduct of Interview will take place after the questionnaire would be filled up by the respondent .In a mail questionnaire there is hardly any possibility of achieving complete response from different categories of a sample .Thus ,interview produces better response rate than a questionnaire as it is more personal than a questionnaire method.

An interview was conducted with faculty members and students .The interview method was used mainly to gain insight into certain aspects not covered in the questionnaire. An interview is called personal when the Interviewer asks the questions face-to-face with the Interviewee. In interview, there is always a possibility to achieve an excellent communication between a respondent and a researcher. A researcher can personally explain and clarify the questions If needed, a respondent can amplify or qualify his answer.

As the questionnaire became too lengthy, therefore, some questions couldn't be incorporated. It was thought that these questions could be handled in the interviews. Therefore, the interview were undertaken to supplement the data gathered through the questionnaire, both qualitatively and quantitatively. The questions for the interviews were carefully chosen, covering some important areas relating to the topic. The detailed interview with some of the experienced and good users of the library was carried out to gather supportive data for the data collected through questionnaire.

Objectives of Interview

Some of the objectives of interview are :

1. To collect information for research work
2. To assess human behavior
3. To explore the unknown forces acting behind a problem.
4. To formulate hypothesis.
5. To help project evaluation
6. To supplement the data collected through the questionnaire.

IMPORTANCE OF INTERVIEW

Interviewing may be used either as main method or as a supplementary one. Interviewing is the only method of gathering information from illiterate or less educated respondents. It is useful for collecting a wide range of data from factual demographic data to highly personnel and intimate information relating to a person's opinion, attitudes, etc. Where area covered for the survey is compact, or when a sufficient number of qualified interviewers are available, personal interview is feasible.

Interview is often superior to other data collecting methods. People are usually more willing to talk than write. It permits the investigator to seek clarification for those questions, that one reason or other, respondent do not want to answer.

Advantages of Interviewing

Some of the advantages of interview are:

1. If the respondent lacks reading skills to answer a questionnaire in it, there is always a possibility to achieve an excellent communication between respondent and a researcher.
2. Interviewer can obtain supplementary information used to appraise user verbal fluency.
3. The interview may be modified as needed to gather important information.
4. The Interviewer can probe deeper into a response given by an interviewee.
5. Interview produces better response rate than a questionnaire.
6. Interview is a very effective means to reveal the truth.
7. One of the major advantages of interview is flexibility.
8. To find the fact, cross checking questions can be included in an interview.
9. Interview is a direct method for collecting data in which personal barriers are eliminated and as a result findings of an interview are reliable.
10. This method is simple and easy to perform.
11. Numbers of questions can be clarified by dialogue with the respondent.
12. It is possible to achieve complete response from the respondents. A researcher can personally explain and clarify the questions. It is difficult to obtain complete results in case mail questionnaire.
13. This method provide better response rate than other methods.

14. Researcher has greater control over interview. He has also control over the sequence in which can be asked questions
15. Personnel information can be obtained easily in this method.
16. The interviewer can gather other supplemental information.

Disadvantages of Interviewing

Some of the disadvantages of interviewing are :

1. The interviewer can affect the data if he/she is not consistent.
2. Always there is a possibility that interview process can be influenced by the biases of the interviewer.
3. Preparation for the interview, setting up, interviewing, transcribing, analyzing, feedback, etc.
4. Interview and interpretation of the responses required much time which make the interview method time consuming.
5. Inefficiency of an interviewer can lead to misleading results.
6. Subjective evaluations are made.
7. Not as reliable as tests.
8. Supervision is required.
9. This method is not very suitable where population is large and geographical dispersed.
10. This method is expensive and time consuming.
11. Interview may be biased due to age, religion, caste, etc.
12. For conducting interview proper training is required.
13. Sometimes information collected from interview is difficult to analyses.
14. There is a possibility of bias of interviewer as well of respondent.

TYPES OF INTERVIEWING

The interview can be classified into :

1. Structured direct interview and
2. Unstructured interview.

1. Sructured Direct interview : This method of collecting information through personnel interview, usually carried out in structured way. This interview is known as structured interview. Such interview involve the use of a set of predetermined questions .This is an interview made with a detail standardized schedule .The same questions are put to all the respondents and in the same order. This type of interview is used for large scale formalized survey.

Advantages

Some of the advantages are:

1. The data from one interview to the next are easily comparable.
2. Recording and coding data do not pose any problem, and greater precision is achieved.
3. Attantion is not diverted irrelevant and time consuming conversation.

Limitations

Some of the limitations are :

1. It tends to lose the spontaneity of natural conversation.
2. The scope for exploration is limited.

2. Unstructured interview or non directive interview

The unstructured interviews are characterized by flexibility of approach to questioning. The interview encourages the respondent to talk freely about a given topic with minimum of guidance. In this type of interview, a detail pre planned schedule is not used. Only a broad interview guide is used. Questions are not standardized and not in a order in a particular way. Unstructured questionnaire do not follow a system of pre determined questions. In non structured interviews, the interview is not allowed much freedom to ask. Unstructured interviews is the main technique of collecting information in case of exploratory or formularize research studies. But in case of descriptive studies we often use the technique of structured interview because it is more economical and require lesser skills.

This interview is more useful in case studies rather than in surveys. It is particularly useful in exploratory research where the line of investigation are not clearly defined. It is also not useful for gathering information on sanative topics such as social discrimination, drug edition etc.

Advantages

1. It is less prone to interviewers' bias.
2. It provides greater opportunity to explore the problem in an unrestricted manner.

Limitations

1. One of the major limitation is that the data obtained from the interview is not comparable to the data from the next. Hence , it is not suitable for surveys.
2. Time may be wasted in unproductive conversations
3. As there is no particular order or sequence in the interview, the classification of responses and coding may require more time.
4. This type of interview greater skill is required as compared to formal survey interview.

Interviewing Process

The interviewing process consists of following stages:

1. Preperation
2. Introduction

3. Developping report
4. Carrying the interview forward
5. Recording the interview
6. Closing the interview

1. Preparation : The interview require some pre planning. He should have list of names, addresses of respondents in order to save the time. The interviewer should keep the copy of the interview schedule ready for use.

2. Introduction : The investigator is stranger to the respondent. He should be properly introduced to each of the respondent. When making the study of the organization or institution, the head of the organization should be approached first and his cooperation before contacting the staff.

After getting himself introduced to the respondent in the most appropriate manner, the interviewer can follow the sequence of procedure as under :

- With smile greet the respondent
- Identify the respondent by name
- Mention the name of the organization conducting the research.
- Assure the confidential nature of the interview.
- Explain the usefulness of the study.

3. Developing Rapport : Before starting the research interview, the interviewer should established a friendly relationship with the respondent. This is described as "rapport". It means establishing a relationship of confidence and understanding between the interviewer and the respondent. Start the conversation with general topic of interest such as weather, current news, sports etc. Such initial conversation may create a friendly relationship and mutual understanding of one another.

4. Carrying the interview forward : After establishing rapport, the technical task of asking questions from the interview schedule starts. This task requires skills and ability to listen with understanding.

In carrying this task , the following guidelines should be followed:

1. Starts the interview with informal and natural conventional style.
2. Ask all the questions in the same order as they appear on the schedule without any change.
3. If questions are not understood, repeat it slowly.
4. Neither argue nor dispute.
5. Listen quietly with undivided attention.
6. Should not reveal your own opinion or reaction.
7. When there is pause in the flow of information, do not hurry the interview.
8. At the time of interview "run dry" and need re-stimulation. Then use such expression as "that's interesting" or "I see" "can you tell me more about this" etc.

5. Recording the interview : It is important to record responses as they take place. If not recorded properly, a good deal of information may be lost. With the pre coded structured questions, the interviewer task is easy. He has to simplify ring the appropriate code or tick the appropriate box, as the case may be. He should not make mistakes by ringing or ticking a wrong item.

6. Closing the interview : After the interview is over, take leave off the respondent, thanking him with a friendly smile.

7. Editing : At the close of the interview, the interviewer must edit the schedule to check that he has asked all the questions and recorded all the questions and there is no inconsistency between answers.

Interview Problems

In interview method, the researcher generally face two main problems:

1. Inadequate and non response
2. Interviewer bias

Inadequate response : It may be in the following form:

1. The respondent may give relevant but incomplete answer (partial response).
2. The respondent may remains silent or refuse to give answers the question (non response).
3. When the respondent's answer is not relevant to the question asked (irrelevant response).

One possible approach to deal with inadequate response is to allow a brief pause. Another way to encourage the respondent is to use such expressions as " I see" " is it" or to put a supplementary question "what do you mean".

The problem of inaccurate response is common in economic surveys. The respondent have difficulty in furnishing accurate information on sensitive matters such as income, expenditure, saving, investment etc. It is difficult to deal with this problem.

Interviewers bias : The interviewer is an important cause of response bias. The interviewer can influence the responses by incorporating suggestions etc. He may resort to cheating by 'cooking up' data without actually interviewing. As interviewers are human beings, such biasing factor can never be overcome completely, but their effects can be reduced by careful selection and training of interviewers, proper motivation, standardization of interview procedures.

Non Response : Non response refers to failure to obtain responses from some sample respondent. There are many sources of non response; non availability, refusal, inaccessibility.

Non availability : Some respondents may not be available at home at the time of call. It depends upon the nature of the respondent and the time of call. For example employed person may not be available during working hours. The selection of appropriate timing for calls could solve this problem. Evenings and weekends may be favorable interviewing hours for such respondents.

Refusal : Some respondents may refuse to furnish information because they approached at the wrong hour.

Inability : May refers to illness which prevents a response during the entire survey period. This may also arise on account of language barrier.

Inaccessibility : Some respondents may be inaccessible. Some may not be found due to migration and other reasons.

2. Telephone interviewing

Telephone interviewing is a non personnel method of data collection. It may be used as main method or supplementary method. This method involve the conducting interview through telephone itself.

Uses

It may be useful in following situations:

1. When the universe is composed of those persons whose names are listed in telephone directories, e.g. business houses, executives, doctors etc.
2. When the study requires responses to five or six simple questions e.g. television programme survey.
3. When the survey is to be conducted in a very short period of time, provided the units of study are listed in the telephone directory.
4. When the respondents are widely scattered and when there are many call backs to make.

Advantages

It is not a widely used method of data collection but playing important part in industrial survey.

Some of the advantages of this method are:

1. It is more flexible as compared to mailing method.
2. It is cheaper than personnel interview method, the cost per response is low. It does not involve travel time and cost and all calls can be made from the single location.
3. Higher rate of response as compared to mailing method.
4. Clarification is easier.
5. It does not involve field work.

Disadvantages

Some of the disadvantages are:

1. It is limited to persons with listed telephone. The sample will be distorted, if the universe includes persons not on phone.
2. There is limit to the length of the interview. Usually the a call cannot last over five minutes. Only five to six sample questions can be asked. Hence, telephone cannot be used for a longer questionnaire.
3. The type of information to be collected is limited to what can be given in simple, short answer of few words. Hence telephone is not suitable for complex surveys, and is difficult to obtain detail information.
4. If the questions cover personnel matter, most respondents will not cooperate with the interviewer.

Selection and training of interviewers

The quality of data collected depends upon the capabilities of interviewers. Hence, careful selection and proper training of interviewer is essential.

3. OBSERVATION METHOD

The observation method is the most commonly used method of data collection specially studies related to behavioral science. Observation become scientific method of data collection for the researchers. In this method the investigator collect the information by direct observation without asking from the respondent. Information is collected by observing the process at work. For example: In a study relating to user behavior in the library , the investigator instead of asking the name of the journal used by the user, may himself observe the use of journal by the user.

Observation

Meaning : Observation means viewing or seeing. Observation is a fundamental and highly important method in all qualitative inquiry. Systematic noting and recording of events, behaviors, and artifacts (objects) in the social setting chosen for study. Observation may be defined as a systematic viewing of a specific phenomenon in its proper setting for the specific purpose of gathering data for a particular study.

"Observation" is one way to collect primary data. In this method the researcher observes an activity and note down the information /data observing from a close distance. It is a purposeful, systematic and selective way of watching and listening to an interaction or phenomenon as it takes place. Complete and detailed data is collected and recorded through observation or a phenomena or behavior. Observation is a method of data collection in which the situation of interest is watched and the relevant facts, actions and behavior of the users are recorded. Originally, observation method involved the basic technique of simply watching the phenomena until some hunch or insight was gained. "A data collection method in which a Person (usually trained) observes subjects or phenomena and records information about characteristics of the phenomena (Sproull, 1988, p.166)[74]

Krishna Swami[46] defined observation as a systematic viewing of a specific phenomenon in its proper setting for the specific purpose of gathering data for a particular study. Observation means watching carefully. This method is very correctly described as the classic method of scientific enquiry. It helped a great deal in collecting various types of useful clues in the reference process as being displayed at the reference desk. Since Questionnaire was structured with the objective of studying the electronic services, the observation came as a very handy tool. So observation is the best approach to collect required information.

The technique of observation involves the watching and recording of data. This method is also important method of data collection. In this method we study the actual behavior of the user at various service points such as periodical and reference area. We can observe the borrowers' records, observation of recommendation records, observation of reference records etc. There are two types of observations-1.participant and 2. non-participants observation. When the observer participates with group under study, it is called participant observation and when the observer observes the activities of a person from a close distance. It is called non-participant observation. A particular observer makes himself a part of the group and observes them in their natural behavior without allowing the individuals in the group to know that they are being observed. A non-participant observer on the other hand, observes a selected number of users from a close distance and keeps a record of their activities such as type of sources he consulted, time spent in the library etc. Data gathered from the observation finally analyzed.

Observation also plays a major role in formulating and testing hypothesis in social sciences. Individual observation of various information seeking activities taken for collection of data. For example study of use of reference collection by the users, etc. We observe the use of various resources used by them. Observing at information desk in a reference section can clarify the important questions, if users are to be asked to evaluate the reference service.

Reliability of observation increases, if the observations are repeated by observer himself and or the same observations are recorded by a number of persons simultaneously. Validity of the data increases if the setting is kept as natural as possible. It is not influenced by the presence of the observer.

While using this method researcher should keep in mind the following things:

1. What should be observed?
2. How the observation should be recorded?

CHARACTERSTICS OF OBSERVATION

Some of the characteristics are:

1. Observation is purposive and not casual. It is made for specific purpose of noting things relevant to the study.
2. It capture the natural social context in which person's behavior occur.
3. Observation is selective. A researcher does not observe anything and everything, but selects the range of things to be observed on the basis of the nature, scope and objectives of the study.
4. It is both physical and mental activity. The observing eye catches many thing which are slighted but attention is focused on the data that are pertinent to the given study.

TYPES OF OBSERVATION

The observation can be classified into :

1. Structured Observation and Unstructured Observation

2. Participant and Non-participant Observation.

But in terms of mode of observation, it may be classified into 1. Direct observation and 2. Indirect observation.

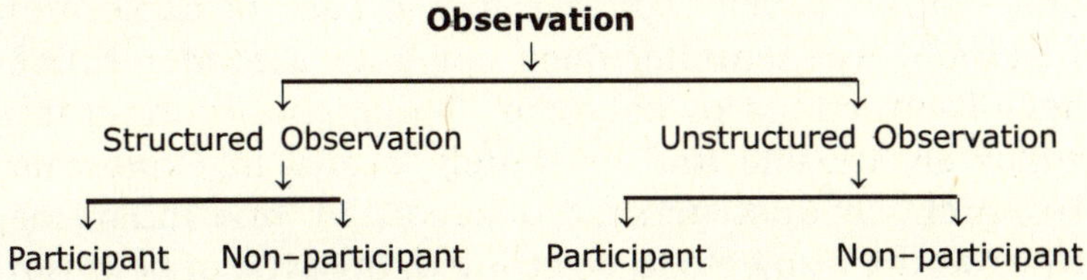

1 (a) Structured Observation

Structured observation works according to a plan and involves specific information of the units that are to be observed and also about the information that is to be recorded. The units to be observed have to be carefully defined. It is often used to provide systematic description or test casual hypotheses .It can be applied in field studies and laboratory type settings, where focus being on certain aspects of behavior.

The operations that are to be observed and the various features that are to be noted or recorded are decided well in advance. Such observations involve the use of especial instruments for the purpose of data collection that are also structured in nature. In this type, the categories of observation have to be developed .It is subjected to high levels of control and differentiation.

Structure observation is considered appropriate in descriptive studies, where as in exploratory study the observational procedure is most likely to be relatively unstructured. The main pitfall of non controlled observation is that of subjective interpretation.

Generally, controlled observation takes place in various experiments that are carried out in a laboratory or under controlled conditions, where as uncontrolled observation is restored to in case of exploratory researches.

1 (b). Unstructured Observation

In unstructured observation, observer has the freedom to note down what he or she feels is correct and relevant to the point of study and also this approach of observation is very suitable in the case of exploratory research. A researcher does not have a predetermined set of categories of behavior. Thus, this technique is relatively flexible and extremely useful in exploratory research. In unstructured observation, one must keep in view, the subjects to be studied, the type of behaviors to be observed, the setting, duration and frequency of the behaviors.

2(a). Participant Observation

In participant observation the investigator become a part of the group or phenomenon. He act as both an observer and a participant. Participation by the observers with the various types of operations of the group under study refers to the participant type of observation. He participates in all the activities and functions of the group and simultaneously observes the behaviors of the group. In participant observation, the degree of the participation is largely affected by the nature of the study and it also depends on the type of the situation and also on its demands.

Merits

Some of the merits of participant observations are:

1. The researcher is enabled to record the natural behavior of the group.
2. The researcher even can gather information which could not easily be obtained if he observe in a distinguished fashion.
3. The researcher can even verify the truth of the statement made by the informants in context of a questionnaire.

4. Data more reliable and free from respondent bias
5. Easier to note the effects of environmental influences on the specific outcome
6. Easier to observe certain groups of individual

Demerits

Some of the demerits are:

1. The observer may lose the objectivity of the extend he participates emotionally; the problem of observation –control is not solved.
2. The participant observer narrow his range of observation.
3. An other limitation of this method is the dual demand made on the observer. Recording on the spot is not possible and it has to be postponed until the observer is alone.
4. Observer must be present
5. Low collecting data
6. Needed to be trained Focus Groups

2(b). Non–Participant Observation

In non-participant observation, the observer, gets detached with the group and does not participate or intervene in their activities. Naturally, there is no emotional involvement on the part of the observer. This method require certain skills in recording observation. Non participant type of observation, no participation of the observer in the activities of the group takes place and also there occurs no relationship between the researcher and the group. In this method the facts are collected in more formal manner. May be as a non-participant observer it is difficult to maintain the quality of information.

3. Controlled and uncontrolled observation

a. Controlled Observation : This involve standardization of observational techniques and excursive of maximum control over extrinsic and intrinsic variables. Controlled observation is carried out either in the laboratory or in the field. It is primarily use for inferring causality and testing casual hypothesis.

b. Uncontrolled observation : This does not involve control over extrinsic and intrinsic variables. It is primarily used for descriptive research .Participant observation is a typical uncontrolled one.

Controlled vs Uncontrolled observation

If the observation takes place in the natural setting, it may be termed as uncontrolled observation, but when observation takes place according to defined pre-arranged plan, involving external procedure, the same is called controlled observation. In non controlled observation, no attempt is made to use precision instruments. The major aim of this type of observation is get a spontaneous picture of persons.

Advantages of Observation Method

The main advantage of this method is that subjective biased is eliminated, if observation is done accurately. The information obtained in this method is related to what is currently happening. This method is independent of the respondents willingness to response.

Some of the advantages of observation method are:

1. Observation method is simple to use.
2. It can be used to verify data by questionnaire or interview method.
3. It produces verifiable observations, thus it has a potentially high degree of reliability.
4. It gives firsthand information.

5. It can be used to study subjects who are not able to communicate verbally properly.
6. Observation is a natural process we do it all the time.
7. A key advantage of observation research is that often the respondent is unaware that they are being observed, allowing their behavior to be observed naturally.
8. This method is very useful method for study the actual behavior of the uses at various points in the library as it occurs.
9. This method is not biased.
10. This method can be useful to verify data obtained by other methods such as interview and questionnaire.
11. Reliable method of data collection.

Disadvantages of Observation method

However, observation method has various limitations also. It is an expensive method. The information provided in this method is very limited.

1. The major problem with observation is the fact that the observer have feeling, aspirations, fears, and biases and any one of these can influence and distort that which is being observed.
2. It may require skilled observer.
3. Validity and reliability may be problematic.
4. Cost is the final disadvantage of the observation method.
5. This method is time consuming and costly as compared to questionnaire method.
6. Duration of activity may be so long, thus difficult to observe. Sometimes the activity is too short such as consultation of catalog, it is difficult to observe.

7. Sometimes it is difficult to quantify the data obtained from this method. Measurement of human behavior is complex.
8. A major limitation of this method is that the observer normally must be at the scene of the event when it takes place. Yet it may not be possible to predict where and when the event will occur e.g. road accident etc.
9. Observation is a slow process , require human observers and /or costly surveillance equipments.
10. Observation can not be used as and when the researcher find it convenient to use it. He has to wait for the event to occur.
11. It is not suitable for studying opinions and attitudes.

OBSERVATION TOOLS AND RECORDING DEVICES

The systematic observation requires the use of observation schedule, diary, and various mechanical recording devices.

1. Scedule : A schedule to be constructed covering items such as definitions of the concept, hypothesis, investigative questions etc. It should be constructed in such a manner as to make it possible to record the necessary information easily and correctly. Enough space should be provided for recording observations for each item. The items should be appear in the order in which the observer would observe them.

Field observation log : This may take the form of a diary or cards. Each item should be recorded under appropriate sub headings. At the time of observation, rough noting may be made and at the end of the day a full log may be made. The card system is flexible and the arrangement of items can be made in desired order.

Mechanical Devices : These may include camera, tape recorder, CCTV, etc. They give permanent record of events.

Suitability and Applications of observation methods

Observation is suitable for a variety of research studies. It may be useful in studying

a. Behavior of human beings and social groups
b. The behavior of other living creatures such as animals etc.
c. Physical characteristics of inanimate things such as factories, stores, residences etc.

It may be use in exploratory research to gain insights that will be subsequently tested as hypothesis. It may be used to collect supplementary data that may interpret or qualifying findings obtained by other methods. Observation may be used as the primary method e.g. anthropological studies of communities, behavioral studies of small group.

3. OTHER METHODS

Indirect Methods

Indirect methods includes the analysis of already existing records such as loan records, reference query request records, etc. An analysis of these records can provide a view of information needs of the user. The analysis of these questions can indicate about their requirements for information. On the basis of this analysis a good reference collection can be developed. This method also includes citation analysis.

Citation Analysis Method

Citation analysis is the technique of secondary analysis also shows the user dependence on libraries and their preference for a particular channel for getting the information. The main objectives of citation analysis are to evaluate and to interpret citations received by articles, authors, institutions and other aggregate of scientific activities. It is also used as a tool for measuring communication links in the sociology of science. (Ravichandra Rao,1983,p.199)[59]

Usefulness

- The bibliographic citations in articles contributed by an author in a journal articles, provides very useful data on the type of documents cited.
- This citation analysis is very useful for determining the acquisition policy of journals, and in weeding out less important ones.
- Citation analysis provides useful data about the non-use of considerable proportion of periodicals in our libraries. It is a matter of great concern because of the heavy cost of periodical subscription. We can review and update the subscription list.
- The citation analysis method is useful for producing a rank list of journal titles which help the library staff to take decision relating to acquisition of important journals. The journal which is most cited can be useful for the library. This will help the library staff to take decision related to acquisition, selection and rejection of source material for developing information products such as indexing and abstracting periodicals. Because these are costly journals, care should be taken while selecting them.
- It is technique for user study. Citations or references provided by authors in their documents become the basis of citation analysis. The document which is more cited by the in a particular journal, supposed to be more useful. Citation analysis also shows the extent of users dependence and their preference for a particular journal for getting information.

Merits

- This method is unbiased method.
- Citation analysis method is popular indirect method that can be used as a technique for user study.

- Citation analysis is important method for producing a rank list of journal titles, which is useful for taking decision relating to acquisition.

Demerits

- Citation analysis can provide only rough idea about the use of documents other sources such as secondary, tertiary and non-documentary sources etc. The authors are not generally cited.
- The possibility of citing reputed author's title. This title may not be really used by the author.

Case Study Method

Case study method is a very popular form of qualitative analysis and it involves the complete and careful observation of social unit. The unit may be person, a family, an institution, a cultural group or even the entire community. The case study give more emphasis on the full analysis of a limited number of events and their interrelations. The case study is intensive investigation of the particular unit under consideration. The case study method is a technique by which individual factor is analyzed in its relationship to any other in the group.

It is a comprehensive study of a social unit be that unit a person, a group, a social institution, community etc.

It is a form of qualitative analysis wherein careful and complete observation of an individual or an institution is done. The study of each and every aspects of the concerning unit in minute details.

Method of systematic gathering of enough information about a person to permit one to understand how he or she functions as unit of society.

The case study is a form of qualitative analysis involving the very careful and complete observation of a person, situation or institution.

Characteristics of case study method

Some of the characteristics of case study method are:

1. Under this method the researcher can take one single social unit or more of such units for his study purpose.
2. Here selected unit is studied in minute details. Case study attempts in depth and detailed study of a unit.
3. In this method we make complete study of the social unit covering all facets.
4. Under this method the approach happens to be qualitative and not quantitative.
5. Under case study method the behavior pattern of the concerning unit is studied directly and not by indirect approach. The case study method deals with both what and why of the subject.

The scope of the case study method

The case study method is widely used systematic field research technique in sociology these days. The anthropologists, historians, novelists, and dramatists have used this method concerning problems pertaining to their areas of interests. Even management experts use case study methods for getting clues to several management problems. We can say that case study method is being used in many disciplines.

Basic Assumptions

In this method, the unit of the study which may be an individual or a social group is studies as a unit.

Advantages of case study Method

The case study method is very old and popular method of collecting data about personnel life of individuals and groups.

Some of the advantages of case study method are:

1. Intensive and deep study of the problem is possible. The case study method is enables one to understand fully the behavior pattern of the concerned unit.

2. Study of the subjective aspects : Through case study a researcher can obtain a real and enlighten record of personnel experience.

3. Comparative study : In this method, all aspects of life of an individual are studied. Through this study the characteristics of one particular group or individual may be differentiated from the characteristics of another.

4. Formulation of valid hypothesis : Once the various cases are extensively studied and analyzed, the researcher can deduce various generalizations, which may be developed into useful hypothesis.

5. Useful in framing questionnaire and schedules : Case study is of great help in framing questionnaire, schedules and other forms.

6. Sampling : Case study is helpful in stratification of the sample. By studying the individual unit the researcher can put them in definite classes or types and thereby facilitate the perfect stratification of the sample.

7. Use of several research method : The researcher can use one or more of several research methods under the case study method depend ending upon the prevalent circumstances.

8. The case study methods has proved beneficial in determining the nature of units to be studied along with the nature of the universe.

Limitations of the case study Method

1. Unrealastic assumption : Case study method is based on several assumptions which may not be very realistic at times as such the usefulness of a case is always subject to doubt.

2. False generalization : Generalization is formulated on the basis of data collected. If the data collected are wrong , the generalization shall be wrong.

3. Difficult to test reliability of validity of the data collected : If the information furnished by the individual or a person is wrong, there is no method on the basis of which researcher can test the reliability of the information.

4. Not possible to apply sampling method : In this method individual is recognized as unit and the entire study is concentrated on that unit. It is necessary that the unit may be representative of the universe. Through the study of a particular unit it is not possible to apply the knowledge to other units.

5. Lack of quantitative study : It is not possible to quantify the feelings, emotions, values etc.

6. Prejudice and bias : people generally suffer from prejudices, tendency to give negative reply due to their own psychological makeup. This makes difficult to obtain the prejudice free data.

Procedure of case study

The procedure include the following:

1. Statement of the problem : In this the problem is selected and studied.

2. Description of the course of event : It requires that the investigator should describe the course.

3. Determinant or factors : In every event there are certain factors that are responsible for that event. In case study method these factors are also studied. These factors may be classified under two heads:

1. General factors and
2. Particular factors

Sequence of case study Method

1. Observation unrecorded.
2. Anecdotal record recorded.
3. Anecdotal summary: A brief summary of observation.
4. Rating Scale and descriptive items marked on the basis of previous observation.
5. Development record card: significant information mostly from questionnaire and other sources is collected and recorded.
6. Development record folder: more description is collected and recorded.

METHODS FOR COLLECTING SECONDRY DATA COLLECTION

The secondary data may either be published or unpublished data.

1. Various publications of the central, state and local government.
2. Variuos publications of foreign governments or of international bodies and their related organizations.
3. Technical and trade journals.
4. Books, magazines and newspapers.
5. Reports and publications of various associations connected with various fields.
6. Reports prepared by research scholars, etc. in different fields.

The sources of unpublished data are many. They may be find in diaries, letters, unpublished biographies, and autobiographies and also may be available with scholars and research workers, trade associations, public/private individuals and organizations.

But before using secondary data, the researcher must ensure the reliability, suitability and adequacy of data.

6

Processing and Analysis of Data

INTRODUCTION

The process of evaluating data using analytical and logical reasoning to examine each component of the data provided. This form of analysis is just one of the many steps that must be completed when conducting a research experiment. Data from various sources is gathered, reviewed, and then analyzed to form some sort of finding or conclusion. There are a variety of specific data analysis method, some of which include data mining, text analytics, business intelligence, and data visualizations. Authenticity and reliability of a research investigation is based on assurance of error free qualitative reliability of the collected data.

Data processing is an intermediary stage of work between data collection and data interpretation. The data gathered in the form of questionnaire/interview etc. is mostly in the form of a large volume of research variables. Processing of data requires advance planning and this planning may cover such aspects as identification of variables, hypothetical relationship among the variables and the tentative research hypothesis.

WHY DO WE ANALYZE DATA?

The purpose of analyzing data is to obtain usable and useful information. The analysis, irrespective of whether the data is qualitative or quantitative, may:

1. Describe and summaries the data 2. Identify relationships between variables 3. Compare variables 4. Identify the difference between variables 5. Forecast outcomes (Rao p 112)[59] For investigating a research problem statistically, the following methods and procedures can be adopted in accordance with the nature of the data:

1. Classification and tabulation 2. Measures of central tendency and dispersion 3. Association of attributes 4. Simple correlation and regression 5. Multiple correction and multiple regression 6. Interpolation and extrapolation.

Processing of Data : Processing consists of task of editing, coding classification and tabulation. In spite of careful collection by a researcher there may be possibility of error. It is therefore, process of editing is necessary. Authenticity of data is very important. There is no room for factious data to creep in. For the purpose of classification of data into useful and meaning full classes, the procedure of coding has to be used. Manual processing and analysis can be carried out by using measures of central tendency, dispersion, correlation, regression and other statistical methods if the volume of data is not very large. If the volume of data is large than it is important to use computer processing.

1. Collection of data

2. Organisation of collected data : Involves process of classification and tabulation

3. Presentation of the organized data : After organization of data, the next step is presentation of data in a systematic way. Data may be presented in diagrammes or graphs. These graphs and diagrammes are easy to present and understand, also facilitates comparison. The diagrammes are of various types such as bar diagramme, pie diagramme, pictographs etc. Graphs are also various types such as time series graphs, histogram, frequency polygon etc.

4. Analysis of presented data

STEPS IN PROCESSING OF DATA

After the data is collected, we have to proceed in the following manner:

The various steps in processing the data are as follows:

1. Identify the data structure
2. Editing the data
3. Coding and classifying the data
4. Transcription of data
5. Tabulation of data

1. Identify the data structure

In the data preparation step, the data are prepared in the data format, which allows the analysis to use modern analysis software such as SPSS. The major criterion in this is to define the data structure. A data structure is the dynamic collection of related variables. Most data structure can be graphically presented to give clarity as to the framed research hypothesis. A simple structure could be linear structure , in which one variable leads to an other and finally to the resultant end variable.

2. Editing

Editing is the process of examining errors and omissions in the collected data and making necessary corrections in the same. Data editing happens at two stages. One at the time of recording the data and second at the time of analysis of data. Data editing is also requisite before the analysis of data is carried out. This ensure that the data is complete in all respect for subjecting them to further analysis.

A few examples will indicate how editing can be helpful.

1. The respondent has marked two answers instead of one for a particular question. In such a case, the editor has to carefully examine which of the two answer would be more accurate.
2. The respondent has answered a question by checking one of the many possible categories contained in the questionnaire.

In all such cases the where editorial corrections are to be made, it is necessary that these should be kept distinct from the changes made either by the respondent or by the interviewer.

An editor should be well versed with the editing of questionnaire. It may be emphasized that editing a manuscript is different from the editing of a questionnaire. Person with long experience and having special aptitude for editing data should be given performance over others. The editing step checks for the completeness, accuracy and uniformity of data set created by the researcher.

Completeness : The first step of editing is to check whether there is an answer to all the questions/variable set out in the data set. If the information is vital and has been found to be incomplete , then the researcher can take the steps of contacting the respondent personally again.

Accuracy : The accuracy of each recorded answer should be checked. A random check process can be applied to trace the errors at this step. The reliability of the data set would heavily depend upon this set of error correction. The fake responses should be dropped from the data set. The cross verification to a few related responses would help in checking for consistency in responses.

Uniformity : In editing the data set , another keen look out should be for any lack of uniformity in interpretation of questions and instructions by the data recorders. In all, uniformity checks for consistency in coding throughout the questionnaire/interview schedule response/data set.

3. Coding

Coding is the procedure of classifying the answers to a question into meaningful categories. The symbols used to indicate these categories are called codes.

Coding is necessary to carry out the subsequent operations of tabulating and analyzing data. If coding is not done it will not be possible to reduce a large number of heterogeneous responses into meaningful categories with the result that analysis of data would be weak and ineffective and without proper focus.

Coding involve two steps:

Step 1. The first is to specify the different categories or classes into which the responses are to be classified.

Step 2. The second step is to allocate individual answer to different categories.

The problem of coding is not so simple, especially in respect of an open ended question. He response to such a question is in a descriptive form, in the words of respondent himself.

For example, the respondent may asked: what is your opinion regarding the sources and services of a particular library? The respondent may give a lengthy answer indicating what he feels about the sources and services of a library. In case of such responses, coding needs extra care in framing the possible categories in which various responses can be classified.

CLASSIFICATION AND TABULATION OF DATA

Introduction

In any statistical investigation, the collection of the numerical data is the first and the most important matter to be attended. Often a person investigating will have to collect the data from the actual field of inquiry. For this he may issue suitable questionnaires to get necessary information or he may take actual interviews; personal interviews are more effective than questionnaires, which may not evoke an adequate response.

Sometimes the data may be available in publications of Government bodies or other public or private organizations. Such data, however, is often so numerous that one's mind can hardly comprehend its significance in the form that it is shown. Therefore, it becomes very necessary to tabulate and summarize the data to an easily manageable form. For a layman, presentation of the raw data in the form of tables or diagrams is always more effective.

Classification

When open ended responses have been received, classification is necessary to code the responses. For example, the income of the respondent could be open ended question. For all responses, suitable classification can be arrived at.

Meaning

The process of dividing the data into different groups (viz. classes) which are homogeneous within but heterogeneous between themselves, is called a classification. Classification is the process of sorting similar things from among the group of objects with different characteristics. In other words heterogeneous data is divided into separate homogeneous classes according to characteristics that exist among different individuals or quantities constituting the data.

"Classified and arranged facts speak of themselves, and narrated they are as dead as mutton" This quote is given by J.R. Hicks.

The main object of classification is to present data in a simplified and quickly intelligible form, a mass of complex data. Without classification it is difficult to compare quickly and analyze properly different set of qualitative and quantitative phenomenon.

Basic Requirements

The basic requirements of good classification are stability, non ambiguity, flexibility and comparability.

It helps in understanding the salient features of the data and also the comparison with similar data. For a final analysis it is the best friend of a statistician.

Methods of Classification

The data is classified in the following ways:

1. According to the characteristics of data
   a. Descriptive and
   b. Numerical
2. According to attributes or qualities, this is divided into two parts:
   a. Simple classification
   b. Multiple classifications.
3. According to variable or quantity or classification according to class intervals. -
   a. Number of classes
   b. Length of class interval

1. According to characteristics of data

a. **Descriptive :** Descriptive characteristics are those that can be described in words and are expressible in qualitative terms. For example literacy, sex, religion etc.

b. **Numerical characteristics :** Numerical characteristics are quantitative in nature such as age, income, weight etc.

2. Simple and Multiple classifications: (Qualitative Classification) : When facts are grouped according to the qualities (attributes) like religion, literacy, business etc., the classification is called as qualitative classification. It may be simple or multiple classifications.

Classification based on attributes may be either simple or multiple.

a. **Simple classification :** In case of simple classification, only single attribute is studied. Data is classified into two separate classes under a single attribute. For example data collected on literacy in the country can be classified into two distinct classes – literate and illiterate. Since this process is quite simple, it is known as simple classification. When data (facts) are divided into groups according to their qualities, the classification is called as 'Simple Classification'.

Qualities are denoted by capital letters (A, B, C, D ......) while the absence of these qualities are denoted by lower case letters (a, b, c, d, ... etc.) For example,

Population(N)
↓
Male (A) 9 (a) Female

2. Manifold or multiple classifications : On the other hand, analyzing and classifying collected data under several attributes in different classes is called manifold or multiple classification. In this method data is classified using one or more qualities. For example, if each of two classes, literate and illiterate, is divided into male and females, then there would be four classes. Such a process of classification of data into a number of classes and classes within classes is known as manifold classification or multiple classifications. First, the data is divided into two groups (classes) using one of the qualities. Then using the remaining qualities, the data is divided into different subgroups. For example, the population of a country is classified using three attributes: sex, literacy and business.

3. Classification according to class intervals or variables : The data which is expressed in numbers (quantitative data), is classified according to class-intervals. While forming class-intervals one should bear in mind that each and every item must be covered. After finding the least value of an item and the highest value of an item, classify these items into different class-intervals. For example, if in any data the age of 100 persons ranging from 2 years to 47 years, is given, then the classification of this data can be done in this way:

Table 6. Classification according to class intervals

Age in years	No. of Persons
0 - 10	5
10 - 20	9
20 - 30	32
30 - 40	34
40 - 50	20

a. **Number of classes :** The number of classes into which particular data should be classified depends upon the mass of data. The larger the mass the more should be the number of classes. Usually the data is classified into not less than six classes and not more than 20 classes, depending upon the mass and size of the data and the length of the class intervals.

b. **Length of the class interval :** The uniform length of class intervals depends upon the difference between the extreme items in the data –the length item and the smallest item and the number of classes required. For example if in the data on marks secured by 250 candidates in the subject at an examination, 0 and 93 are the lowest and the highest marks respectively and 10 classes are required, each class would then have a class interval length of 10. Ordinary class intervals are fixed in such a way as to enable easy calculation and precision.

According to the class-intervals in classification the following terms are used:

(i) Class-limits : The choice of class limit is determined by mid value of a class interval, which should as far as possible be identical with the arithmetic average of the items occurring in that class interval. A class is formed within the two values. These values are known as the class-limits of that class. The lower value is called the lower limit and is denoted by l1 while the higher value is called the upper limit of the class and is denoted by l2. In the example given above, the first class-interval has l1 = 0 and l2 = 10.

(ii) Magnitude of the class-intervals : The difference between the upper and lower limits of a class is called the magnitude or length or width of a class and is denoted by 'i' or 'c'. Thus i ° (l2 - l1).

(iii) Mid-value or class-mark : The arithmetical average of the two class limits (i.e. the lower limit and the upper limit) is called the mid-value or the class mark of that class-interval. For example, the mid-value of the class-interval (0 - 10) is :

$$\frac{\ell_1 + \ell_2}{2} = \frac{0+10}{2} = 5 \text{ of } (10-20) \text{ it is } \frac{10+20}{2} = 15$$

and so on.

METHODS OF CLASSIFICATION

Exclusive Method : In this method, all items, the value of which are less than 5, equal to 0 or more than zero are classified in the class 0-5. All those quantities that are equal to 5 or less than 10 are classified in the class 5-10, and so on.

In this method the upper limit of a class becomes the lower limit of the next class. It is called 'Exclusive' as we do not put any item that is equal to the upper limit of a class in the same class; we put it in the next class, i.e. the upper limits of classes are excluded from them. For example, a person of age 20 years will not be included in the class-interval (10 - 20) but taken in the next class (20 - 30), since in the class interval (10 - 20) only units ranging from 10 - 19 are included. The exclusive-types of class-intervals can also be expressed as :

0 and below 10 or 0 - 9.9

10 and below or 10 - 19.

20 and below 30 or 20 - 29.9 and so on.

It is the process of condensation of the data for convenience, in statistical processing, presentation and interpretation of the information.

Inclusive Method

Here, quantities that are equal to 4, less than 4, equal to or more than zero are classified in the class 4-9 and so on.

Table 7. Inclusive method

Exclusive Method	*Inclusive Method*		
Class	*Frequency*	*Class*	*Frequency*
0-4	5	0-49	5
5-9	7	5-9.9	7
10-14	9	10-14.9	9
20-24	12	15-19.9	12
25-29	14	20-24.9	11
		25-29.9	14

Tabulation (Tabular Presentation)

The transcription of data can be used to summaries and arrange the data in a compact form for further analysis. This process is called tabulation.

Meaning

Tabulation is the process of arranging quantitative data based on similarities and common characteristics in certain rows and columns so that data can easily be understandable and comparable. Data are generally presented in tabular form, a table is systematic presentation of statistical data in columns and rows. In rows data are arranged horizontally and in columns data are arranged in vertically.

Table may be general purpose table and specific purpose table. The general purpose table usually displays data of historical interest such as census data. The specific purpose table usually answer a specific question. Usually the general purpose table are found in appendices and the specific purpose tables are presented in the text.

Presentation of data

Easy-to-understand tables and graphics will greatly enhance the readability of the written research report. As a general rule, all tables and figures should contain:

1. Identification number corresponding to the list of tables and the list of figures.
2. A title that conveys the content of the table or figure, also corresponding to the list of tables and the list of figures, and
3. Appropriate column labels and row labels for tables, and figure legends defining specific elements in the figure.

There are a number of ways to produce tables and figures. When typing a report on a typewriter or word-processor, it is sometimes easiest to type a table out by hand. However, when complicated tables have to be produced, it is advisable to use spreadsheet software like Lotus 1-2-3 or Excel.

Data can be presented in :

1. Textual presentation
2. Tabular presentation
3. Graphic presentation

1. Textual presentation : Textual presentation is mostly used in media for presenting the data. This type of presentation is also often used in digests, especially in management digests for executives.

Presentation of data

↓

↓	↓	↓
Textual presentation	Tabular presentation	graphic presentation

2. Tabular presentation : Data are often presented in tabular form. In tabular form data is organized in columns and rows. Rows are horizontal arrangement and columns are vertical arrangement. The table usually simplifies the presentation of data and facilitates the comparison of two or more data sets.

Features of good table **:** A good table is one which has the following features:

1. It should present the data clearly, highlighting important details.
2. It should save space but attractively designed.
3. The table number and title of the table should be given.
4. Row and column headings must explain the figures therein.
5. Averages or percentages should be close to the data.
6. Units of the measurement should be clearly stated along the titles or headings.

7. Abbreviations and symbols should be avoided as far as possible.
8. Sources of the data should be given at the bottom of the data.
9. In case irregularities creep in table or any feature is not sufficiently explained, references and foot notes must be given.
10. The rounding of figures should be unbiased.

Types of Tabulation

There are three types of tabulation:

1. One way tabulation (single tabulation)
2. Two way tabulation (double tabulation)
3. Three way tabulation (triple tabulation)
4. Higher order table (manifold tabulation)

1. One way tabulation : A one way table gives answer to the question about one character of data. For example population data of a state.

2. Two way table : Two way table gives information about two interrelated characteristics of a particular type of data. Such as male and female population in a given data.

3. Three way table (triple tabulation) : A three way table answer question relating to three interrelated characteristics of a given data. Such as literate, illiterate of male and females in a state.

4. Higher order table (manifold tabulation) : This table gives information under several main heads and sub heads and questions relating to number of interrelated characteristics.

One way table

A one way table gives answer to the questions about one characteristic of data.

Example of one way table:

Users of different libraries in Delhi

Table 8. One way table

Libraries	*users*
Total	

Two way table

A two way table gives information about two interrelated characteristics of a particular type of data.

Table 9. Two way table

Libraries	*Users*		*Total*
	Male	*Females*	
Total			

Table 10. Three way table

Libraries	*Population*			*Males*			*Females*		
	Literate	*Illiterate*	*total*	*Literate*	*Illiterate*	*Total*	*Literate*	*illiterate*	*Total*

Three way table

A three way table answers questions relating to three interrelated characteristics of a given data.

COMPONENTS OF STATISTICAL TABLE

The table generally consists of following parts: title, sub-title, if any, stub, caption, body of the data, foot notes etc.

(1) Table : (2) frequency of use of sources

(1) Table 11. Frequency distribution (2)

	Frequency (3)	*Students*		
		No.	*%*	
(4)	Daily	131	59.5	(5)
	Once in a week	13	5.9	
	2 times a week	14	6.3	
	Once in a fortnight	08	3.6	
	Once in a month	09	0.4	
	Occasionally	45	20.4	

1. Table number, 2. Title of the table 3. Stub head 4. Stub entries 5. Body

Table 12. Frequency distribution

Use of E- Resources	*Frequently*		*Sometime*		*Never*	
	No.	*%*	*No.*	*%*	*No.*	*%*
Internet website	153	69.5	38	17.2	29	13.1
E-Journals (Back Volumes)	17	7.7	41	18.6	162	73.6
E-Journals (current)	35	15.9	39	17.7	146	66.3
E-Books	37	16.8	54	24.5	129	58.6
E-Data Archives	08	3.6	30	13.6	182	82.7
E-Manuscripts	12	5.4	31	14.0	177	80.4
E-Maps	26	11.8	48	21.8	146	66.3

Use of E- Resources	*Frequently*		*Sometime*		*Never*	
	No.	*%*	*No.*	*%*	*No.*	*%*
E-Thesis/ Dissertations	16	7.2	33	15.0	171	77.7
E-Magazines	26	11.8	42	19.0	152	69.0
WWW	96	43.6	39	17.7	85	38.6
E-Newspaper	35	15.9	35	15.9	150	68.1
E-Mail	107	48.6	30	13.6	83	37.7
E-Research Reports	16	7.2	38	17.2	166	75.4
CD-ROM/ DVD ROM	57	25.9	59	26.8	104	47.2
Indexes /abstract	23	10.4	40	18.1	157	71.3
Online Database	24	10.9	46	20.9	150	68.1
Online Public Access catalogue	45	20.4	34	15.4	141	64.0
Reference sources e-form	36	16.3	31	14.9	153	69.5
Statistical Sources e-form	09	4.1	32	14.5	179	81.3
Sound Recordings	26	11.8	40	18.1	154	70.0
Video cassettes	26	11.8	32	14.5	162	73.6
Search engines	113	51.3	23	10.4	84	38.1
E- articles	33	15.0	28	12.7	159	72.2
Journal articles (full text)	21	9.5	33	15.0	166	75.4
Journal articles (abstract)	24	10.9	41	18.6	155	70.4

Guidelines and rules for the construction of table

1. The title of the table should be placed at the top
2. Do not plan the size and shape without preliminary layout.
3. Give importance to certain parts of the table
4. In order to show important part of the data distinctly,

it is necessary to draw thick double or multiple ruled lines

5. The entire arrangement of data should be appropriate, compact and self explanatory so that it is not necessary to rearrange the data in any manner.
6. Comparison between different figures such as totals averages are easier if they are arranged vertically and not horizontally.
7. The caption should be clear and brief.
8. Every table should have a title. It should be in brief. It should be placed above the body of the table.
9. A number to facilitate easy references should identify each table. The number can be centered above the title. The table numbers should run in a consecutive serial order. Alternatively tables in chapter 1 be number as 1.1, 1.2, 1.3.... in chapter 2 as 2.1, 2.2,2.3.... and so on.
10. Abbriviations should be avoided whenever possible.

Computerized Tabulation

Computerized tabulation is easy with the help of software package. The input requirement will be the columns and raw variables. The software package than computes the number of records in each cell of the row/ column categories. The most popular package is the statistical package for social Sciences (SPSS). It is integrated set of programmes suitable for analysis of social science data. This package contains programmes for a wide range of operations and analysis such as handling missing data, recording, variable information, cross tabulation, etc.

2. GRAPHS/CHARTS/DIAGRAMS

Visual Aspects of Report:

The main role of graphics in a report is:

1. To make the report more attractive.
2. To emphasize key points.
3. To save time.
4. To support text to communicate report contents.
5. To help the reader to remember main points.

The main objective of graphic presentation of data is to summarize clearly the facts and conclusion drawn from the data. The presentation of data in graphic is important because the data can be easily understood and interpreted.

The graphic presentation is important for evaluation of library services, to identify the change in library services by comparing the various operations over a period of time.

In presenting the data of frequency distributions and statistical, it is often desirable to use appropriate form of graphic presentation. These forms reduces large masses of statistical data to a form that can be quickly understood at a glance. The graphic presentation is particularly useful when the readers are non technical people or general public.

Graphic forms used should be simple, clear and accurate and also be appropriate to the data. In planning this work , the following questions should be considered:

1. What is the purpose of the diagramme?
2. What facts are to be emphasized?
3. What is the educational level of the audience?
4. How much time is variable for the preparation of the diagramme?

There are different types of graphical presentation such as pie chart, bar chart, histogram, etc.

Types of Graphics : The common types of visuals used in communicating data are:

1. Pie charts
2. Bar charts
3. Pictogram
4. Pictorial diagrammes

1. Pie chart

The pie chart is the most common method of presentation of the data. Data is presented in partitions in a circle. The circle chart is usually a percentage chart. The data are converted to percentage of the total and the proportional segments, therefore give a clear picture of the relationship among the components parts. Each partition of the data is presented as a portion of a pie. Pie charts are the commonly used visual aids. Use a pie chart when we want to compare a number of elements to each other and in relation to a whole. Pie charts are drawn for the nominal data. The pie chart is commonly used for presenting the sectoral distribution of national income, or any other type of simple percentage distribution.

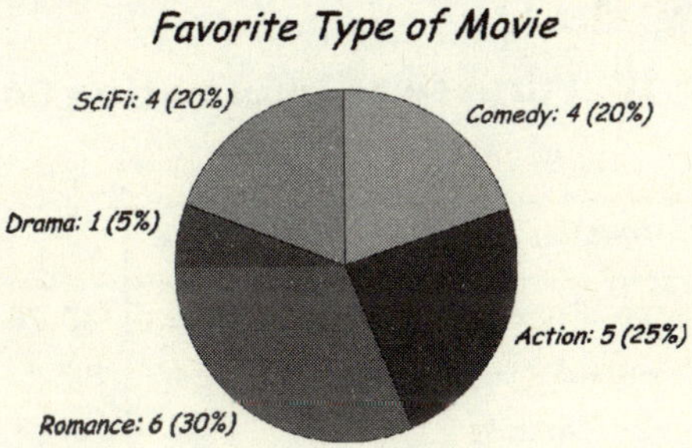

Features

1. Easy to draw
2. Good for making comparison
3. Familiar to all

The disadvantage of pie chart is that it is not possible to show any category that has zero frequency.

When to use?

Use pie chart when you want to compare a number of elements to each other and in relation to a whole. One of the fundamental rule of using pie chart is "never include more than 6 elements"

The pie chart can be made more attractive by:

1. Adding pattern to each part
2. Using colour
3. Adding depth

2. Bar chart

Qualitative data is usually represented in the form of bar chart diagram. A bar chart consists of number of bars of equal width arranged vertically or horizontally. The length of each bar varies with the magnitude of data collected over a period of time. Simple bar charts consists of number of single bars, each representing the magnitude of some variables. If one wants to compare the magnitude of one variable with another, over a period of time, one can use group of double bars. The double bars usually has no gap between the two bars but between each group of bars, there should be a gap.

Table 13. Purpose of Information Search

N=96

Purpose of Information Search	*Yes*	%	*No*	%
For doing Research work	42	43.75	54	56.25
For Seminar/ workshop presentation	81	84.37	15	15.62
For writing books/ article	66	68.75	30	31.25
For Class Lectures	87	90.62	09	09.37
Recreational	18	18.75	78	81.25
Reference and information services	39	40.62	57	59.37
General Awareness/knowledge	63	65.62	33	34.37
Updating knowledge	42	43.75	54	56.25

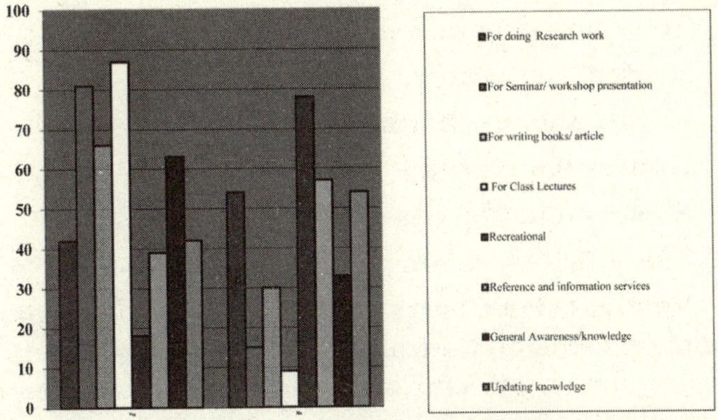

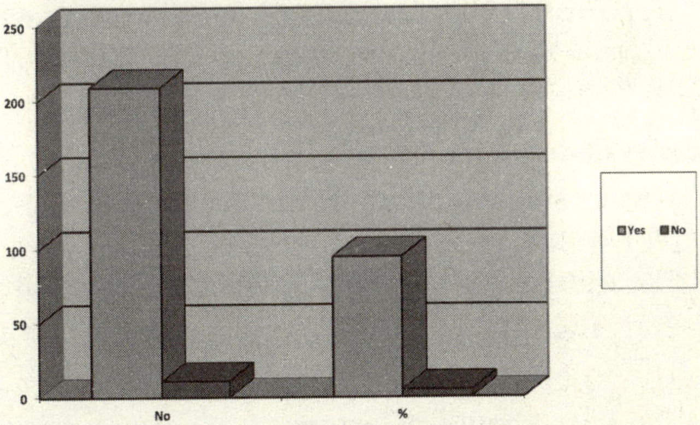

Features

1. Shows frequency of each data category.
2. Summarizes large data set in a visual form.
3. Shows how variable or group of variables change over time.
4. Can be use to explain how quantities changes or differ to a lay man.
5. Easy to draw.
6. Familiar to all.
7. Good for making comparison.

TYPES OF BAR CHARTS

These are generally following types:

1. Vertical Bar Charts
2. Horizontal bar charts
3. Groups bar charts
4. Sketched bar charts

These two types are generally used :

Vertical Bar Charts : Consists of vertical bars or columns erected on horizontal line and the values of the bars are shown on Y-axis .Above bar diagrammes are vertical bar diagrammes.

Horizontal Bar Charts: Are commonly used for presenting qualitative and geographical distribution .They are also used for discrete quantitative distribution.

Principles of designing bar charts

While using bar charts the following points should be kept in mind:

1. The width of all the bars should be kept same
2. Start the vertical axis at zero(0) , if possible
3. The order of the category should be logical
4. The bars should be arranged in some systematic order such as in chronological order in a presentation of time series; according to magnitude, starting with the largest, in other cases.
5. A scale should be included in every bar chart. The intervals should be indicated in round numbers.

3. Pictogram

A chart on which symbols are used to represents values. A pictogram is variation of the bar charts .In it the values are represented by identical symbols or pictures. Each one represents a fixed size of the variable. The symbol used may be appropriate to the type of data.

For example, a picture of human being can be used for depicting population data.

Rules for developing a pictorial chart

The following rules should be observed in developing pictorial chart:

1. The symbols should be self explanatory.
2. The chart should be made as simple and clear as possible.
3. The chart should be given only an overall picture and not the minute details.
4. Comparision in terms of one dimension only should be charted.

HISTOGRAM

This is an other forms of line chart used for presenting a frequency distribution. A histogram is a diagram consisting of rectangles whose area is proportional to the frequency of a variable and whose width is equal to the class interval. It is constructed by erecting vertical lines on the limits of the class intervals marked on the base line. The vertical lines so drawn from a series of continuous rectangle or columns. The width of each rectangle represents its class interval and the height represents the class frequency.

A histogram represents the class frequencies in a frequency distribution with vertical bars. Each bar represents a class interval whose area is proportional to the class frequency in the interval. Class intervals are plotted along the x axis and frequencies are plotted along the y axis. Each class is represented by a distance along the scale that is proportionate to its class interval. The distances are the width of the bars.

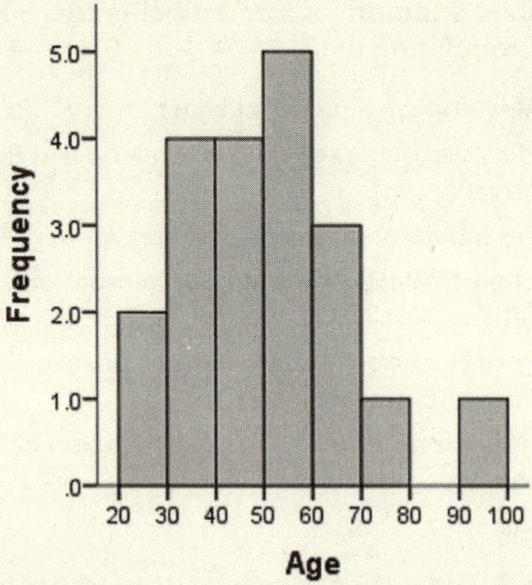

How it is used?

Histogram assists in decision making, communicate information to persons, compare measurements to specifications, summarize large data sets graphically.

Parts of histogram

Histogram is made up of five parts- 1.Title: the title briefly describe the information that is contained in the histogram. Horizontal: or x axis: The horizontal or x-axis shows you the scale of value into which the measurements fits.

Bars : The bars have two important characteristics, height and width. The height represents the number of times the value within an interval occurred. The width represents the length of the interval covered by the bars.

Vertical of y axis : The vertical or Y-axis is the scale that shows you the number of times the values within an interval occurred. The number of times is also referred to as "frequency"

Steps of Histogram

Step 1 - Count number of data points

Step 2 - Summarize on a tally sheet

Step 3 - Compute the range

Step 4 - Determine number of intervals

Step 5 - Compute interval width

Step 6 - Determine interval starting points

Step 7 - Count number of points in each interval

Step 8 - Plot the data

Step 9 - Add title and legend

7

Statistical Analysis And Interpretation of Data

INTRODUCTION

When statistical data is properly classified and condensed into a frequency distribution, it is easy for us to study the different characteristics of that data. Measure of central tendency (statistical average) tell us the point about which items have a tendency to cluster. Such a measure is considered as the most representative figure for the entire mass of data. Measure of central tendency is also known as statistical average such as mean, median, and mode are most popular average.

STATISTICAL ANALYSIS

Analysis means a critical examination of the assembled data for studying the characteristics of the object under study. Statistical analysis is useful for determining the patterns of relationship among the variables relating to it. Both quantitative and non quantitative methods are used.

PURPOSE OF STATISTICAL ANALYSIS

Statistical analysis of data serve many purposes:

1. It summarizes large mass of data into understandable and meaningful form.
2. Statistics makes exact descriptions possible.
3. Statistical analysis facilitates identification of the casual factors underlying complex phenomenon.
4. Statistical analysis aids the drawing of reliable inferences from observational data.
5. Statistical analysis also help in making estimation or generalization from the results of sample surveys. This is an other function of inferential statistics.
6. Statistical analysis is useful for assessing the significance of specific sample results under assumed population conditions. This type of analysis is called hypothesis testing.

TYPES OF STATISTICAL ANALYSIS

Statistical analysis is used for estimating the value of unknown characteristics of the population and for testing hypothesis for drawing inferences. Analysis therefore, may be broadly classified into:

1. Descriptive analysis
2. Inferential analysis

1. Descriptive Analysis

This type of analysis describes the nature of an object or phenomenon under study. This sort of analysis may describe data on one variable, two variable or more than two variables. Accordingly, it is called univariate analysis, bivariate analysis and multivariate analysis respectively.

Multivariate analysis consists of : a. Multiple regression analysis b. Multiple discriminate analysis c. Canonical analysis d. In multivariate analysis of variance e. Factor analysis.

b. Multiple regression analysis : It is made when

one dependent variable is presumed to be function of two or more independent variables.

c. Multiple Discriminant Analysis : is appropriate when the dependent variable cannot be measured but can be identified with a particular group on the basis of several predictor variables.

d. Canonical Analysis : is used for simultaneously predicting a set of dependent variables from their joint covariance with a set of independent variables.

e. In multivariable analysis of variance : the ratio of 'among group variables' to 'within group variables' is worked on a set of variables.

f. Factor Analysis : is useful for grouping a large number of variables into a few independent factor dimensions.

INFERENTIAL ANALYSIS

Inferential analysis is concern with drawing inferences and conclusions from the findings of a research study. There are two areas of statistical inferences1. Statistical estimation and 2.the testing of hypothesis

1. Statistical estimation : involves estimation of the population parameters from the results of sample data analysis. In order to arrive at accurate estimates of parameters, the researcher the researcher has to effectively deal with three problems 1.the precise definition of population 2.the determination of adequate sample size and 3. The selection of a representative sample.

2. Testing Hypothesis : Hypothesis are tested with test of significance. The testing involves the assessment of the probability of specific sampling results under assumed population conditions. Inferential analysis enable us to make decisions and draw conclusions from studies which could otherwise not be feasible because of the size of the universe or of the cost of census survey.

TYPES OF STATISTICAL MEASURES

The statistical measures used in statistical analysis may be categorized into:

1. Measures of central tendency: mean median, mode
2. Measures of dispersion: standard deviation
3. Measures of associations/relations: correlation, regression ,chi-square test, etc.
4. Analysis of variance
5. Time series analysis

MEASURES OF CENTRAL TENDANCY AND DISPERSION (Mean, median, Mode)

A useful way to describe a set of observations is to find out a single value that represents the 'average' characteristic of its frequency distribution. Such a value is known as a measure of central tendency since it is generally located towards the center of the distribution. The three most commonly used measures of central tendency are the mode, median and the arithmetic mean.

The mean (often called the average) is most likely measure of central tendency that you are most familiar with, but there are others, such as the median (middle score) and the mode(most frequently occurring).The mean, median and mode are all valid measures of central tendency, but under different conditions, some measures of central tendency become more appropriate to use than others.

A statistical average is a single expression that sum up the characteristics of an entire group of figures or complex data. Descriptive measures such as these generally throw light on the central characteristics of the data and are therefore, present in its central part. Hence, they are also known as 'measures of central tendency'.

Need of measure of central tendency

The measures of central tendency is generally

needed for the following reasons:

1. The average represents all the measurements made on a group and gives a concise description of the group as a whole.
2. When two or more groups are measured, the central tendency provides the basis of comparison between them.

TYPES OF STATISTICAL AVERAGE

The different types of statistical averages area :

1. Arithmatic mean
2. Median
3. Mode
4. Geometric mean
5. Harmonic mean
6. Quadric mean
7. Moving average
8. Progressive average

All these grouped into three separate groups. Arithmetic mean, geometric mean, harmonic mean and quadric mean are known as mathematical averages because they are calculated by using certain mathematical procedures. Mode and median are known as averages of position since the position of certain items in the data is taken into consideration while finding these.

Mean or Arithmetic mean

The mean (or average) is the most popular and well known measure of central tendency. It can be used with both discrete and continuous data, although its use is most often with continuous data . It is the average of all values in a distribution.

The mean is equal to the sum of all the values in the data set divided by the number of values in the data sct. It may be defined as the value which we get by dividing the total of values of various given items in a series by the total number of items. For example the mean of the series 2, 4, 6, 7, 11 is 30/5 = 6. It is designated by the symbol $\bar{X}$ (read as x-bar) and the formula is:

$$\bar{X} = \frac{\Sigma(fx)}{n}$$

Where $\bar{X}$ = arithmetic mean

x = any value; f = frequency of value; Σ = the total of all the categories; n = number of values

Arithmetic mean =

$$\begin{bmatrix}\text{Assumed} \\ \text{mean}\end{bmatrix} + \frac{\text{sum of the deviations of items from the assumed mean}}{[\text{total number of items}]}$$

So, if we have n values in a data set and they have values $x_1, x_2, \ldots, x_n$, the sample mean, usually denoted by $\bar{x}$ (pronounced x bar), is:

$$\bar{x} = \frac{(x_1 + x_2 + \ldots + x_n)}{n}$$

$$\text{Mean} = \frac{10 + 12 + 8}{3} = 10$$

This method of finding A.M. is called direct method. It is very simple and does not required any mathematical skills. But is useful only when the items are few and size of the data is small. If the items are many and size is large, it would be difficult to calculate the A.M. with this method.

To remove this difficulty a short method is used. We can assume one of the items as an arbitrary (assumed) mean and find out how much the items derived from this assumed mean.

This formula is usually written in a slightly different manner using the Greek capitol letter, Σ, pronounced "sigma", which means "sum of...":

$$\bar{X} = \frac{\Sigma x}{n}$$

Where $\bar{X}$ = simble for mean

Σ = simble for summation

Xi = value of the ith item X, i= 1,2,....,n

n = total number of items

If we used assumed average than mean would be:

MEAN ($\bar{X}$)

FORMULA : Ungroup Data $\bar{X} = \frac{x_1 + x_2 + ... + x_n}{n}$

Group Data : $\bar{X} = \frac{\Sigma fx}{n}$

where f = frequency in each class; x = midpoint of each class; n = total number of scores

It is noticed that the above formula refers to the sample mean. So, why have we called it a sample mean? This is because, in statistics, samples and populations have very different meanings and these differences are very important, even if, in the case of the mean, they are calculated in the same way. To acknowledge that we are calculating the population mean and not the sample mean, we use the Greek lower case letter "mu", denoted as μ:

$$\mu = \frac{\Sigma x}{n}$$

The mean is essentially a model of your data set. It is the value that is most common. You will notice, however that the mean is not often one of the actual values that you have observed in your data set. However, one of its important property is that it minimizes error in the prediction of any one value in your data set. That is, it is the value that produces the lowest amount of error from all other values in the data set.

Calculation of arithmetic mean- discrete series

There are two methods of calculating arithmetic mean:

1. Direct method
2. Shot cut method

Table 14. Direct method of Calculation of Arithmetic mean

Marks obtained (X)	*No. of students (f)*	*Xf*
20	3	60
25	5	125
30	8	240
35	14	490
40	10	400
45	6	270
50	4	200
Total	**N= 50**	**ΣfX = 1785**

$$\bar{X} = \frac{\Sigma fx}{n} = \frac{1785}{50} = 35.70$$

Hence average marks are 35.70

f = frequency of each class

Σ = summation

n = total number of items

Shortcut method : To minimize the calculations in case of frequency distribution, it is better to use the shortcut method. In this method, the derivation of the quantities from an assumed mean are first calculated; these derivations than multiplied by their respective frequencies..Than the frequency obtained by dividing the sum of these products(derivation X frequency) by the total number of frequencies is added to the assumed mean.

The resulting figure is actual A.M.

$$\text{Mean} = A + \frac{\Sigma fd}{n}$$

A = assumed mean

Σfd = sum of the products of the deviations and their respective frequencies.

n = total number of frequencies

Table 15. Calculation of mean by shortcut method

Marks	*No of students*	*deviation from assumed mean*	*D*
X	*f*	*d (X-35)*	*fd*
20	3	-15	-45
25	5	-10	-50
30	8	-5	-40
35	14	0	0
40	10	+5	+50
45	6	+10	+60
50	4	+15	+60
Total	**N= 50**		**Σfd= +35**

Arithmetic Mean as

$$\bar{X} = A + \frac{\Sigma fd}{N} = 35 + \frac{35}{50}$$

$$= 35 + 0.70 = 35.70$$

Average marks = 35.70

Continuous Series

In case of continuous series, items are grouped in certain class interval , the common factor 'i' is the length of the class interval. For instance , the length of the class interval 10-15 is 5.In continuous series, arithmetic mean may be computed by applying any of the methods:

1. Direct method
2. Short cut method
3. Step division method

The A.M. is calculated as:

1. First find out the mid value of the respective class interval
2. This mid value is taken as assumed mean
3. From the this step the working procedure and formula for calculating A.M. is exactly the same as in case of the discrete series. Multiply the respective frequencies of each class by b these d values and obtained the total Σfd. Mid point= lower limit Upper limit/2.

   AM. = a+ Σfd/nxi

Table 16. Calculation of Arithmetic mean in continuous series

Marks obtained	***No of students***
0-10	6
10-20	11
20-30	14
30-40	20
40-50	15
50-60	9
60-70	5
Total	**80**

Marks	*Class*	*No. of students* *f*	*Mid Value* *d – 35* *d*	*d*	*fd*
0-10	5	6	-30	-3	-18
10-20	15	11	-20	-2	-22
20-30	25	14	-10	-1	-14
30-40	35	20	0	0	0
40-50	45	15	+10	+1	+15
50-60	55	9	+20	+2	+18
60-70	65	5	+30	+3	+15
Total N =		**80**			**Σfd= -6**

N = 80 i = interval = 10 mid-value (d) = 35

Mean = a + Σfd/n × i

35 + – 6/80 × 10

= 35 - 0.75 = 34.25

This is short cut method

Merits and Limitations of Arithmetic mean

Merits

Arithmatic mean is most widely used in practice because:

1. It is simple, reliable, easy to understand and compute.
2. It is effective by the value of every item in the series.
3. It is defined by the rigid formula with the result that everyone who computes the average get the same answer.

Limitations

1. Since the value of mean depends upon each and every item of the series, extreme items, i.e. very small and very large items, unduly effects the valuc of the average.

2. The arithmetic mean is not always a good measure of central tendency. The mean provides a "characteristic" value, in the sense of indicating where most of the value lie, only when the distribution of variable is reasonably normal (bell shape) in case of U-shaped distribution the mean is not likely to serve a useful purpose.
3. In distribution with open ended class the value of mean cannot be computed without making assumptions regarding the size of the class interval of the open-end class.

Weighted Arithmetic Mean

When the different items are assigned weights according to their significance (relatively), the average then calculated is called weighted arithmetic average. One of the limitations of arithmetic mean discussed above is that it gives equal importance to all the items. But there are classes where the relative importance of the different items is not the same. When it is so, we compute weighted arithmetic mean. The term wighted stands for the relative importance of the different items.

The formula for computing weighted arithmetic mean is $\bar{X} = \Sigma WX/\Sigma W$

Where X represents the variable values i.e. X_1, X_2,....X_n

Symbolically the weighted average of n items X_1, X_2, X_3, ... X_n whose weights are W_1, W_2, W_3, ...W_n respectively is :

$$\frac{X_1W_1 + X_2W_2 + X_3W_3 + \ldots + X_nW_n}{W_1 + W_2 + W_3 + \ldots + W_n}$$

For example , if a person buys three different books for Rs. 12, Rs. 18 and Rs. 30 respectively, than the average price of the book that he purchases is:

$$\frac{12 + 18 + 30}{3} = \text{Rs. } 20$$

If he purchase five copies of the books at rate Rs. 12 each, three copies at Rs. 18 each and two copies at Rs. 30 each -10 books in all- the average price of book would be ;

$$Xw = \Sigma WX/\Sigma W$$

$$\frac{12 \times 5 + 18 \times 3 + 30 \times 2}{10} = \frac{60 + 54 + 60}{10} = 17.40$$

This is called weighted average since it has been calculated by giving the weights 5, 3 and 2 to the respective prices of the book.

Table 17. Calculation of simple and weighted arithmetic mean

	Delhi			*Mumbai*			*Kolkata*		
University Cource of study	***Pass %***	***No. of students in 100***		***Pass %***	***No. of students in 100***		***Pass %***	***no of students in 100***	
	X	***W***	***WX***	***X***	***W***	***WX***	***X***	***W***	***WX***
BCom (P)	71	3	213	82	2	164	81	2	162
Bcom (H)	83	4	332	76	3	228	76	3.5	268
B.A.(H) Economics	73	5	365	73	6	438	74	4.5	333
B.A.(H) PolSc.	74	2	148	76	7	532	58	2	116
B.A.(H) History	65	3	195	65	3	19	70	7	490
BSc	66	3	198	60	7	420	73	2	146
	ΣX 432	ΣW 20	ΣWX 1451	ΣX 432	ΣW 28	ΣWX 1977	ΣX 432	ΣW 21	ΣWX 1513

Simple and weighted arithmetic mean

$\bar{X} = \Sigma X/N = 432/6 = 72$

$\bar{X}w = \Sigma WX/\Sigma W = 72.55$; Delhi = 72.55

$\bar{X} = \Sigma X/N = 432/6 = 72$

$\bar{X}w = \Sigma WX/\Sigma W = 1977/28 = 70.6$; Mumbai = 70.6

$$\bar{X} = \Sigma X/N = 432/6 = 72$$

$$\bar{X}w = \Sigma WX/\Sigma W = 1513/21 = 72.05;\ \text{Kolkata} = 72.05$$

When not to use the mean

The mean has one main disadvantage: it is particularly susceptible to the influence of outliers. These are values that are unusual compared to the rest of the data set by being especially small or large in numerical value. For example, consider the wages of staff at a factory below:

Staff	1	2	3	4	5	6	7	8	9	10
Salary	15k	18k	16k	14k	15k	15k	12k	17k	90k	95k

The mean salary for these ten staff is $30.7k. However, inspecting the raw data suggests that this mean value might not be the best way to accurately reflect the typical salary of a worker, as most workers have salaries in the $12k to 18k range. The mean is being skewed by the two large salaries. Therefore, in this situation, we would like to have a better measure of central tendency. As we will find out later, taking the median would be a better measure of central tendency in this situation.

Another time when we usually prefer the median over the mean (or mode) is when our data is skewed (i.e., the frequency distribution for our data is skewed). If we consider the normal distribution - as this is the most frequently assessed in statistics - when the data is perfectly normal, the mean, median and mode are identical. Moreover, they all represent the most typical value in the data set. However, as the data becomes skewed the mean loses its ability to provide the best central location for the data because the skewed data is dragging it away from the typical value. However, the median best retains this position and is not as strongly influenced by the skewed values. This is explained in more detail in the skewed distribution section later.

2. MEDIAN

The median is the middle score in any distribution. Half of the scores are above the median value and half are below it. The median is the value of the middle item of series when it is arranged in ascending or descending order of magnitude. It divide the series into two halves; in one half all items are less than median whereas in other half all items have value higher than median. In other words, the value of the variable greater than the median have the same frequency as the values of the variable less than it.

The median is positional average that divides a distribution into two equal parts so that one half of items fall above it and the other half below it. For example, in the series 2, 4, 6, 7, 9, 10, 12, the median is 7. If the number is odd , the median is the middle item.

The median can be found by:

1. Determining whether N is odd or even
2. Arrange the scores in order from the lower to the highest
3. And then counting off to find the middle score.

The median of the following 7 items :

40, 10, 70, 50, 30, 60, 20

If the values of items arranged in the ascending order: 10, 20, 30, 40, 50, 60, 70 than the value of 4th item is 40 is value of median.

For example:

Find the median of the following scores: 5, 3, 13, 4, 11, 6 and 10.To start the score have to put in numerical order as: 3, 4, 5, 6, 10, 11, and 13. The count shows that there are 7 scores which is an odd number. When n is odd there will be one middle score with an equal number of scores above and below it. To find the score of middle score, divide N by 2 and round the result up-in to the next higher number this example n = 7 divided by 2 produces 3.5 that is rounded to 4. Therefore, the median id, fourth score from the top or bottom.

The value of the middle item of a series that is ordered either in the ascending order either in searching or descending order of magnitude is called the median. To determine the median it is necessary to arrange the items first either in ascending order or descending order.

For example the median of the following number 12, 15, 16, 14, 22, 31, 32, 30, 28, 19, is 21, since 21 is the middle number are written in ascending order as under:

12, 14, 15, 16, 19, 21, 22, 28, 30, 31, 32

In symbols, if n stands for number of items in a data than the median is :

Median (M) = value of :

$$\frac{\{n+1\}\text{ th item}}{2}$$

When the number are written either in ascending or descending order of magnitude. If n is an odd number, than the median can be located at once. But if n is even number, than the median is equal to the value of A.M. of the two central items.

Median is used only in context of qualitative phenomenon such as intelligence etc.

Median is not useful where items need to be assigned relative importance and weights. It is not frequently used in sampling statistics.

For example: The median of the numbers 17, 18, 21, 26, 28, 31, 33, 36, is $\frac{26+28}{2} = 27$

Discrete series

The following is the procedure for finding the median in the case of a desecrate series:

1. Items are arranged either in ascending order or descending order of magnitude and their respective frequencies are written against them.
2. These frequencies are cumulated.
3. The value of the items, where n= total number of frequencies, is determined by mere inspection of the cumulative frequencies. An important property of the mean is that it includes every value in your data set as part of the calculation. In addition, the mean is the only measure of central tendency where the sum of the deviations of each value from the mean is always zero.

Table 18. Calculation of Median

Value	*frequency*	*c.f.*
0-10	4	4
10-20	12	16
20-30	24	40
30-40	36	76
40-50	20	96
50-60	16	112
60-70	8	120
70-80	5	125
	N = 125	

Median = size of N/2 th item = size of 125/2 =62.5th item

Hence median lies in the class 30-40

Median = L + N/2 – C.F/f × i

L = 30, N/2 = 62.5, c.f. = 40, f = 36, i = 10

Median = 30+ 62.5-40/36 × 10 = 30 + 6.25 = 36.25

Advantages of median

1. It is very easy to calculate in case of discrete series.
2. The median is of immense use while estimating

qualities such as honesty, intelligence etc. and prove to be a good representative.

3. It is possible to find the median by knowing only the values of the central items and the number of items. It means the value of the extreme items are not necessary for finding the median.

Disadvantages

1. Arrangement of data either in ascending or descending order of magnitude is the pre requisite. This process is tedious when the data is large.
2. It absolutely fails to be of any use in cases where it is necessary to give large weights to extreme items.
3. Sometimes the median may exist between two values, thus involving the work of estimation.
4. Unlike the arithmetic mean, it is not possible to find the total value of all items if we know the value of the median and the number of items.

3. MODE

The mode is simplest of all averages. It is a measure that occurs most frequently in a distribution.

Mode is that item around which there is maximum concentration. In other words, it is the value of the item that occurs most frequently in the data. The value of the item in a variable that is repeated the greatest number of times is called the mode. It is said to be the most prominent item. It is easy to determine the mode in case of desecrate series that is regular- that is, where frequencies are not distributed irregularly. In case of continuous series that is regular, the model class can be determined at once and the interpolation formula can be used.

Mode is the value of variable for which the frequency is maximum. In other words, for y = f(x) is a frequency function, x is said to be a mode of the frequency distribution if the value of y is maximum.

The procedure for finding the mode of a set of a group data is:

1. Find the category or the class interval which has the greatest frequency.
2. The mid point on this category is mode.

Advantages and Disadvantages of Mode

Advantages

1. It is easy to find it in the case of discrete series.
2. It is possible to find the median by knowing only the value of the central items and the number of items. The value of the extreme items are not necessary for finding the median.
3. Median is very useful while estimating qualities such as: honesty, intelligence etc.

Disadvantages

1. Arangement of data in ascending or descending order is difficult when the data is large. It is the pre-requirement in median calculation.
2. It does not satisfy some of the conditions laid down for an ideal average.
3. In case of irregular series it is not very easy to determine the mode.
4. It is likely that in certain instances there may be two or more values for the mode.
5. It may fail to be representative average in the case of certain types of data.

CALCULATION OF MODE

For example:

Journal A is used 5 times

Journal B is used 4 times

Journal C is used 5 times

Journal D is used 2 times

Journal E is used 5times

Journal F is used 2 times

Journal G is used 4 times

Journal H is used 5 times

Journal I is used 3 times

Journal J is used 1 time

The frequency distribution of 10 journals is :

Table 19. Calculation of Mode

Number of times Journal used (X)	*Number of journals f(x)*
1	1
2	2
3	1
4	2
5	4
Total	10

The mode of the frequency distribution of use is 4 since most of the journals used 4 times.

Mode is the most commonly or frequently occurring value in a series. The mode in a distribution is that item around which there is maximum frequency, but at times such an item may not be mode on account the effect of frequencies of the neighboring items. Like median, mode is a positional average and is not affected by the values of extreme items.

Formula for Mode :

$$Z = l_1 + \frac{f_1 - f_0}{2f_1 - f_0 - f_2} \times i$$

where, Z = value of Mode

l_1 = Lower limit of model class

f_0 = Frequency of preceeding model class

f_2 = Frequency of subsquent model class or post model class

i = Class interval of the model class

Compute the mode for the following data:

Table 20. Calculation of mode

Price of books in (Rs.)	*Number of books*
0-24	6
25-49	18
50-74	18
75-99	21
100-124	7
125-149	10
Total	80

The model class is 75 - 99

Thus, l = 75, i = 25, fm = 21, fi = 18, m f2 = 7

Mode = l + I

$$\left\{\frac{\{Fm - fi\}}{(fm - fi) + (fm - f2)}\right\}$$

$$= 75 + 25\ \frac{3}{3+14} = 75 + \frac{75}{17} = 75 + 4.4118$$

Mode = 79.4118

Use of Mode

The mode is especially useful measure for qualitative data. It is the only appropriate measure of central tendency for nominal level of data. For finding out the typical category, the mode is the appropriate measure.

The mode is easily calculatable, but it is quite

unstable, because its position shifts when categorization is altered.

It is positional average and is not affected by extreme items. It is a dead end statistic as it is not amenable for any further arithmetic manipulation.

MEASURES OF DISPERSION

The measure of central tendency indicate the central value of a distribution. However, the central value alone is not sufficient to fully describe the distribution. In addition to the measures of centrality, we require a measure of the spread of the actual scores. The extent of such spread may vary from one distribution to another. For example, two income distributions may have the identical mean, but they may present different pattern of distribution. It means one distribution has less variability than other. The extend of such variability is measured by measures of dispersion.

The most common measures of dispersion are:

1. The range
2. Quartile deviation
3. Mean deviation or average deviation
4. Standard deviation or root mean square deviation
5. Variance
6. Cofficient of variation

Some of the main measures of dispersion are given below:

1. Range

The range (R) measures the difference between the highest and lowest scores of a distribution. For example, in a set of values 3, 5, 7, 9, 12, the range is the difference between 12 and 3i.e.12 – 3 = 9. The measures requires ordering of scores according to size. It can thus be applied in cases where the distribution is at least on an ordinal level of measurement.

Advantages and disadvantages of Range

Advantages

1. The range is easy to compute and understand.
2. It is useful device for gaining a quick impression of dispersion.
3. It is useful for computation of the standard deviation.

Disadvantages

1. As it based on two extreme values only, even if one of the extreme value changes, the range will fluctuate sharply. It is thus sensitive to extreme values.
2. The range cannot be compared with each other unless they are based on a similar number of observations.
3. The range does not give us any information about the pattern of variation.

2. VARIANCE

The variance is the mean of the squared deviations from the mean of distribution.

The formula for computing variance is:

$$\sigma^2 \text{ or } S^2 = \frac{\Sigma x^2}{n} = \frac{\Sigma (X - \bar{x})^2}{n}$$

Where σ^2 or s^2 = variance;

σ or s = standard deviation

x = deviation of each score from the mean $(X - \bar{x})$

n = number of observations

Advantages and disadvantages

The variance expresses the average dispersion not in the original units of measurement but in squared units. This problem is solved by taking the square root of variance. This transforms the variance into the standard deviation.

STANDARD DEVIATION (SD)

It is similar to that of the mean deviation method. The only difference is that individual deviations from the arithmetic mean are squired. It is denoted by sigma. The standard deviation, represented by the letter σ (sigma).It is simply a square root of the variance. When the square root is taken from one side of an equation, the same operation has to be performed on the other side in order to maintain the equality of two sides. When the square root is taken from both sides of the equation, σ^2 become ó and square root is taken of the value for calculation from the formula. Standard deviation (SD) is the square root of the mean of the squared deviation from the mean of distribution. It is denoted by the symbol σ, the Greek letter sigma or S.

Steps for calculating SD :

Step 1 : Find the mean.

Step 2 : For each data point, find the square of its distance to the mean. Calculate the deviation of each item from the arithmetic mean and squire it.

Step 3 : Sum the values from Step 2. Divide the sum of these squires by the number of items in the given data.

Step 4 : Divide by the number of data points.

Step 5 : Take the square root. The squire root of this quantity gives the standard deviation.

Calculation of SD:

There are two methods

1. By taking deviation from the actual mean
2. By taking deviation from the assumed mean

1. By actual mean

$$\sigma = \sqrt{\frac{\Sigma(X - M)^2}{N}}$$

$$X - M = d$$

$$SD = \sigma = \sqrt{\frac{(\Sigma d^2)}{N}}$$

Mean and Standard Deviation

When we report mean, it is good practice to report the corresponding standard deviation as well. The mean indicates the central tendency of the distribution of the variable; the standard deviation shows the extent to which the values for the variable are clustered around the mean. A small standard deviation means that the values are closely clustered around the mean; a large standard deviation says that the values are spread out farther from the mean.

1. Calculate the actual mean

Steps

1. Take the deviation of the items from the mean i.e. find $(X - \bar{X})$
2. Square these deviations and obtain the total ΣX^2
3. Divide ΣX^2 by the total number of observations, i.e. N, and extract the square root. This gives us the value of standard deviation.

Deviation taken from the Assumed mean

When the actual mean is in fraction such as 123.23, it would be too cumbersome to take deviation from it and than obtain square of these standard deviation.

2. Formula for standard deviation from assumed mean

$$S.D. = \sigma = \sqrt{\frac{\Sigma d^2}{N} - \left(\frac{\Sigma d}{N}\right)^2}$$

Steps

1. Take the deviation of the items from the assumed mean i.e. obtain (X-A), denote these deviation by d. Take the total of these deviations, i.e. obtain Σd
2. Square these deviations and obtain the total Σd^2
3. Subsitute the value of Σd^2, Σd and N in the above formula.

It is the term used to denote the squire of the standard deviation.

Calculate the SD of the following data:

Table 21. Calculate of SD from the assumed mean

Roll numbers	*Marks (x)*	*(X-50)=d*	*d^2*
1	43	-7	49
2	48	-2	4
3	65	15	225
4	57	7	49
5	31	-19	361
6	60	10	100
7	37	-13	169
8	48	-2	4
9	78	28	784
10	59	9	81
N = 10	**ΣX = 526**	**Σd = 26**	**Σd^2 = 1826**

$$S.D. = \sigma = \sqrt{\frac{\Sigma d^2}{N} - \left(\frac{\Sigma d}{N}\right)^2}$$

$$= \sqrt{\frac{1826}{10} - \left(\frac{26}{10}\right)^2} = \sqrt{182.6 - 6.76}$$

$$= \sqrt{175.84} = 13.26$$

Table 22. Calculation of standard deviation from the actual mean

Marks (x)	*no of students (f)*	*xf*	*d (X–A)*	*d²*	*fd²*
2	2	4	-4	16	32
5	3	15	-1	1	3
6	8	48	0	0	0
7	5	35	1	1	5
9	2	18	3	9	18
	20	120		27	58

$$\frac{\Sigma xf}{n} = \frac{120}{20} = 6$$

$$\sigma = \sqrt{\frac{(\Sigma fd^2)}{N}}$$

$$\sqrt{\frac{(\Sigma fd^2)}{N}} = \sqrt{\frac{58}{20}} = \sqrt{2.9} = 1.703$$

Advantages and disadvantage of standard deviation

Advantages

The standard deviation is more useful than other measures of dispersion because of following reasons:

1. It is rigidly defined.
2. Individual deviations are squired in its calculations.
3. SD is more stable from sample to sample.

4. Its mathematical properties makes it possible to obtain SD for two or more groups combined.
5. It is more useful in more advanced statistical analysis especially in statistical inferences.

Disadvantages

Since the individual deviations are squared, its value is effected a great deal by the value of each item in the data.

MEASURES OF SKEWNESS

What is skewness?

In probability theory and statistics, skewness is a measure of the asymmetry of the probability distribution of a real-valued random variable about its mean. The skewness value can be positive or negative, or even undefined. The qualitative interpretation of the skew is complicated. Measures of Skewness and Kurtosis, like measures of central tendency and dispersion, study the characteristics of a frequency distribution. Averages tell us about the central value of the distribution and measures of dispersion tell us about the concentration of the items around a central value. These measures do not reveal whether the dispersal of value on either side of an average is symmetrical or not. If observations are arranged in a symmetrical manner around a measure of central tendency, we get a symmetrical distribution, otherwise, it may be arranged in an asymmetrical order which gives asymmetrical distribution. Thus, skewness is a measure that studies the degree and direction of departure from symmetry.

When a series is not symmetrical it is said to be asymmetrical or skewed. It is lack of symmetry in the shape of a frequency distribution. When the distribution is not symmetrical it is called skewed distribution.

A distribution is said to be skewed when the mean and the median fall at different points in the distribution.

A skewness is positive: the frequencies in the distribution are spread out over a greater range of values on the high value end of the curve (the right hand side) than they are on the low –value end.

If the curve is normal, the spread will be the same on both sides of the center point and the mean, median and mode will all have the same value.

A symmetrical distribution, when presented on the graph paper, gives a 'symmetrical curve', where the value of mean, median and mode are exactly equal. On the other hand, in an asymmetrical distribution, the values of mean, median and mode are not equal. When two or more symmetrical distributions are compared, the difference in them are studied with 'Kurtosis'. On the other hand, when two or more symmetrical distributions are compared, they will give different degrees of Skewness. These measures are mutually exclusive i.e. the presence of skewness implies absence of kurtosis and vice-versa. But in a skewed distribution, the mean, median, and mode are all different values. A skewed data distribution or bell curve can be either positive or negative. A positive skew means that the extreme data results are larger.

Definition of Skewness

Skewness in statistics represents an imbalance and asymmetry from the mean of a data distribution. If we look at a normal data distribution using a bell curve, the curve will be perfectly symmetrical. Now, this doesn't happen all that often! In order to fully understand when a data distribution is imperfect and skewed, let's look at a normal data distribution and symmetrical bell curve.

A few basic terms :

- Mean is the average of the numbers in the data distribution.
- Median is the number that falls directly in the middle of the data distribution.

- Mode is the number that appears most frequently in the data distribution.

In a normal data distribution, the mean is directly in the middle (and top point) of the bell curve.

Properties of Skewed Bell Curves

A skewed data distribution or bell curve can be either positive or negative. A positive skew means that the extreme data results are larger. This skews the data in that it brings the mean (average) up. The mean will be larger than the median in a skewed data set. A negative skew means the opposite: that the extreme data results are smaller. This means that the mean is brought down, and the median is larger than the mean.

1. Systamatic distribution
2. Positively skewed distribution
3. Negatively skewed distribution

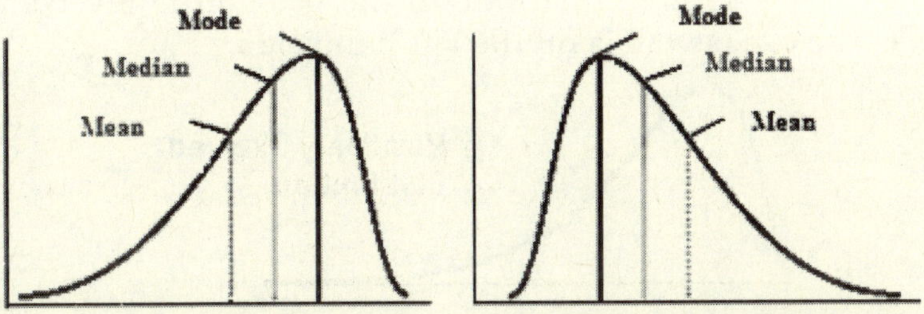

Left-Skewed (Negative Skewness) **Right-Skewed (Positive Skewness)**

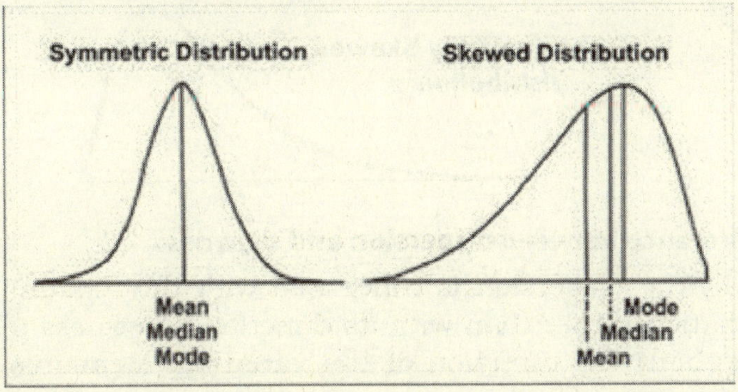

1. Simmetrical distribution : In symmetrical distribution the value of mean, median and mode coincide. The spread of frequencies is the same on both sides of the center point of the curve.

A distribution which is not symmetrical is called a skewed distribution and such a distribution could either be positively skewed or negatively skewed.

2. Positively skewed distribution or skewed to right : In this distribution the value of mean is maximum and that of mode least the median lies in between the two. In positively skewed distribution the frequencies are spread out over a greater range of values on the high value end of the curve(the right hand side) than they are on the low value end.

3. Negatively skewed distribution or skewed to left : In this the value of mode is maximum and that of mean least the median lies in between the two. In the negatively skewed distribution the position is reversed i.e. the excess tail is on the left hand side.

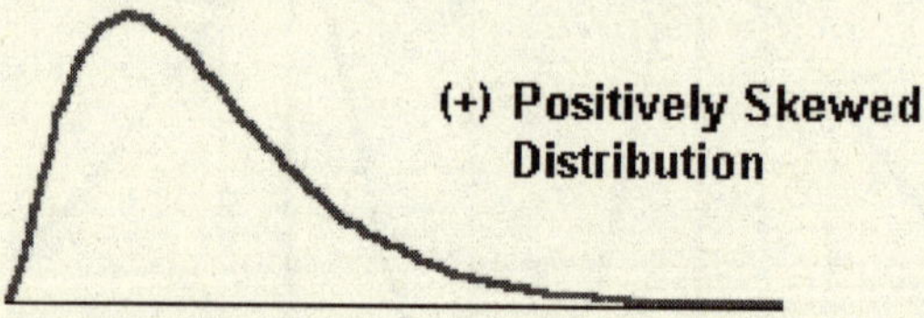

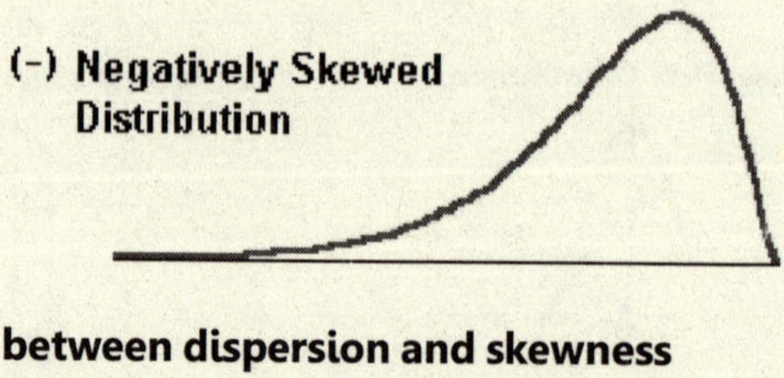

Difference between dispersion and skewness

The dispersion is concerned with the amount of variation rather than with its direction. Skewness tells us about the direction of the variation. Measures of skewness are dependent upon the amount of dispersion. It may be noted that although skewness is an important characteristics for defining the precise pattern of distribution, it is rarely calculated in business and economics series.

Tests of Skewness

There are certain tests to know whether skewness does or does not exist in a frequency distribution.

They are:

1. In a skewed distribution, values of mean, median and mode would not coincide. The values of mean and mode are pulled away and the value of median will be at the centre. In this distribution, mean-Mode = 2/3 (Media Mode).
2. Quartiles will not be equidistant from median.
3. When the asymmetrical distribution is drawn on the graph paper, it will not give a bell shaped curve.
4. Sum of the positive deviations from the median is not equal to sum of negative deviations.
5. Frequencies are not equal at points of equal deviations from the mode.

Characteristic of a good measure of skewness

1. It should be a pure number in the sense that its value should be independent of the unit of the series and also degree of variation in the series.
2. It should have zero-value, when the distribution is symmetrical.
3. It should have a meaningful scale of measurement so that we could easily interpret the measured value.

MEASURES OF SKEWNESS

Measures of skewness tells us the direction and extend of asymmetry in a series, and permit us to compare two or more series with regard to these. The skewness can be measured in absolute term by taking the difference between the men and mode symbolically.

$$\text{Absolute Sk} = \bar{X} \text{ -Mode}$$

Methods of ascertaining Skewness

Skewness can be studied graphically and mathematically. When we study skewness graphically, we can find out whether skewness is positive or negative or zero. This can be shown with the help of a diagram.

Mathematically skewness can be studied as :

(a) Absolute Skewness

(b) Relative or coefficient of skewness

When the skewness is presented in absolute term i.e. in units, it is absolute skewness. If the value of skewness is obtained in ratios or percentages, it is called relative or coefficient of skewness. When skewness is measured in absolute terms, we can compare one distribution with the other if the units of measurement are same. When it is presented in ratios or percentages, comparison become easy. Relative measures of skewness is also called coefficient of skewness.

Mathematical measures of skewness can be calculated by :

(a) Bowley's Method

(b) Karl-Pearson's Method

(c) Kelly 's method

a. Bowley's Method : Bowley's method of skewness is based on the values of median, lower and upper quartiles. This method suffers from the same limitations which are in the case of median and quartiles.

b. Karl Pearson's Method : What is Pearson's Coefficient of Skewness?

Karl Pearson developed two methods to find skewness in a sample.

Pearson measure of skewness

$$= \frac{\text{Mean} - \text{Mode}}{\text{Standard deviation}}$$

Pearson's Coefficient of Skewness

1. Uses the mode. The formula is:

$$Sk_1 = \frac{\bar{X} - Mo}{s}$$

Where $\bar{X}$ = the mean

Mo = the mode and s = the standard deviation for the sample.

Pearson's Coefficient of Skewness

1. Uses of Median.

The formula is:

2. $$Sk2 = \frac{3\left(\bar{X} - Md\right)}{S}$$

Where $\bar{X}$ = the mean, Md = median and s = the standard deviation for the sample.

It is generally used when you don't know the mode.

Sample problem : Use Pearson's Coefficient #1 and #2 to find the skewness for data with the following characteristics:

Mean = 70.5

Median = 80

Mode = 85

Standard deviation = 19.33

Pearson's Coefficient of Skewness

1. Mode

Step 1: Subtract the mode from the mean: 70.5 – 85 = -14.5

Step 2 : Divide by the standard deviation: -14.5 / 19.33 = -0.75

Pearson's Coefficient of Skewness

2. Median

Step 1 : Subtract the median from the mean:

70.5 – 80 = -9.5

Step 2 : Divide by the standard deviation:

-9.5 / 19.33 = -1.47

The significance of skewness lies in the fact that through it one can study the formation of series and can have the idea about the shape of the curve, whether normal or otherwise, when the items of given series are plotted on a graph.

MEASURING CORELATION AND REGRESSION

The numerical relationship between two series is called correlation.

The following are some of the related variables ; height and weight, income and expenditure etc. Correlation is direct or positive if two variables changes in the same direction; it is inverse or negative, if the variables change in opposite direction.

Correlation is a statistical measure that indicates the extent to which two or more variables fluctuate together. A positive correlation indicates the extent to which those variables increase or decrease in parallel; a negative correlation indicates the extent to which one variable increases as the other decreases.

MEASURING CORELATION OR CORRELATION ANALYSIS

When both the independent and dependent variables are interval or ratio level measures correlation analysis is used for measuring relationships and testing hypothesis.

The correlation coefficient measures the degree of association between variables. The correlation could be positive or negative. When two variables move in same direction their association is said to be positive correlation.

When they move in opposite direction, their association is said to be negative correlation. There are also other types of correlation such as linear correlation, non linear correlation, simple correlation, multiple correlations.

Linear correlation refers to negative or positive straight line relationship. Non linear correlation refers to the curve line type relationship. Simple correlation shows the relationship between two variables, whereas multiple correlations is concern with simultaneous correlation among three or more variables.

The correlation analysis involves three main aspects:

1. Measuring the degree of association between the two variables
2. Testing whether the relationship is significant
3. Establishing the cause and effect relationship if any

We can study the correlation between two sets of figures through the following methods:

1. By drawing graph of the data
2. By drawing scattered diagram
3. By calculating coefficient of correlation

1. Graphical method

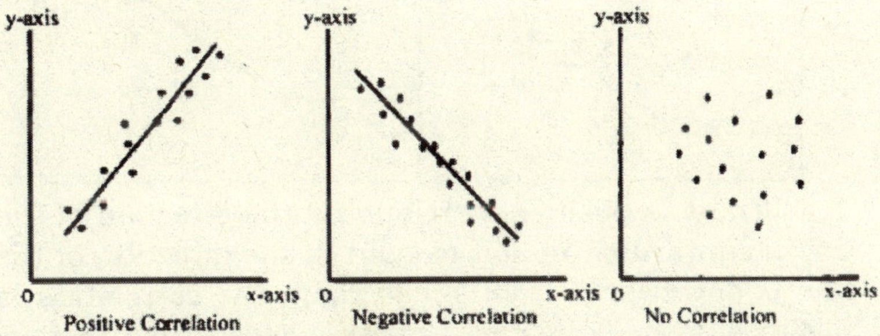

Here we represent each of two sets of figures by plotting the relevant points on the graph and then joining these points. If the two curves move in the same direction, then the correlation between the two sets of figure is positive. If the curve move in opposite direction, than it is correlation is negative.

2. Scattered Diagram

Each numerical value in two sets of figures can be represented by a point on a graph. By taking values for the first series along the x- axis and the values for the second series along the y-axis, the entire data can be plotted on the graph. The figure obtained by plotting the points is called scatter diagram.

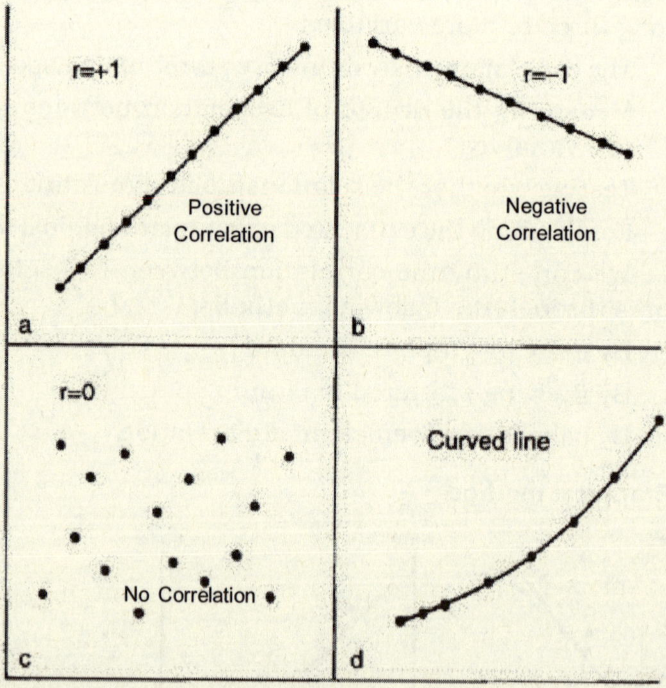

There is positive correlation if the direction of the line is upwards from left to right .If the direction of the line is downwards from left to right, the correlation is negative. If the points are scattered widely then there is no correlation.

3. Coefficient of Correlation

The Karl Pearson devised a formula for this coefficient, which is as follows:

$$r = \frac{\Sigma xy}{N\sigma x\sigma y}$$

$x = (X - \bar{X})$

$y = (Y - \bar{Y})$

σx = standard deviation of series X

σy = standard deviation of series Y

N = number of pairs of observation

r = correlation coefficient

This method is to be applied only where the deviation of items are taken from the actual means and not from assumed mean.

The value of the coefficient of correlation as obtained by the above formula shall always lie between ± 1 where r = +1, it means that there is perfect positive correlation between the variables.

When r = –1 it means that there is perfect negative correlation between the variables. When r = 0, it means that there is no relationship between the variables. However in practice such values of r as +1 , -1, and 0 are rare.

We normally get values, which lie between +1 and –1 such as -0.3

The coefficient of correlation describe not only the magnitude of correlation but also its direction.

The above formula of computing Pearson coefficient of correlation can be transformed in the following form which is easier to apply.

$$r = \frac{\Sigma xy}{\sqrt{\Sigma x^2 x \ \Sigma y^2}}$$

$x = (X - \bar{X})$

$y = (Y - \bar{Y})$

We have to calculate separately the standard deviation of X and Y series.

Steps

1. Take the deviations of X series from the mean of X and denote these deviations by x.
2. Square these deviations and obtained the total i.e. Σx^2.
3. Take the deviation of Y series from the mean of Y and denote these deviation by y.
4. Square these deviations and obtained the total i.e.Σy^2.
5. Multiply the deviations of X and Y series and obtained the total Σxy.
6. Substitute the value of Σxy, Σx^2, and Σy^2 in the above formula.

   Example:

Table 23. Calculation of coefficient of correlation

X	*$(X-\bar{X}) = x$*	*x^2*	*Y*	*$(Y - \bar{Y}) = y$*	*y^2*	*xy*
	x			*y*		
9	+4	16	15	+3	9	+12
8	+3	9	16	+4	16	+12
7	+2	4	14	+2	4	+4
6	+1	1	13	+1	1	+1
5	0	0	11	−1	1	0
4	−1	1	12	0	0	0
3	-2	4	10	-2	4	+4
2	-3	9	8	-4	16	+12
1	-4	16	9	-3	9	+12
$\Sigma X = 45$	$\Sigma x = 0$	$\Sigma x^2 = 60$	$\Sigma Y = 108$	$\Sigma y = 0$	$\Sigma y^2 = 60$	$\Sigma xy = 57$

The coefficient of correlation is said to be a measure of covariance between two series. The covariance of two series X and Y is written as:

$$\text{Covariance} = \frac{\Sigma xy}{N}$$

Where x and y stands for deviations of X and Y series from their respective means. In order to find out the value of correlation coefficient, first we calculate covariance and then we divide the covariance by the standard deviation of the two series. The ratio so obtained is called Karl Pearson's coefficient of correlation.

$$r = \frac{\Sigma xy}{N\sigma x\sigma y}$$

$$\sigma x = \sqrt{\frac{\Sigma x^2}{N}}$$

$$\sigma y = \sqrt{\frac{\Sigma y^2}{N}}$$

$$r = \frac{\Sigma xy}{\sqrt{\frac{\Sigma x^2}{N} \times \frac{\Sigma y^2}{N}}} = \frac{\Sigma xy}{\sqrt{\Sigma x^2 \times \Sigma y^2}}$$

$$x = (X - \bar{X})$$
$$y = (Y - \bar{Y})$$

$$\bar{X} = \frac{45}{9} = 5$$

$$\bar{Y} = \frac{108}{9} = 12$$

$$\Sigma xy = 57,\ \Sigma x^2 = 60,\ \Sigma y^2 = 60$$

$$r = \frac{57}{\sqrt{60 \times 60}} = \frac{57}{60} = 0.95$$

CALCULATION OF COEEFICIENT OF CORRELATION USING THE RANK DIFFERENCES METHOD FOR FOLLOWING DATA:

X 43, 56, 29, 81, 96, 34, 73 62, 48, 76

Y 15, 26, 34, 86, 19, 29, 83, 67, 51, 5

Table 24. Calculation of coefficient of correlation using the rank differences

X	*Rx*	*Y*	*Ry*	*d*	d^2
43	08	15	10	02	04
56	06	26	08	02	04
29	10	34	06	04	16
81	02	86	01	01	01
96	01	19	09	08	64
34	09	29	07	02	04
73	04	83	02	02	04
62	05	67	03	02	04
48	07	51	05	02	04
76	03	58	04	01	01
					106

Coefficient of correlation =

$$r = \frac{\sigma\Sigma d^2}{n\left(n^2 - 1\right)}$$

$$= 1 - \left(\frac{6 \times 106}{10\,(100 - 1)}\right)$$

$$= 1 - \left(\frac{636}{990}\right) = +0.35$$

Spearman's Rank Correlation

Table 25. Computation of rank correlation coefficient

Rank according to the Number of items used	*Rank according to the citation, if received*	*Di*	*Di²*
1	1	0	0
2	4	-2	4
3	3	0	0
4	2	2	4
5	10	-5	25
6	6	0	0
7	7	0	0
8	8	0	0
9	9	0	0
10	5	5	25
11	11	0	0
12	12	0	0
			58

$$\rho = 1 - \frac{6\Sigma Di^2}{N\left(N^2 - 1\right)}$$

$$\rho = 1 - \frac{6 \times 58}{12\left(144 - 1\right)} = 1 - \frac{348}{1716} = 0.80$$

Since the value of ρ = near to +1, It means X and Y are correlated. It is also called Spearman's rank correlation.

REGRESSION ANALYSIS

Unlike the coefficient of correlation, which indicated the extent of the relationship between two sets of figures, a regression equation enables us to calculate the amount of change in one variable corresponding to a change in other.

In social sciences, most relationships are linear in nature and can be fitted into a linear function. A function is said to linear when pairs of X, Y values fall into a function that can be plotted as straight line. This line is represented by the following equation:

$$Y = a + bX$$

Where X and Y = value of X and Y variables respectively.

a = Y intercept or the place at which the line crosses the Y axis or the amount of Y when X = 0

b = slope of the line across the group , expressing the number of units of changes in Y accompanying one unit of change in X.

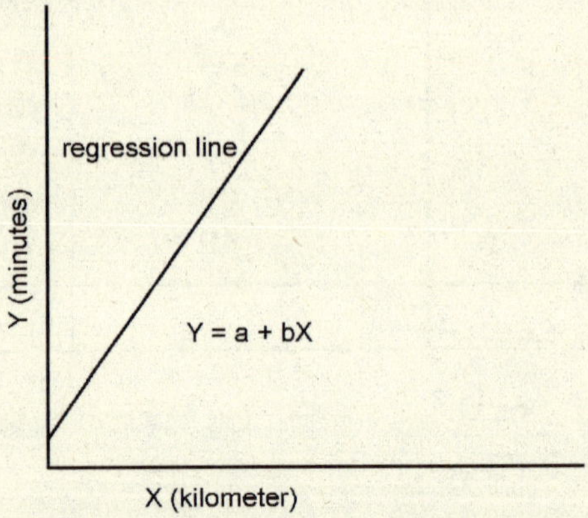

For example there is a perfect linear relationship between the distance and time that a bus travels at a fixed speed. The above diagramme shows the interrelationship between distance and time.

The regression equation

The relationship can be represented by a simple equation called the regression equation. In this context "regression" (the term is a historical anomaly) simply means that the average value of y is a "function" of x, that is, it changes with x.

The regression equation representing how much y changes with any given change of x can be used to construct a regression line on a scatter diagram, and in the simplest case this is assumed to be a straight line. The direction in which the line slopes depends on whether the correlation is positive or negative. When the two sets of observations increase or decrease together (positive) the line slopes upwards from left to right; when one set decreases as the other increases the line slopes downwards from left to right. As the line must be straight, it will probably pass through few, if any, of the dots. Given that the association is well described by a straight line. We have to define two features of the line if we are to place it correctly on the diagram. The first of these is its distance above the baseline; the second is its slope.

Correlation describes the strength of an association between two variables, and is completely symmetrical, the correlation between A and B is the same as the correlation between B and A. However, if the two variables are related it means that when one changes by a certain amount the other changes on an average by a certain amount. For instance, in the children described earlier greater height is associated, on average, with greater anatomical dead space. If y represents the dependent variable and x the independent variable, this relationship is described as the regression of y on x.

The regression equation performs some functions. First it describe the nature of association. The slope of regression line (Y on X) is geometric representation of the rate of change of Y with respect to X. Second the regression equation is useful for predicting or estimating an unknown value of one variable for a given value of the other variable. The goal is to construct such a equation that the error of prediction will be minimum.

According to criteria 'a' and 'b' in the regression equation can be calculated by the following formula:

$$\frac{N(\Sigma XY) - (\Sigma X)(\Sigma Y)}{N\left(\Sigma X^2\right) - (\Sigma X)^2}$$

They are expressed in the following *regression equations :*

Regression Equation of Y on X

The regression equation that enables us to find out the amount of change in Y corresponding to a change in X is called the regression equation of Y on X .If this regression equation responded by Y =a' +b'x, than the constant a' and b' are determined from the two normal equations:

$$\Sigma Y = Na' + b''\Sigma X$$

$$\Sigma XY = a' \Sigma X + b'\Sigma X^2$$

Regression Equation of X on Y

The regression equation that enables us to find out the amount of change in X corresponding to a change in Y is called the regression equation of X on Y .If this regression equation responded by X =a' +b'Y, than the constant a' and b' are determined from the two normal equations:

$$\Sigma X = Na' + b''\Sigma Y$$

$$\Sigma XY = a' \Sigma Y + b'\Sigma Y^2$$

From the graph of two regression lines, the following conclusion can be drawn:

1. The two regression lines intersects at the point x, y, where x = arithmetic mean of the items in X series, y = arithmetic mean of the item Y series.
2. If two regression lines are close to each other than the correlation between X series and Y series is very high.
3. If the two regression lines coincide than there is perfect correlation.
4. If the two regression lines are at a distance from each other than the degree of correlation between the X series and Y series is less.

5. If the two regression lines intersect at right angle than there is no correlation between X series and Y series.

From the data find out the :

1. Karl Pearson's coefficient of correlation
2. The two regression equations
3. The two regression coefficient
4. The most likely value of X when Y= 41
5. The most likely value of Y when X=-45

Table 26. Calculation of Regression

X	x	x^2	Y	y	y^2	xy
52	4	16	40	-9	81	-36
60	12	144	46	-3	9	-36
58	-10	100	43	-6	36	-60
39	-9	81	54	-5	25	-45
41	-5	49	49	0	0	0
53	5	25	55	6	36	36
47	-1	1	48	-1	1	1
34	-14	196	57	5	64	-112
384		612	392		252	-258

$$\text{A.M.} = \bar{X} = \frac{384}{8} = 48$$

$$\text{S.D.} = \sigma x = \sqrt{\frac{\Sigma x^2}{n}} = \sqrt{\frac{612}{8}} = \sqrt{76.5} = 8.746$$

$$\text{S.D.} = \sigma y = \sqrt{\frac{\Sigma y^2}{n}} = \sqrt{\frac{392}{8}} = \sqrt{31.5} = 5.612$$

$$\text{Coeficient of correlation } r = \frac{xy}{n \,.\, \sigma x \,.\, \sigma y}$$

$$= \frac{258}{8(8.7346)(5.612)} = 0.66$$

The regression equation

The regression equation of Y on X

$$y - \bar{y} = r\frac{\sigma y}{\sigma x}(X - \bar{x})$$

$$\sigma y = 5.612$$

$$\sigma x = 8.746$$

$$Y - 49 = -066 \times \frac{5.612}{8.746}(x - 48)$$

$$Y = -0.42 + 69.16$$

$$SD = \sigma x$$

The regression equation of X on Y

$$X - \bar{X} = r\frac{\sigma x}{\sigma y}(Y - \bar{y})$$

$$X - 48 = \frac{8.75}{-66x\ 5.61}(Y - 49)$$

$$r = \frac{\Sigma xy}{\sqrt{\Sigma x^2\ \Sigma y^2}} = \frac{258}{\sqrt{612 - 252}} = -0.66$$

$$X - 48 = -1.02y + 49.98$$

$$X - \bar{X} = \frac{r\ \Sigma x}{\sigma y}(Y - y)$$

$$X - 1.02 + 97.98$$

Regression coefficient

The regression coefficient of Y on X is

$$r = \frac{\sigma y}{\sigma x} = -0.66x \frac{5.61}{8.75} = -0.42$$

The regression X on Y is

$$r = \frac{\sigma x}{\sigma y} = -0.66 \times \frac{8.75}{5.61} = -1.02$$

The most likely value of X when Y =41

X = – 1.02Y

X = (–1.02) X 41 + 97.98

X = 41.82 + 97.98

X = 56.16

The most likely value of Y when X = 45

Y = – 0.12X + 69.16

Y = – 41X 45 + 69.16

Y = –18.90 + 69.16

Y = 5026

8

Hypothesis and Testing the Hypothesis

INTRODUCTION

Hypothesis is generally considered as basic instrument in research. Once the problem has been formulated, literature reviewed, research approach selected, then the researcher is ready to state his hypothesis. Hypothesizing is done only after survey of relevant literature and learning the present status of the field of research. It can be formulated based on previous research and observation.

Hypothesis is tentative propositions relating to the phenomenon under study. They have to be tested empirically before we can accept or reject them.

To formulate a hypothesis the researcher should acquire enough knowledge in the topic of research and a reasonably deep insight about the problem. In formulating a hypothesis construct operational definitions of variables in the research problem. Hypothesis is due to an intelligent guess or for inspiration which is to be tested in the research work rigorously through appropriate methodology. Testing of hypothesis leads to explanation of the associated phenomenon or event.

DEFINITIONS

What is?

The Oxford Reference dictionary defines hypothesis as "a proposition or supposition made from known facts as the basis for reasoning or investigation(plural: hypotheses)" Hypotheses has a provisional characteristic till the time it is established as true. Examples:

1. "Users of college libraries mainly depends upon the textbooks for their information seeking"
2. "Journals are the main source of information for the researchers"

Depending upon the subject matter of investigative research, appropriate hypothesis or hypotheses can be framed.

"A hypothesis is a shrewd guess or inference that is formulated and provisionally adopted to explain observed facts or conditions and to guide in future investigation" (Goods and Scates, 1954, p.90)[34]

According to Chambers Twentieth Century Dictionary, hypothesis is a supposition, a proposition assumed for the sake of argument, a theory to be proved by reference to facts, a provisional explanation of anything."

"A hypothesis then, could be defined as an expectation about events based on generalizations of the assumed relationship between two variables." (Tuckman, 1978, p.27)[78]

"... the hypothesis is meant to provide the researcher with an opportunity, in advance of the actual data collection, to predict the results of the study. These predictions of the results are called the hypothesis of the study". (Fox, 1969, p.48)[26]

For researcher point of view hypothesis is a formal question that he intends to resolve. Thus, a hypothesis may be defined as a proposition or a set of proposition set forth as an explanation for the occurrence of some specified group of phenomena either asserted merely as a provisional conjecture to guide some investigation or accepted as highly probable in the light of established facts.

Quite often a research hypothesis is a predictive statement, capable of being tested by scientific methods, that relates an independent variable to some dependent variable. For example

1. "Library A is performing better than B library."
2. "Users of university mainly depends upon the primary sources to fulfill their information needs".

These are the hypotheses capable of being verified and tested.

From the above definitions it can be concluded that:

1. Hypothesis is shrewd guess or inference
2. A tentative generalization
3. Predition of the result of the study

Every type of enquiry began with some guess or supposition. If road accident has taken place, one may guess the cause of accident as rash driving. This guess has to be studied by careful observation, investigation of various facts of accident.

Which includes:

1. What is the cause of event accident?
2. How and why did the event occured?
3. When?
4. Was there any lapse on the part of the signal system?

Proper answer to these questions and other related questions will have to be obtained without bias. Only than the guess is deemed as realistic. It is such a variable or provable guess that can be classified as a "hypothesis"

Depending upon the subject matter of investigative research, appropriate hypothesis or hypotheses can be framed. There is no fixed formula for framing hypothesis. A hypothesis is tentative generalization about the relation between two or more variables.

Researchers do not carry out work without any aim or expectation. Research is not of doing something and presenting what is done. Every research problem is undertaken aiming at certain outcomes. That is, before starting actual work such as performing an experiment or theoretical calculation or numerical analysis, we expect certain outcomes from the study. The expectations form the hypothesis. Hypotheses are scientifically reasonable predictions. They are often stated in terms of if-then sentences in certain logical forms. A hypothesis should provide what we expect to find in the chosen research problem. That is, the expected or proposed solutions based on available data and tentative explanations constitute the hypothesis.

In Social Sciences where direct knowledge of population parameter(s) is rare, hypothesis testing is the often used strategy for deciding whether a sample data offer such support for a hypothesis that generation can be made.

Thus, hypothesis testing enables us to make probability statements about population parameter(s).

NATURE OF HYPOTHESIS

Hypothesis may be of single variable (univartiate proposition). It involves two variables (bivariate proposition). If it involves more than two variables than it is a multivariate proposition. A proposition that has been proved and verified becomes a validated hypothesis leading to a theory or scientific law.

SOURCES OF HYPOTHESIS

Some of the sources of hypothesis are:

1. Earliear researches carried out by researchers on a subject or area.
2. Review of literature in various sources, books and journals.
3. Observation of various problems pertaining to various organization.
4. Various issues that may arise while tackling one's own professional problems.
5. Studies pertaining to the impact of technological changes.

CRITERIA FOR A GOOD HYPOTHESIS

What are the criteria of a good hypothesis?

An hypothesis should have conceptual clarity and a theoretical orientation. Further, it should be testable. It should be stated in a suitable way so that it can be tested by investigation. A hypothesis made initially may become incorrect when the data obtained are analyzed. In this case it has to be revised. It is important to state the hypothesis of a research problem in a research report. We note that if a hypothesis withstands the experiments and provides the required facts to make it acceptable, not only to the researchers performing the experiments but to others doing other experiments then when sufficiently reinforced by continual verification the hypothesis may become a theory.

According to Poincar´e, a scientific hypothesis which was proved untenable can still be very useful. If a hypothesis does not pass an empirical test, then this fact means that we have neglected some important and meaningful element. Thus, the hypothesis gives us the opportunity to discover the existence of an unforeseen aspect of reality. As a consequence of this point of view about the nature of scientific theories, Poincar´e suggested that a scientist must utilize few hypotheses, for it is very difficult to find the wrong hypothesis in a theory which makes use of many hypotheses.

Some of the criterias of good hypothesis are :

1. It should be specific, concise and meaningfully presented. If the hypothesis is not clear and precise, the inferences drawn on its basis cannot be taken as reliable.
2. It should not contain contradictory statements.
3. It should be based directly on the existing data.
4. A hypothesis can be framed as a descriptive statement relating to the pertinent issue of a problem.
5. A hypothesis relating to problem in a social science must be relevant and scientifically realasting and verifiable.
6. The hypothesis should state relationship between variables, if it happens to be a relational hypothesis.
7. Hypothesis should be limited in scope and must be specific.
8. Hypothesis should be stated as far as possible in most simple terms so that the same is easily understandable by all concern.
9. Hypothesis should be consistent with most known facts.
10. Hypothesis should be amenable to testing within a limited time. One cannot spend a life time collecting data to test it.

TYPES OF HYPOTHESIS

Depending upon the nature of hypothesis, can be classified into following categories:

1. Working hypothesis
2. Research hypothesis

3. Scientific hypothesis
4. Statistical hypothesis consisting of null hypothesis and alternate hypothesis

1. Working hypothesis : When a researcher assumed temporarily certain facts in the course of his preliminary study of a problem, then he may make a tentative proposition that is not final. Such a course of action makes him frame a working hypothesis.

2. Research hypothesis : It arises out of the finalization of a working hypothesis.

3. Scientific hypothesis : When a hypothesis is framed on the basis of available, adequate data, for the purpose of empirical verification and systematic justification than it becomes a scientific hypothesis.

4. Statistical hypothesis : These are propositions that express quantitative relationship. A statistical hypothesis consists of null hypothesis and alternate hypothesis. When the researcher is interesting in finding the existence or non existence of a quantitative relationship then he proceeds in an unbiased manner by assuming the non existence of a relationship. A null hypothesis is the one indicating expectation of no difference 'between or among' the variables. Such an assumption is called "Null hypothesis". It is used primarily for statistical testing. The objective of null hypothesis is to avoid the personnel bias of investigator during the gathering of data. If he supposes the contrary, that is, the existence of a relationship, than his hypothesis would be "Alternate Hypothesis".

If the null hypothesis is accepted as true on the basis of empirical verification, than the alternate hypothesis is rejected and vice-versa. Null hypothesis should always be specific hypothesis .It should not state about or approximately a certain value.

It is the null hypothesis that is always tested.

NEED AND IMPORTANCE OF HYPOTHESIS

The hypothesis need to be established as a scientifically accurate only after proper observation and experimental verification. It depends upon the subject matter of the research. Hypothesis is a guiding instrument for conducting research work. There is no fixed formula for framing hypothesis. Its main function is to suggest new experiments and observations.

Researchers do not carry out work without any aim or expectation. Research is not of doing something and presenting what is done. Every research problem is undertaken aiming at certain outcomes. That is, before starting actual work such as performing an experiment or theoretical calculation or numerical analysis, we expect certain outcomes from the study.

Hypotheses are scientifically reasonable predictions. They are often stated in terms of if-then sentences in certain logical forms. A hypothesis should provide what we expect to find in the chosen research problem. That is, the expected or proposed solutions based on available data and tentative explanations constitute the hypothesis.

IMPORTANCE OF HYPOTHESIS

1. A well formulated hypothesis provides an essential basis for a researcher to began his in quisite enquiry without wastage of much time and energy.
2. If researcher is confused and lost his way, it is the hypothesis that guide him and show him the direction to the path along he has to proceed for carrying out his investigation.
3. Hypothesis is very helpful in enabling a researcher to know exactly as to what type of information would be most suitable for tackling the problem which he is facing. By collecting the essential facts and figures and using the right methodology, the researcher would be able to draw reliable conclusions.

4. A non hypothesized research would be an aimless search of everything about anything. Hence, the importance of hypothesis in establishing the relevance of research.
5. In the age of modern information technology, no researcher should take the risk of wasting a lot of precious time neglecting the guidance provided by a well framed hypothesis.

FORMULATION OF HYPOTHESIS

The hypotheses are formulated before the collection of data. These are based on literature or experience of the researcher. If it has no basis in the literature or experience, then it need not to be stated. When the hypothesis is tested, it can be either supported or rejected. Hypothesis should represent researcher's thinking about the problem before the start of the study.

TESTING THE HYPOTHESIS

The testing of hypothesis means the test the validity of the data that the researcher has collected. Whether or not hypothesis is valid or not. The main question is whether to accept the null hypothesis or not to accept the null hypothesis.

We make certain suppositions known as hypothesis about population parameters. These hypotheses are our expectations. The hypothesis testing determines the validity of the assumption (technically described as null hypothesis) with a view to choose between two conflicting hypotheses. Hypothesis testing helps the researcher to decide on the basis of sample data, whether the hypothesis about the population is likely to be true or false.

We test by finding out the difference between our observation of some statistics of a sample with the corresponding parameters of the population. This process of testing is known as significance of statistical hypothesis.

Hypothesis testing is a procedure, based on sample evidence and probability theory, used to determine whether the hypothesis is a reasonable statement and should not be rejected, or is unreasonable and should be rejected.

What is Hypothesis Testing?

Hypothesis testing means subjecting a hypothesis to an appropriate empirical scrutiny and statistical test to determine its validity. A researcher has to do number of things as pre requirement for testing a hypothesis. He should see that the hypothesis is testable. The variables used in the hypothesis should be amenable to measurement. He has to select a real social situation that will be sufficient as a reasonable testing ground for the hypothesis.

For example, if the hypothesis is concerned with study of user behavior, the researcher should select a sample of users, and collect the relevant data needed for verifying the his hypothesis, and analyze them. All these are the pre requirement for hypothesis testing.

Approaches to Hypothesis Testing

There are two approaches to hypothesis testing :

1. The classical or sampling theory approach and
2. Bayesian approach

The classical approach is an established one and is widely used in research. In this approach, the decision making ret totally upon an analysis of sampling data. A hypothesis is set up and tested on the basis of sample data.

The Bayesian approach is based on an older theorem known as Bayes Theorem. It is also uses sampling data, but it goes beyond them, and takes into consideration all other available information for making decisions. Decision rules are established, and cost and other estimates are made.

On the basis of them, decision alternatives are judged. The Bayesian approach has emerged as an alternative testing procedure since the mid 1950s.

Inferences on the population characteristics (or parameters) are often made on the basis of sample observation, especially when the population is large and it may not be possible to enumerate all the sampling units belonging to the population. In doing so, one has to take the help of certain assumptions (or hypothetical value) about the characteristics of the population, if such information is available. Such hypothesis about the population is termed as statistical hypothesis and the hypothesis is tested on the basis of the sample values.

"A claim or hypothesis about the population parameters or values is known as Null Hypothesis and is written as H_0"

This hypothesis is then tested with the available evidence and the decision is made whether to accept this hypothesis or reject. If this hypothesis is rejected, there we accept the alternate hypothesis.

The hypothesis is denoted as H_1

Statisticians have developed several tests of hypothesis for the purpose of testing the hypothesis. These tests can be classified as:

1. Parametric test or standard test of hypothesis
2. Non parametric tests or distribution free test of hypothesis.

Parametric tests usually assume certain properties of the parent population from which we draw samples. But when there are situations when researcher cannot or does not want to make such assumptions. In such case we use statistical methods for testing hypothesis which are called non parametric tests because such tests do not depends upon any assumption about the parameters of the parent population.

Important parametric tests are:

1. z-test 2. t-test 3. ξ^2 test and 4. F-test.

Chi square test is an important test amongst the several tests developed by the statisticians.

BASIC CONCEPT CONCERNING TESTING HYPOTHESIS

1. Null hypothesis and alternative hypothesis

Null hypothesis : If we are to compare with library A with B about the superiority and if proceed on the assumption that both are equally good, than this assumption is termed as the null hypothesis. It is generally symbolize as H_0. As against this, we may think that that the library A superior or B is inferior, we may stating this term as alternate hypothesis (kothari p.225)[45]. Alternate hypothesis as H_0. Suppose we want to test the hypothesis that the population mean (μ) is equal to the hypothesized mean (μH_0)= 100. Then we say that the null hypothesis that the population mean is equal to the hypothesized mean 100 and symbolically we can express as :

$$H_0 : \mu = \mu H_0 = 100$$

If our sample results do not support this null hypothesis, we should conclude that something else is true. The set of alternatives to the null hypothesis is referred to as the alternative hypothesis.

Alternative hypothesis is usually the one which one wishes to prove and the null hypothesis is one wishes to disapprove. Thus, null hypothesis represents the hypothesis we are trying to reject, and alternative hypothesis represents all other possibilities.

2. Null hypothesis should always be specific hypothesis i.e.it should not state about or proximity a certain value.

Generally, in hypothesis testing we proceed on the basis of null hypothesis, keeping the alternative hypothesis in view. It is because that null hypothesis is true, one can assign the probabilities to different possible sample result, but this cannot be done if we proceed with the alternative hypothesis.

The null hypothesis and the alternative hypothesis are chosen before the sample is drawn(the researcher must avoid the error of deriving hypothesis from the data that he collects and then testing the hypothesis from the same data).

In the choice of null hypothesis, the following considerations are usually kept in view:

1. Alternative hypothesis is usually the one which one wishes to prove and the null hypothesis is one which one wishes to disapprove. Thus, a null hypothesis represents the hypothesis we are trying to reject , and alternative hypothesis represents all other possibilities.
2. If the rejection of a certain hypothesis when it is usually true involve great risk, it is taken as null hypothesis because then the probability of rejecting it when it is true is á (the level of significance) which is chosen very small.
3. Null hypothesis should always be specific hypothesis i.e. it should not state about or approximately a certain value.

3. The level of significance : This is very important concept hypothesis testing. It is always some percentage (usually 5%) which should be chosen with great care. The 5% level of significant means that researcher is willing to take as much as a five percent risk of rejecting the null hypothesis when (H_0) happen to be true. It is determined in advance before testing the hypothesis.

4. Test of hypothesis : Given a hypothesis H_0 and an alternative hypothesis Ha, we make a rule which is known as decision rule according to which we accept H_0

(i.e. reject H_a) or reject H_0 (accept H_a).This sort of basis is known as decision rule.

5. Type I and type II error : In hypothesis testing there are two types of errors we generally make. We may reject H_0 when H_0 is true and we may accept H_0 when H_0 is not true. The former is known as type I error and later as type II error. Type I error means rejection of hypothesis which should have been accepted and type II error means accepting the hypothesis which should have been rejected.

PROCEDURE FOR TESTING THE HYPOTHESIS

Our first task is to state the hypothesis in statistical terms. Suppose we are studying the impact of automation on the services of academic libraries. The hypothesis may be stated as "the efficiency of the library services has increased due to automation". We draw a random sample of users of academic libraries and collect data for testing the hypothesis.

We develop a null hypothesis (H_0) for statistically testing the hypothesis. The null hypothesis is especially formulated for testing for possible rejection or nullification. Hence, the name null hypothesis. It is accompanied by alternative hypothesis (H_a). It means our regular research hypothesis which is the logical apposite of the null hypothesis.

The null hypothesis is based on a negative inference in order to avoid the fallacy of affirming the consequent. That is, it is easy to reject a false hypothesis rather than to accept a real hypothesis.

Since a sample is likely to vary somewhat from its population, the sample result is subject to sampling error and therefore, it does not always reflect the true population value; a decision rule is needed to enable us to reject or accept a hypothesis on the basis of a sample result.

The statistical testing of a hypothesis consists of following steps :

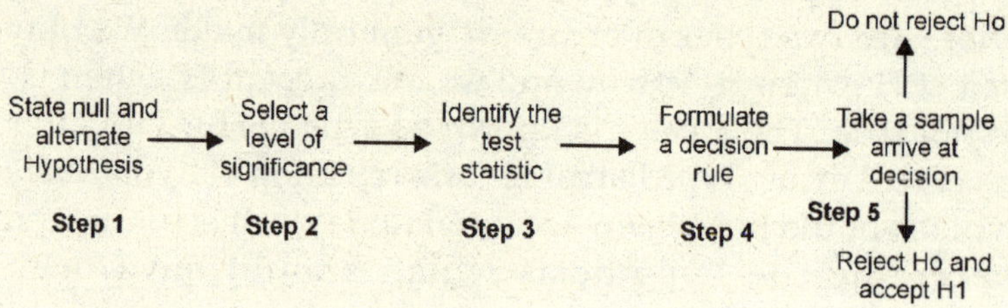

A Hypothesis should be able to meet the test of its validity. Validity is established in two stages:

Stage 1: use the test of logic

Stage 2: employs an empirical test

Stage 1 : From the hypothesis, the researcher develops certain implications. These implications are stated in operational terms. If these implications come in conflict with accepted knowledge, then the hypothesis rejected or modified.

Stage 2 : If the hypothesis passes the test of logic, than it is put under an empirical test by means of experiment or subject to certain kinds of measurements.

STEPS IN HYPOTHESIS TESTING

The various steps involved in hypothesis testing are stated below:

Step 1 : State the Null Hypothesis and the Alternate Hypothesis

Example: H_0: educated and uneducated have the same level of political awareness.

Ha: educated persons have higher level of political awareness than uneducated persons. It means that hypothesis should be clearly stated, considering the research problem.

Let us assume the population mean = 50 and set up the hypothesis as:

Null hypothesis, Ho : u = 50 Null hypothesis, Ho: u= 50

Alternate hypothesis, H1 u ≠ 50 Null hypothesis, H1: u < 50

Example 2 : The average score of UGC national level test is 90 and the average score of 100 of states's students selected on random basis are 80.The states wants to know is there any difference between local scores and national scores.

In such cases the hypothesis may be stated as:

Null hypothesis: H1: μ= 90

Alternative hypothesis : H1: $\mu \neq \Sigma 90$

Step 2 : select a level of significance (prior to sampling) : The hypothesis are tested on predetermined level of significance and it should be defined. Generally, in practice either 5 % level or 1% level is adopted for the purpose. The level of significance must be adequate in the context of the purpose and nature of enquiry.

The level of significance signifies the probability of committing type 1 error α and is generally taken as equal to 0.05. Sometimes, the value α is established as 0.01, but it is at the discretion of the investigators to select its value, depending upon the sensitivity of the study.

Step 3 : Select the appropriate statistical test : There are various tests of significance such as chi-square test. An appropriate test must be selected with reference to the nature of the population studied. The method of sampling used, the level of measurement of data and the like.

This step is to select a random sample and compute an appropriate value from the sample data concerning the test statistic utilizing the relevant distribution. A random sample has to be selected as per the sample design decided, and for the collected data, the appropriate measures (mean, standard deviation, or correlation) with reference to the research question, type of hypothesis to be tested and the level of measurement of data.

For the purpose of selecting and rejecting or accepting the null hypothesis, a suitable statistics called 'Test Statistics", this mean H_0 is assumed to be really true. If the difference is large enough, one suspects the validity of the assumption and rejects the null hypothesis (H_0). On the other hand, if the difference may be assumed due to sampling (random) fluctuation and hence the null hypothesis (H_0) is accepted.

Step 4 : fixing up the level of significance and defining the critical (rejection) region : Based on the sampling distribution of the statistic, the probability of obtaining a difference equal to or greater than the observed difference is calculated on the assumption that the null hypothesis is true.

It is important to note that a hypothesis is never proved, it is merely supported or conformed sustained or rejected. Even if a hypothesis is confirmed, it is always tentative, which can be revised or rejected.

If we select the value of α level of significance = 0.05, and we use the standard normal distribution as our test statistic for testing the population parameter μ, than the value of difference between the assumption of null hypothesis (assumed value of the population parameter) and the value obtained by the analysis or the sample results is not expected to be more than 1.96 at α 0.05.

The relationship can be shown by the diag. is given below :

The hypothesis should be evaluated with regards to :

$$z = \frac{\text{observed value of statistic } (\overline{X}) - \text{ expected value } (\mu)}{\text{Standard error of the estimate}}$$

Calculated value of z = as given by the formula above = (Absolute value)

Step 5 : Critical (or Tabulated value) : Find out the critical(or Tabulated) value of the statistic (z or t or f etc.). One has to calculate the probability that the sample result would diverge as widely as it has from expectations, if the null hypothesis were in fact true.

We must locate the critical value in the table concerned with the selected probability distribution for the given level of significance for the appropriate number of degree of freedom. The critical value so located in the table is commonly known as table value.

Step 6 : If the calculated value of the statistic< the tabulated value : Reject Null hypothesis H_o and accept H1 otherwise accept the Null Hypothesis, if the difference may be assumed due to sampling (random) fluctuation and hence the Null Hypothesis (H_0) is accepted.

Step 7 : make the decision : For most tests, if the calculated test value is larger than the corresponding critical (i.e. table) value, we reject the null hypothesis and conclude that the research hypothesis is supported. If the table value is larger than the calculated value, the research hypothesis is not supported.

TEST OF SIGNIFICANCE USED FOR HYPOTHESIS TESTING

The test of significance used for hypothesis testing are of two types. The parametric and non parametric test. The parametric test are more powerful , but they depend on the parameters or characteristics of the population. They are based on following assumptions:

1. The observation or value must be independent.
2. The population from which the sample is drawn on a random basis should be normally distributed.
3. The population should have equal variances
4. The data should be measured at least at interval level so that arithmetic operations can be used.

The important parametric test are: z-test, the t-test and F-test, chi-square test.

1. The z -test

Prof. R.A. Fisher has developed the z-test. It is based on the normal distribution; it is widely used for testing the significance of several statistics such as mean, median, mode etc. This test is used even when binominal distribution or 't' distribution is applicable on the presumption that such a distribution tends to approximate normal distribution as the sample size (n) become larger.

The relevant test statistic, z is calculated and compared it with probable value (to be read from the normal distribution table) at a specified level of significance for judging the significance of the measures concerned.

Research example : In one of the study on role conflict among employed housewives computed Z values pertaining to the differences between mother role and other sub roles of housewives (overall) and also for each occupational group. The Z value showed that respondents experienced difficulty in their role as mother and also in their relationship with parents and relatives.

2. Chi-Square Test

Introduction : The chi-square test is the most popular non-parametric test of significance in social science research. It is used to make comparisons between two or more nominal values. The chi-square is used to make comparisons between frequencies rather than between mean scores.

Chi-square is a statistical test commonly used to compare observed data with data we would expect to obtain according to a specific hypothesis. For example, if, according to Mendel's laws, you expected 10 of 20 offspring from a cross to be male and the actual observed number was 8 males, then you might want to know about the "goodness to fit" between the observed and expected.

Were the deviations (differences between observed and expected) the result of chance, or were they due to other factors. How much deviation can occur before you, the investigator, must conclude that something other than chance is at work, causing the observed to differ from the expected.

The chi-square test is always testing what scientists call the null hypothesis, which states that there is no significant difference between the expected and observed result.

Meaning : The chi square test is an important test developed by the statisticians. This test evaluated whether the difference between the observed frequencies and expected frequencies under the null hypothesis can be attributed to chance or actual population differences.

It is a statistical measure used in context of sampling analysis for comparing a variance to a theoretical variance. As a non parametric test, it can be used to determine if categorical data shows dependency or the two classifications are independent. The chi square test is applicable to large number of problems.

The test is a technique through the use of which it is possible for all researcher to :

1. Test the goodness of fit
2. Test the significance of association between two attributes and
3. Test the homogeneity or the significance of population variance.

A chi-squared test, also written as χ^2 test, is any statistical hypothesis test wherein the sampling distribution of the test statistic is a chi-squared distribution when the null hypothesis is true. Without other qualification, 'chi-squared test' often is used as short for Pearson's chi-squared test. It is a statistical measure used in the context of sampling analysis for comparing a variance to a theoretical variance.

The formula for chi-square test is :

$$\chi^2 = \Sigma \frac{(f_0 - f_e)^2}{f_e}$$

where f_0 = the observed frequency

f_e = the expected frequency in terms of null hypothesis

That is, chi-square is the sum of the squared difference between observed (*o*) and the expected (*e*) data, divided by the expected data in all possible categories.

To compute the expected frequency for any cell, the following formula is used:

$$f_e = \frac{(\text{row total})\,(\text{column total})}{n\,(\text{total number})}$$

The chi-square is applicable in large number of problems. It can be used to make comparisons between theoretical populations and actual data when categories are used.

The test is in fact a technique through the use of which it is possible for all researchers to :

1. test the goodness of fit
2. test the significance of association between two attributes, and
3. test the homogeneity or the significance of population variance.

Chi-square as a test for comparing variance:

The chi square value is often used to judge the significance of population variance. It means we can use the test to judge if a random sample has been drawn from a normal population with mean (μ) and with a specified variance (σ).

The test is based on chi square distribution. Such

a distribution we encounter when we deal with collection of values that involves adding up squares.

Variance of samples require us to add a collection of squared quantities and, thus, have distributions that are related to χ^2 distribution.

If we take each one of a collection of sample variances, divide them with the known population variance and multiply these quotients by (n – 1), where n means the number of items in the sample, we shall obtain a χ^2 distribution.

Thus, $\frac{\sigma_s^2 (n-1)}{\sigma_p^2} = \frac{\sigma s^2 \sigma^2}{\sigma_p^2}$ (d.f.) would have the same distribution as χ^2 with (n – 1) degree of freedom.

The χ^2 distribution is not symmetrical and all the values are positive.

Chi-square as a non parametric test

Chi-square is an important non parametric test and as such no right assumptions are necessary in respect of the type of population. We need only the degree of freedom for using this test. The chi square test can be used as: 1. the test of goodness of fit 2. As the test of independence.

1. As a test of goodness of fit, χ^2 test enable us to see how well does the assumed theoretical distribution fit to the observed data. When some theoretical distribution is fitted to the given data, we are always interested in knowing as to how well this distribution fits with observed data. The chi-square test give answer to this.
2. **As a test of independence :** Chi-square test enable us to explain whether or not two attributes are associated. For example, we may be interested in knowing whether a new medicine is effective in controlling flue or not we Chi-square test help us in deciding this issue. In such situation we proceed

with the null hypothesis that the two attributes (new medicine and control of flue) are independent which means that new medicine is not effective in controlling flue. We first calculate the expected frequencies and then work out the value of chi square.

Condition for the application of chi square test

The following conditions should be satisfied before the chi square applied:

1. Observations recorded and used are collected on random basis.
2. All the items in the sample must be independent
3. No group should contain less than 10 items
4. The overall number of items must also be reasonably large. It should be at least 50.
5. The constraints must be linear.

Steps involved in applying chi square test

Various steps involved are :

1. First of all calculate the expected frequencies on the basis of given hypothesis or on the basis of null hypothesis. The expected frequency for any given cell is worked out to be as under;

   Expected frequency of any cell :

   $$= \frac{(\text{row total for the row of that cell}) \times (\text{column total for the column of the cell})}{(\text{Grand total})}$$

2. Obtain the difference between observed and expected frequencies and find out the squares of such differences i.e. calculate $(0ij\text{-}Eij)^2$
3. Divide the quantity $(0ij\text{-}Eij)^2$ obtained as stated above by the corresponding expected frequency to get and this should be done for all the cell frequencies or group frequencies.

$$\frac{(0_{ij} - E_{ij})^2}{E_{ij}}$$

4. Find the summation of $\frac{(0_{ij} - E_{ij})^2}{E_{ij}}$

Values or what we call $\frac{\sum(0_{ij} - E_{ij})^2}{E_{ij}}$

This is required chi-square value. The chi-square value obtained as such should be compared.

With relevant table value of chi square and then inference is drawn as stated above.

Example: Find out the chi square value for the following information:

Table 27. Calculate the Chi Square value

Class	A	B	C	D	E
Observed Frequency	8	29	44	15	4
Expected frequency	7	24	38	24	7

Class	*Observed frequency Oi*	*Expected frequency Ei*	*Oi-Ei*	*(Oi-Ei)²/Ei*
A and B	(8 + 29) = 37	(7 + 24) = 31	6	36/31
C	44	38	6	36/38
D and E	(15 + 4) = 19	(24 + 7) = 31	-12	144/31

$$\chi^2 = \sum\frac{(0_i - E_i)}{E_i} = 6.76 \text{ appxt.}$$

Example : Weight of 10 students is as follows:

S.No.	1	2	3	4	5	6	7	8	9	10
Weight (kg.)	38	40	45	53	47	43	55	48	52	49

If variance of 10 students drawn is equal to 20 kgs than test this as 5 percent and 1 percent level of significance.

Solution : First of all we should work out the variance of the sample data or σ_s^2 and the same can be calculated as under;

Table 28. Calculation of Variance of Sample data

S.N.	*X_i (Wt in kgs)*	*(Xi-X)*	*$(Xi\text{-}X)^2$*
1	38	-9	81
2	40	-7	49
3	45	-2	04
4	53	6	36
5	47	0	00
6	43	-4	16
7	55	8	64
8	48	1	01
9	52	5	25
10	49	2	04
n = 10	$\Sigma X_I = 470$		$\Sigma(X_i - X)^2$

Important characteristics of Chi square test

1. This (as non parametric test) is based on frequencies and not on the like mean and standard deviation.
2. It is used for testing the hypothesis and is not useful for estimation.
3. This test possesses the additive property as has already been explained.
4. This test can also be applied to a complex contingency table with several classes and as such is very useful test in research work.

5. This test is important non parametric test as no rigid assumptions are necessary in regard to the type of population, no need of parameter values and relatively less mathematical details are involved.

Cautions in using chi-square test

Chi-square test is no doubt is most frequently used test, but its correct application is a very difficult task.

It should be born in mind that the test is to be applied only when the individual observations of sample are independent which means that the occurrence of one individual observation has no effect upon the occurrence of any other observation in the sample under consideration.

The other possible reasons of misuse of this test can be:

1. Neglect of frequencies of non occurrence.
2. Failure to equalize the sum of observed and the sum of expected frequencies.
3. Wrong determination of the degree of freedom.
4. Wrong computation and the like.

The researcher while applying this test must remain careful about all these things.

9
Interpretation of Data and Writing Research Report

INTRODUCTION

A research report is a systematic, scientific and consistent presentation of the entire process of research carried out by a researcher. The last step in the research process is the preparation and presentation of the research report which is the most important part of the research process. If the report is not properly presented or poorly written, all the time and effort spend on gathering and analyzing data would not bring any results. The research report may be popular or technical in nature. A technical report is generally intended for other researchers. The popular report is intended for a more general audience.

INTERPRETATION OF DATA

Meaning of interpretation?

The preliminary statistical work consists of collection, classification, tabulation, presentation and analysis of data. The most commonly used statistical tools are: Mean, median, mode, standard deviations, and other measures such as coefficient of correlation, etc .

Before commencing the work of interpretation of data, the researcher should ensure that the following preliminary requirements of interpretation are fulfilled:

1. The data should be adequate for the purpose of drawing reliable conclusions.
2. Data should be homogeneous.
3. The data should not suffer from any biased.

For interpretation of data proper statistical methods should be applied for scientific analysis. The statistical analysis can be classified as:

1. Descriptive and
2. Inferrential

1. Descriptive : Descriptive data provides quantitative information for analytical interpretation. Descriptive statistics provide a description of what the data look like. They provide a means to describe the points of central tendency (mean, mode, median, etc.) and dispersion (standard deviation, variance, inter quartile range, etc.).

2. Inferential : Inferential data relates to statistical inference where conclusions are drawn on the basis of samples taken randomly from a population, which is assumed to be normal. Population parameters are estimated on the basis of sample statistics. Depending upon the nature of the researcher's problem, relevant sampling methods are used for obtaining data.

Inferential statistics allow the researcher to make inferences about populations from smaller samples of the population. Statistics of the sample are used to estimate parameters of the population . A parameter is a constant value representative of the population (such as population mean and standard deviation) while a statistic is any calculation performed on the sample being tested (Leedy and Ormrod, 2001)[51]. Inferential statistics also allow the researcher to test their research hypotheses. Some measures used in inferential statistics include the standard error of the mean, estimators, and the p-value.

The way that the data is interpreted can have varying effects on your conclusions. Absolute honesty in recording and interpreting data is required to maintain the credibility of research. All of the conditions of a situation should be considered and that we make inferences in strict accordance with the data obtained (Leedy and Ormrod, 2001)[51] Using statistics to determine relationships is paramount to the success of good research. Using tools such as ANOVA, correlations, Fisher Exact Tests, regression, etc. can predict whether or not your research hypothesis is satisfied. But, remember to select your p-value before you begin your research project. Doing this will add credibility to your research.

One other important point to remember when doing data analysis is to use parametric statistics instead of nonparametric statistics whenever possible (Leedy and Ormrod, 2001)[51]. Remember that parametric statistics relies on the assumptions of normality, which gives greater power than nonparametric testing.

WHY WE NEED INTERPRETATION?

Interpretation is essential because the usefulness and utility of research findings lies in proper interpretation. The interpretation is useful because research findings lies in the interpretation. It is an important component of research process. The interpretation is important in research process because of following reasons:

1. Through interpretation researcher can linkup his findings with those of similar studies so that he can predict the concrete results of his findings. The continuity of the research can be maintained.
2. It is helpful and serve as research guide for further research studies.

3. It is helpful to make others understand the real significance of research findings.
4. The interpretations of the findings of exploratory research study generally result into hypotheses for experimental research.

Technique of Interpretation

The technique of interpretation requires a great skill, experience and knowledge on the part of the researcher. It is not an easy job. The researcher may seek the guidance from subject expert for interpretation of data.

Following Steps involve in technique of interpretation :

1. Extraneous information, if collected during study, must be considered while interpreting the final results of the research study. It is advisable to consult experienced, knowledgeable or person having insight into the study before reaching the final interpretation. He can helpful in finding the errors and omissions that will result in correct interpretation and thus will enhance the utility of research result.
2. The researcher must be in no hurry while interpreting results, because sometimes the conclusions, which appear to be all right at the beginning, may not at all be accurate. He should avoid false generalization.
3. Researcher must give reasonable explanation of the relations which he found of his diversified research findings.

Precautions in Interpretation

Precautions should be taken while interpreting the data. Even if the data are properly collected and analyzed, wrong interpretation would lead to inaccurate conclusion. It is therefore important that interpretation should be correct one.

The researcher must pay the attention of the following points for correct interpretation:

The researcher must ensure himself that :

1. The data ate appropriate, trustworthy and adequate for drawing inferences.
2. Proper analysis should be done through statistical methods.
3. The researcher must remain cautious about the errors that can arise in the process of interpretation of data. Errors can arise due to false generalization and /or due to wrong interpretation of statistical measures.
4. Precautions concerning the reliability of data, validation and comparison of results should be taken.
5. Broader generalization should be avoided because the coverage may be restricted to a particular time, particular area, and particular condition. Such restrictions, if any must be specified.

RESEARCH REPORT WRITING

The final and very important step in research study is writing its report. The research report is a mean for communicating our research findings to others and adding something new to the knowledge.

What is Research Report ?

A research report is a formal statement of the research process and its result. It narrates the problem studied, methodology, findings, conclusions etc.

Purpose of Research Report

The purpose of research report is to communicate the results to the interested persons the methodology and the results of the study in such a manner as to enable them to understand the research process and to determine the validity of the conclusions. The aim of the report is not to convince the reader of the value of the result, but to convey him what was done, why it was done, what was its findings etc.

Significance of report writing

Research report is a very important part of research study. Without writing research report is of little value unless they are effectively communicated to others. It is an integral part of research process. The purpose of research is not well served unless the findings are made known to others. All these explain the significance of writing research report. The purpose of research is not well served unless the findings are made known to others. Writing research report is the last step in a research study and requires a set of skills somewhat different from those called for in respect of the earlier stages of research. This task should be accomplished by the researcher with utmost care.

Size of the Report

The size of the report will depends upon the subject matter and what is involved in the study. In practice, there is no mandatory length and the researcher should be guided by their project guides on this matter.

Characteristics of Report

Some of characteristics of report are :

1. A research report is a narrative but authoritative document on the outcome of the research efforts.
2. It presents a highly specific information for a clearly designated audience.
3. It is non persuasive form of communication
4. Presentation is subordinated to the matter being presented.
5. It is a simple, readable and accurate form of communication.

Functions or Research Report

A well written research report performs several functions:

1. It serve as means for presenting the problem studied, methods and techniques used for collecting and analyzing data, the findings, conclusion and recommendations in an original form.
2. It serve as a basic reference material for future use in developing research proposals in the same or related areas.
3. A report serve as a means for judging the quality of the completed research project.
4. It is a means for evaluating the researcher's ability and competence to do research.
5. It provides factual base for formulating policies and strategies related to the area studied.
6. It provides systematic knowledge on problems and issues analyzed.

Types of Reports

The research report vary greatly in length and type. It depends upon the problem in hand. For example banks, financial institutions are generally fond of the short balance sheet type of tabulation for their annual report to their customers and shareholders. Students of literature usually write long reports presenting the critical analysis of some writers, or the period or the like. The reports prepared by the government, departments, commissions, and similar other organizations are generally very comprehensive reports on the issues involved.

Similarly the PhD. Theses and dissertations are also a form of research report writing, usually completed by the student/researcher in academic institutions.

The reports are generally of two types:

1. Technical report
2. Popular report

1. Technical report

This is comprehensive full report of research process and its outcome. It primarily meant for academic community for example the researchers. It covers all the important aspects of research process such as objectives, methods and techniques used, tools of data collection, detailed findings, conclusion and suggestions. The technical report is essentially technical in nature and scope and written in technical language.

The technical report generally consists of following outlines:

1. Summery of results 2. nature of study 3. methods employed 4. discussion of data collection. 5. Analysis of data and presentation of findings 6. conclusion 7. bibliography 8. Technical appendices 9. Index

In technical report the main emphasis is on:

1.The methods employed 2. assumptions made in the course of study and 3. the detail presentation of the findings of the study including limitations and supporting data.

1. Summery of the results : A brief review of main findings just in three of four pages.

2. Nature of the study : Description of the general objectives of study, the working hypothesis etc.

3. Methods employed : Specific methods used in the study and its limitations.

4. Data : Explanation of the data collected, their sources, limitations etc. In case of survey, the manner in which data were collected should be fully described.

5. Analysis of data and presentation of findings: The analysis of data and presentation of findings of the study with supporting data in the form of tables and charts be fully explained. This is the main body of the report usually consists of several chapters.

6. Conclusions : A summary of the findings and its implications drawn from the results be explained.

7. Bibliography : Bibliography of various sources consulted be prepared and listed.

8. Appendices : Appendices for questionnaire, interview schedule, etc. should be provided at the end.

The order of the presentation may not necessary be the same in all technical reports. The presentation may vary in different reports.

2. Popular report

The popular report is one which gives emphasis on simplicity and attractiveness. This type of report is designed for the audience of executives, administrators, and other non technical users. The requirement of the audience is different. They are less concerned with methodological details. They are more interested in major findings and conclusion. It consists of minimization of technical, particularly mathematical, detail and liberal use of charts and diagrammes. In such a report more emphasis is given on practical aspects and policy implications. Complicated statistical techniques and tables need not to be used. Instead pictorial diagrammes may be used.

The format of this report is different from technical report. A brief introduction, objectives of the study, findings, conclusion and recommendations is presented. More headlines, pictures and graphs may be used. Paragraphs are small.

The popular report generally consists of following parts:

1. The findings and their implications : Emphasis in the report is given on the findings of most practical interest and on the implications of these findings.

2. Recommendations for action : Recommendations for action on the basis of the findings of the study is made in this section of the report.

3. Objectives of the study : A general review of how the problem arises is presented along with the specific objectives of the project under study.

4. Methods employed : A brief and non technical description of the methods and techniques used in given in the part of the report.

5. Results : This section constitutes the main body of the report in which the results of the study are presented in non technical terms along with illustrations, charts, diagrammes, tables etc.

6. Technical appendices : More detailed information on methods used etc. presented in the form of appendices.

The one important thing about this report is that it gives emphasis on simplicity and policy implications from the operational point of view, avoiding the technical details as par as possible.

DIFFERENT STEPS IN WRITING REPORT

There are following 8 steps in writing research report:

1. Preparation
2. Gathering the information/data
3. Sorting,selecting, arranging and recording the material.
4. Writing the introduction
5. Recording inferences
6. Writing recommendations
7. Preparing the report presentation
8. Typing the report

A research report can be based on practical work, research by reading or a study of an organization or industrial/workplace situation.

1. Preparing

Preparing includes:

- Identify the purpose/the aims of the research/research question.
- Identify the audience – lecturer/supervisor/company/organization management/staff. The amount of background included will vary depending on the knowledge of the "audience".

2. Gathering and organizing information

There are two main sources of information depending on the research task:

1. Reading — theory and other research
2. Research — experiments, data collection questionnaires, surveys, observation, interviews.

Organize and collate the information in a logical order. Make sure you record the bibliographic information of your reading as you go along.

3. Planning

Before writing the report, prepare a detailed plan in outline form. Consider the following:

Logical organization : Information in a report must be organized logically. Communicate the main ideas followed by supporting details and examples. Start with the more important or significant information and move on to the least important information.

Headings

Use headings and suitable sub headings to clearly show the different sections. In longer reports the sections should be numbered.

4. Writing the report

Writing report includes :

1. Draft the report from your detailed plan.
2. Do not worry too much about the final form and language, but rather on presenting the ideas coherently and logically.
3. Redraft and edit : Check that sections contain the required information and use suitable headings, check ideas flow in a logical order and remove any unnecessary information.
4. Write in an academic style and tone.
   - Use a formal objective style.
   - Generally avoid personal pronouns; however, some reports based on your own field experience or work placement can be reflective the first person can be used. For example, "I observed".

Section Purpose

5. Table of contents : Shows the sections of the report.

6. Executive summary : Gives a summary of the whole report.

Outlines -purpose, research method, findings, main conclusions and recommendations mainly past tense

7. Preparing the report presentation

8. Typing the report

DIFFERENT PARTS/ SECTIONS OF RESEARCH REPORT

A research report generally consists of following three parts:

Part 1 : Preliminary pages

Part 2 : Substance of the research (Main text) and

Part 3 : Appendices

1. Part I: Preliminary pages

The report should carry a title and date, followed by acknowledgements in the form of 'preface'. Than there should be table of contents followed by list of tables and illustrations so that the required information can easily be located in the report. The title should be simple, clear and appropriately worded so as to be self explanatory. It should not be too lengthy. The preface should carry briefly the message of the researcher, along with due acknowledgement that sincerely express the thankfulness of the researcher to all those responsible for the successful completion of the research.

It consists of following pages:

1. Title page (Title of report, Student name/student number, Course/subject etc.)
2. Rsearch declaration
3. Research Supervisor/guide certificate
4. Preface and acknowledgement
5. List of tables
6. List of graphs and diagrammes
7. List of contents (page and chapter wise)

Part II : Main text of research report (body of the report)

1. Introduction
   a. Theoretical background of the topic
   b. Statement of the problem
   d. The scope of the study
   e. Objectives of the study
   f. Hypothesis to be tested
   g. Definitions of the concepts
2. Review of literature
3. The design of the study
   a. Methodology

  - b. Sources of data
  - c. Sampling plan
  - d. Data collection instruments (questionnaire etc.)
4. Data Collection (Field work)
5. Data processing and analysis
  - a. An overview of report
  - b. Limitations of the study
6. Findings, Results and discussions
7. Summery, conclusion and recommendations.
8. Terminal items (Part III)
  1. Bibliography
  2. Appendix
  - a. Copies of data collecting instruments (questionnaire, interview)
  - b. Tables
  - c. Glossary of the terms used

The main text provides the complete outline of the research report along with other details. This is the most important part of the research report as it contains the total text of the research work. The following in general should be the sequence of the chapters. The content page should contain the chapter heading in the proper order.

This is the most important part of the research report as it contains the total text of the research. The following is generally the sequence of the chapters.

Chapter 1 : Introduction : 1.The purpose of introduction is to introduce the research project to the readers. It should contain the clear statement of the objectives of the research. A brief summary of the other relevant research may also be stated so that present study can be seen in that context. The hypothesis of the study, if any and the definitions of the major concepts used in the study should be stated in the introduction of the report. The methodology adopted in the study should be explained in the introduction of the report.

This chapter should provide the introductory detail of the research. The purpose of introduction is to introduce the research project to the reader. Enough background should be given to make clear to the reader why the problem was considered worth investigating. It should contain a clear statement of the objectives of the research, hypothesis and methodology. This includes scope of the study, etc. The definitions of the major concepts employed in the study should be stated in the introduction of the report. The methodology adopted in conducting the study must be fully explained. The methods of collecting the data such as questionnaire, interview, observation etc. should be explained. The questionnaire or interview schedule is usually given in an appendix. The various limitations, under which the research project was completed, must also be stated.

The list of tables should be provided in a sequential form. The page number pertaining to each table should be mentioned for quick reference. A list of graphs and diagrams should be provided, in accordance with the sequence of the chapters. The content page should contain the chapter headings in the proper sequence.

Chapter 2 : Review of literature : The research in social sciences is generally based on the extensive study carried out by the researcher. This chapter includes the outcomes of the studies in the present area of research.

Chapter 3 : Collection of data (field work) : Collection of data by different means such as survey method, observation method etc. It includes the statistical or qualitative methods used for data analysis.

Chapter 4 : Analysis of data : The research report should specify the tools and techniques that were used in the analysis of data. In analysis of data appropriate statistical techniques should be used.

Chapter 5 : Findings,. Results and discussion : A detail presentation of the findings of the study, with supporting data in the form of tables, charts, together with the validations of the results, is the next step in writing the main text of the report. This generally comprises the main body of the report, extended into several chapters. The result section of the report should contain statistical summaries of the report. All the results should be presented in a logical way and find the place in the report.

Chapter 6 : Summery, conclusion and recommendations : chapter contains the essence of the research work. Analysis leads to the findings and conclusions. The detailed presentation of the findings of the study, with supporting data in the form of tables, charts, etc. All the results should be presented in the logical sequence and conclusion should clearly be stated.

It has become customary to conclude the research report with a very brief summary of findings.

Chapter 7 : Suggestions and recommendations : After introduction, the research report must contain a statement of findings and recommendations in the non technical language so that it can be clearly understood by all concerns. The research investigation and in depth studies provides new knowledge and experience to a researcher. On that basis researcher made some suggestions and recommendations.

Part III : Appendices : At the end of the report, appendices should be enlisted. The researcher may provide additional information for the purpose of reference such as bibliography, questionnaire, etc. It also includes Questionnaire, list of organizations/institutions and other supporting material. Bibliography of sources consulted should also be given at the end.

PERFACTORY ITEMS

Tile page : Title page is the first page of the research report. It consists of following pages:

1. Title of the study
2. The name of the degree
3. The name of the researcher/author
4. The name of the institution on which the report is submitted
5. Date / year of presentation

Researcher's Declaration

In case of research undertaken by a student in fulfillment of the PhD degree etc.

Sample of Title Page of Ph.D. Thesis :

ACCESS AND USE OF E-RESOURCES AND SERVICES BY STUDENTS AND FACULTY MEMBERS IN SELECTED LIBRARIES OF MANAGEMENT INSTITUTIONS IN DELHI AND NCR

THESIS SUBMITTED
IN FULFILMENT OF THE REQUIREMENTS FOR THE AWARD OF THE DEGREE

OF

DOCTOR OF PHILOSOPHY
in
LIBRARY AND INFORMATION SCIENCE

Guided by
Dr. GURDEV SINGH

Submitted by
Mrs. MONIKA SHARMA
Enrollment No. 11/210

Department of Library and Information Science
NIMS University Rajasthan, Shobha Nagar,
Delhi-Highway, Jaipur- 303121

DECLARATION

I declared that thesis title "...................." is a record of independent research work carried out by me under the supervision of my Guide .... This has not been previously submitted for the award of degree or other similar title.

Place and Date   Research Scholar

CERTIFICATE OF SUPERVISOR

This is to certify that :

a. The candidate, Monika Sharma, has worked to my satisfaction.

b. The Thesis entitled "Access and Use of E-Resources and Services by Students and Faculty Members in Selected Libraries of Management Institutions in Delhi and NCR" is worthy of consideration for the award of Doctor of Philosophy in the subject of Library and Information Science, and

c. This research work is the candidate's original work.

Dated:

(Dr. Gurdev Singh)
Supervisor
Librarian, SGGSCC, University of Delhi,
Pitampura, Delhi

ACKNOWLEDGEMENTS

First and foremost, I am forever indebted and thankful to God for his blessings without which the whole work would not have been possible.

I Express my deep sense of gratitude to my Guru and Guide Dr. Gurdev Singh Ji, for his valuable and expert guidance and suggestions offered to me, throughout the research work. I shall remain grateful to him for his cordial and cooperative attitude, patience and wise knowledgeable counsel, which acted as an impetus in successful completion of my work. I am indeed grateful to him to have worked with him and draw upon his rich experience and scholarly advice. His clear vision and thoughtful criticism has helped in completion of the present research work, in spite of his busy professional schedule of work. Dr. Gurdev Singh has always spared his valuable time which made it possible for me to shape my research work in the present form of the thesis.

My gratitude also goes to the respondents who have participated in this study. The entire project would not been completed without the cooperation of the students and faculty members who have gave their time and effort in answering my questionnaire.

Monika Sharma
Research Scholar
NIMS University Rajasthan
Shobha Nagar Jaipur- 30312

TABLE OF CONTENTS

A table of contents gives an outline of the contents of the report. It contains a list of chapters and their subtitle with page number. It facilitates ready location of the topic in the report. The chapter headings may be typed in capital letters and subtitle in small letters.

LIST OF TABLES

A list of table is given after the list of contents. It is given in the following formats:

1. Table number
2. The title of the table
3. Page number

LIST OF GRAPHS AND CHARTS

If there are number of graphs and charts, they should also be listed after the list of tabes.

1. Number
2. Title of the graph/chart
3. Page number

ABSTRACT

Abstract describe the brief findings of the project. It should brief as possible so that reader can get quick overview of the project. It contains a brief and precise statement of the purpose, scope of the study, methods used, summery of findings etc. More importance should be given to conclusion and findings.

GUIDELINES AND RULES FOR WRITING RESEARCH REPORT

The following guidelines should be followed for writing research report:

1. Make the report clear, use words familiar with the readers, explain all technical words, use figures for easy comparison, usc tables, appendix etc.

2. Physical layout : A margin of at least one and half inches should be allowed at the left hand and of at least half an inch at the right hand side of the paper. There should also be one inch margin, top and bottom. All typing should be double spaced.

3. Footnotes : The footnotes served two purposes:

1. The identification of the material used in quotations in the report and
2. The notice of the material not immediately necessary to the body of the research text but still of supplemental value.

Footnotes are placed at the bottom of the page. Footnotes should be numbered consecutively, usually beginning with 1 in each chapter separately. The consecutive number must be used to correlate the reference in the text with its corresponding note at the bottom of the page, except in the case of statistical tables and other numerical material, where symbols such as asterisk (*) or the like one may be used to prevent confusion.

Such documentary footnotes follow a general sequence. The common order may be described at the end of the chapter.

4. Use of statistics, charts and graphics : A judicious use of statistics in research report is often contributes towards the clarification and simplification of the research results. Statistics are usually presented in the form of tables, charts, bars, pictograms and line graphs.

5. Final Draft : Revising and rewriting the rough draft of the report should be done with great care before writing the final draft. It is very helpful if at least one colleague read the report just before the final revision.

6. Bibliography : Bibliography should be prepared at the end of the study for further readings.

QUALITIES OF GOOD RESEARCH REPORT

The good research report should consists of following details:

1. The information collected in the report must be relevant and focused to derive desired results. Pictorial and graphical presentation of data and related information help to understand the detail easily.
2. Report should follow the exact predefined goals and objectives.
3. The report should always contain the executive summery of the work.
4. It should also contain the methodology of the research which shows the overall process adopted to create the report.
5. The report should contain the description of the questionnaire used in the analysis and the way it has been prepared.
6. The methodology used in the interviews should also be elaborated.
7. The report should be flexible enough to change accordingly.

OTHER IMPORTANT THINGS

1. Grammer : Presentation should be free from spelling and grammatical errors. Each word must be spelled correctly.

2. Carefully observed the rules of punctuation. Some desk dictionaries contain rules of punctuation should be consulted.

3. Principal words of titles and parts of specific works are capitalized. Principal words in captions of tables and exhibits are also capitalized.

4. Active voice is preferable to passive voice.

5. Use the past tense for :

1. Citing findings of others (e.g. Sharma in his study found that....)
2. Describing how you conduct the study (e.g. a structured interview schedule was developed for......)
3. Reporting specific past behavior of your subjects (e.g. some of the sample respondents were not readily available).

USE PRESENT TENSE FOR

1. Presenting the findings of your study (e.g. some of the factors responsible for less use of library are.....)
2. Stating generalizations

Gender : Do not use masculine nouns and pronouns when the contents refers to both genders. The gender of 'man', 'he', 'his' and 'him' refer to both men and women is not only misleading in many instances but also make the readers visualize and think of male persons.

NUMERALS

Arabic numerals and Roman numerals should be used as follows:

1. Use Arabic numerals for : Chapter, edition, figures, footnote number, page, sections, table, volume of periodical etc.

2. Use Roman for Uppercase : Division of paper, part of volume, volume of a book in a series. Lower case: preliminary page, etc.

Words and numerals : when to use numbers and when to use words?

Use words in the following cases:

1. Numbers smaller than one hundred.
2. Round numbers (e.g. multiples of one hundred).

3. A fraction (sixteenth anniversary).
4. Ordinal numbers (e.g. seventeenth anniversary).
5. The numbers at the beginning of the sentence: (fifty of the 300 users were facing the problems), no sentence should begin with a number.
6. Use the percentage (%) symbol only in tables and figures.
7. Use numerals to express page, telephone number, page, etc. combined with abbreviations and symbols. (e.g.1900 B.C).
8. Use Arabic numerals to express decimal and percentage, even when they are smaller than 100.
9. Express references to table and exhibit /figures numbers numerically.

Enumeration

Points can be given special emphasis by listing them in the following form of enumeration:

1. Textual enumeration
2. Tabular enumeration

1. Textual enumeration : is used when the items are so brief that they can easily be woven into the text.

2. Tabular enumeration : is preferred when the length and/or number of items would make a cumbersome sentence if run into the text or when items are long phrases or complete sentences.

Quotations

In research reports generally quotations are used to cite definitions, view point etc. of other writers or authors. The quotations may be direct (verbatim) or indirect (paraphrased)

Direct quotation may be employed when:

1. Giving the wordings of law, official rulings, etc.

2. When citing mathematical, scientific and other formula.
3. When citing the definition of concept.
4. When some significant idea is quoted.

Indirect Quotations : Indirect quotations means paraphrasing a given passage of another writer in our own words. This must involve genuine rephrasing.

Documentation : Every quotation used , either direct or indirect, should be acknowledged through a footnote.

Capitalization and punctuation : Unless the first word of quotation is a proper noun or adjective, it should not be capitalized.

Adding Italics : The italicizing of any part of the a quotation not italicized in the original must be indicated by the insertion of a phrase – italics not in the original – when square brackets ( )

Interpolation : Any corrections or remarks by the person quoting should be inserted in square brackets.

Abbreviations : Do not abbreviate words in the text, spell out them in full. This rule does not apply to materials included in the footnotes, appendices, bibliographies, tables and figures where abbreviations are desirable.

Statistical test results

A researcher may make use of various mathematical and statistical techniques like correlation, regression equation, testing hypothesis etc. When such results mean in terms of the subject matter of the study should be brought out. The statistical limitations of the analysis should be clearly pointed out.

REPORT PRESENTATION (Presentation of Tables, Charts and Graphs etc.)

Presentation of data : Easy-to-understand tables, charts and graphics will greatly enhance the readability of the written research report. Tables, charts, graphs and other forms of visual aids are used to provide in the text or to illustrate the classic points made in the text. These graphs, charts and tables help the readers to understand even the more complex tabulation. Thus, special care is required in presentation of report. This can be achieved by giving accurate, clear and simple headings and footnotes to the tables etc. All these illustrative material should be very clear and simple so that it can be easily understand by the readers. Too much detail in the single table or chart or graph will make it difficult to understand. All the tables, charts and other illustrative material should be numbered.

As a general rule, all tables and figures should contain:

1. Identification number corresponding to the list of tables and the list of figures.
2. A title that conveys the content of the table or figure, also corresponding to the list of tables and the list of figures, and
3. Appropriate column labels and row labels for tables, and figure legends defining specific elements in the figure.

There are number of ways to produce tables and figures. When typing a report on a typewriter or word-processor, it is sometimes easiest to type a table out by hand. However, when complicated tables have to be produced, it is advisable to use spreadsheet software like Lotus 123 or Excel.

Presentation of data
↓
Textual presentation | Tabular presentation | Graphic presentation

1. Textual presentation : textual presentation is mostly used in media for presenting the data. This type of presentation is also often used in digests, especially in management digests for executives.

2. Tabular presentation : Data are often presented in tabular form. In tabular form data is organized in columns and rows. Rows are horizontal arrangement and columns are vertical arrangement. The table usually simplifies the presentation of data and facilitates the comparison of two or more data sets.

Visual Aspects of Report

Many reports require communication of voluminous data. It is not possible to do this job with words only. There is a need of graphic presentation of report.

The main role of graphics in a report is:

1. To make the report more attractive
2. To emphasize key points
3. To save time
4. To support text to communicate report contents
5. To help the reader to remember main points

Types of Graphics : The common types of visuals used in communicating data are:

1. Bar charts
2. Pictogram
3. Pie charts
4. Pictorial diagrammes

1. Bar chart

Features

1. Easy to draw
2. Good for making comparison
3. Familiar to all

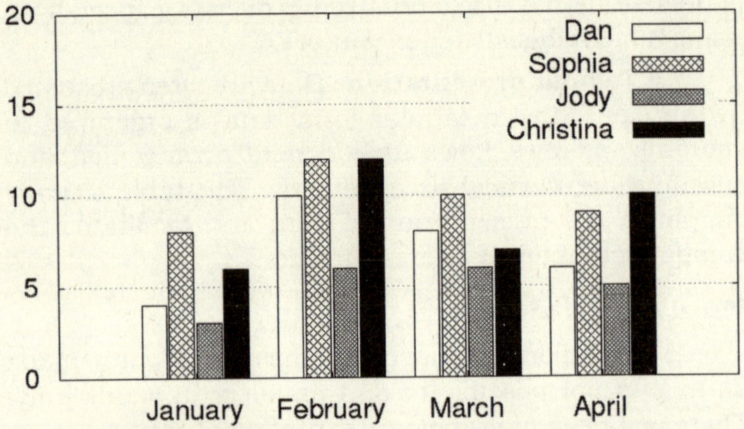

2. Pictogram : A chart on which symbols are used to represents values.

3. Pie chart : Pie charts are the commonly used visual aids. Use a pie chart when we want to compare a number of elements to each other and in relation to a whole.

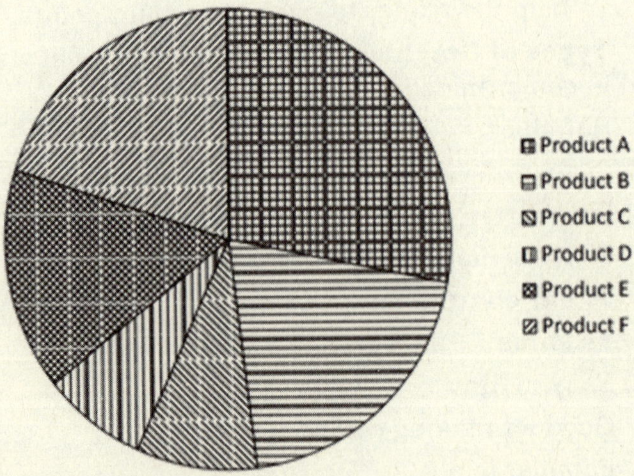

TYPING THE REPORT

For typing the report A4 size paper is used. It is of standard size and will present no difficulty with covers,

binding photocopy and dividing the sections. Sufficient margin should be kept for binding purpose.

- Make sure that each chapter start on new page.
- Indicate where capitals, italics and underlining are required.
- If using DTP, indicate bold, capital, and font size required.
- Indicate where any indentions of the text are required for the ease of reading.
- All headings, sections, sub-sections are clearly indicated.

For example:

Section Headings	1	2	3	4
Sub-sections	1.1	2.1	3.1	4.1
	1.2	2.2	3.2	4.2
	1.3	2.3	3.3	4.3
Paragraph	1.1.1	2.1.1	3.1.1	4.1.1
	1.1.2	2.1.2	3.1.2	4.1.2
Sub-paragraph	1.1.1(a)	2.1.1(a)	3.1.1(a)	4.1.1(a)
	(b)	(b)	(b)	(b)

Ensure that report should contain:

1. Table of contents
2. Table of illustrations, glossary of terms, abbreviations, introduction, main report with chapter plan recommendations and limitations.

Ensure that Appended parts contains :

1. Bibliography
2. Appendix
3. An other source of information

PRECAUTIONS OF WRITING RESEARCH REPORT

It must be prepared keeping the following points in mind:

Research report is a channel of communicating the research findings to the reader of the report. A good report is one which does this task efficiently and effectively. Research report is a channel of communicating the research findings to the readers of the report.

The following precautions should be kept in mind while writing research report :

1. While determining the length of the report, one should keep in view the fact that it should be long enough to cover the subject but short enough to maintain interest.
2. A research report should not be dull, it should be such as to sustain readers interest.
3. The report should be able to convey the matter as simply as possible. It should be in a simple language.
4. Readers are often interested in acquiring a quick knowledge of the main findings and as such the report must provide the ready availability of the findings. For this purpose , charts, graphs and the statistical tables may be provided in the report in addition to the summery of important findings.
5. The layout of the report should be appropriate and must be in accordance with the objectives of the research problem.
6. The report should be free from grammatical mistakes and should be as per the composition of the report writing such as footnotes, use of abbreviations, documentation etc.
7. The report must present the logical analysis of the subject matter.
8. A research report should show the originality and should necessarily be an attempt to solve some intellectual problems.
9. Appendices should be enlisted in respect of al technical data in the report.

10. Bibliography of the sources consulted is must for good report and must necessarily be given.
11. Objectives of the study, nature of the problem, the methods employed and the analysis techniques adopted must all be clearly stated in the beginning of the report in the form of introduction.
12. Index is also considered an essential part of a good report and as such must be prepared and appended at the end.
13. Report must be attractive in appearance, neat and clean, whether typed or printed.

PRECAUTIONS WHILE DRAFTING THE REPORT

No researcher, however experienced, can write research report in final form in one draft. The report needs several revisions and rewritings.

First Draft : In writing first draft, maintaining a flow of ideas is more important than choosing exact words. Hence the entire first draft should be completed any stopping for editing.

The following points should be kept in mind while writing the first draft:

1. Always keep in mind that you are writing for communicating with the target audience.
2. Expand the outline and pull all ideas that occurs on paper.
3. Do not struggle for words and phrases. Write down something that occurs. Inappropriate words can be replaced while revising the draft.
4. When any idea, word or phrase refuses to come to mind, leave it blank. It will arise easily on revision.
5. Write major ideas on separate sheets to facilitate additions and cuttings.
6. Leave double space between lines to provide for corrections.

7. Give appropriate headings to chapters, sections and paragraphs.
8. When first draft is completed, make sure that all research objectives have been analyzed and discussed adequately, all research questions have been answered adequately, and all the hypotheses have been tested adequately.
9. Ensure the correctness of facts and citations.

After first draft is over, it can further be revised with a fresh look.

Revision

The first draft should be read carefully again and again and edited thoroughly and revised. In revising the first draft, the attention should be given to forms, language, readability, clarity and lucidity.

The following points should be kept in mind while revising the research report:

1. Always keep in mind the requirement of research report and principal of report writing.
2. Elimenates gaps in continuity and unclear statements.
3. Simplify the sentences and improve their effectiveness.
4. Cuttoff repetitions by giving cross references.
5. Improve the readability and clarity of writing.
6. Correct the spellings and grammatical errors.

Methodological aspects

The following methdological aspects kept in mind :

1. Does the report fulfill the objectives of the study?
2. Does the title of the research project reflects the core of the problem studied?
3. Have the problem and hypothesis have studied in

scientific terms?

4. Are the hypotheses appropriately and adequately?
5. Are the conclusions logical and based on findings?
6. Are the recommendations flow from findings and conclusions?
7. Does the summery really summaries and point to further research?

Language and Style

1. Does the language conform to prevailing standard of usage?
2. Is the presentation accurate, clear, logical and complete?
3. Are the opening sentences of chapters, sections, and paragraphs attractive?
4. Are the text free from grammatical and spelling errors?
5. Are the findings and conclusion concise?
6. Rectify the flaws, imperfections and weakness discovered in the course of the above critical evaluation and improve the presentation.
7. Get the revised draft read by your colleagues (working in the same area and guide as the case may be and invite their constructive criticism.
8. Revised the draft in the light of valid criticism and suggestions made by the readers.

10

Computer Application : Its Role in Research

INTRODUCTION

Computers can be used for making research more effective. It saves the time of researcher and gives more accurate and fast results. Researchers should also takes the precautions for using computer for better results.

Computers have now become an indispensable part of every profession: so do research. Computers have a very important role to play in all research activities. The importance of computers in scientific research is exceptionally high and the use of a computer can help scientific research immensely, and is an almost invaluable tool.

Computers are used not only in numeric applications but also in non numeric applications such as proving theorems, etc. Computers are being used in scientific research such as for performing computations, research and data analysis, etc.

WHY COMPUTERS?

There are many reasons why computers are so

important in scientific research. Some of the reasons are:

1. Speed : Computer can process numbers and information in a very short time. So researcher can process and analyze data quickly. By saving time researcher can conduct further research. Computers can do calculations very fast and accurately.

(A International Journal of Research in Science And Technology http://www.ijrst.com (IJRST) 2014, Vol. No. 3, Issue No. V, October-December ISSN: 2249-0604 34 INTERNATIONAL JOURNAL OF RESEARCH IN SCIENCE AND TECHNOLOGY calculation that may take a person several hours to process will take computer mere minutes, if not seconds.)

2. Accuracy : Computer is incredibly accurate. Accuracy is very much important in scientific research. Wrong calculations could result an entire research or project being filled with incorrect information. Almost without exception, the error in computing are due to human rather than to technological weaknesses.

3. Organization : We can store millions of pages of information by using simple folders, word processors and computer programs. Computer is more productive and safer than using a paper filing system in which anything can be easily misplaced.

4. Consistency : computer cannot make mistakes through "tiredness" or lack of concentration like human being. This characteristic makes it exceptionally important in scientific research.

Computers has become one of the most useful research tool in modern times. Computers are very useful for data analysis concerning large research projects. Researchers are essentially concern with huge storage of data, their faster retrieval when required. In all these operations computers are of great help. It also enhances the quality of research activity. Computers can perform many statistical calculations very easily and quickly.

Computation of mean, standard deviation, correction coefficient, analysis of variance, multiple regression, factor analysis and various non parametric analysis are just a few of the programmers and sub programmes that are available at almost all computer centers. Software packages are readily available for the various simple and complicated quantitative analyses for the researchers. The only work a researcher has to do is to feed in the data he/she gathered after loading the operating system and particular software package on the computer. The results will be ready within seconds depending upon the quantum of the work. The research work involves a lot of calculations and work of repetitive nature. Computer is best suited for such techniques.

The storage facility which the computer provide is of immense help to a researcher for he can make use of stored up data whenever he requires to do so. Innumerable data can be processed and analyzed with greater ease and speed. The results obtained are generally correct and reliable. Not only this, even the design, pectoral graphing and reports are being developed with the help of computer. Researchers should be trained so that they can use computers effectively and efficiently for their research work.

Researcher must be aware of the following steps while doing data analysis:

1. Data organization and coding.
2. Storing the data in the computer.
3. Selection of appropriate statistical measures/ techniques.
4. Selection of appropriate software package.
5. Execution of the computer programme.

The researcher may face difficulty while analyzing the data if the data are not properly organized. For example regarding sex we can give 1 for male and 2 for female. Once the data is coded, it is ready to be stored in the computer. Input devices to be used for this purpose. After this the researcher must decide the appropriate statistical measures he will use to analyze the data. He will also have to select the appropriate programme to be selected. It may be readymade or can be developed with the help of some specialized agency. Finally the computer may be operated to execute instructions.

The above description shows that how the computers are useful for the researchers in data analysis. Researchers using computers can carry on their research work at a very faster speed and greater reliability.

Now the knowledge of programming language would no longer remain an obstacle in the use of a computer.

Inspite of all these advantages of computers, we should not forget that basically computers are machines that only can compute, they do not think. It can only execute the instructions of a person. If poor data or faulty programme is introduced into the computer, the data analysis would not be worthwhile.

COMPUTERS AND RESEARCHERS

Computers has now become now most useful tools in modern time. Computers are ideally suited for data analysis. Researchers are essentially concerned with huge storage of data, their quick processing and retrieval when required. In all these operations computers are very helpful and will add to the quality of research activity.

Computers can perform many statistical calculations very easily and quickly. Commutations of mean, standard deviation, correlation coefficient, multiple regression etc. can easily be done with the help of some programmes available in the computer center or market. Many Software packages are available for simple and complicated calculations. The only work a researcher has to do is feed in the data he gathered after loading the operating system and required software package on the computer. The output or the result will be ready within few minutes depending upon the quantity of data.

The research process generally involves a lot of calculations and work of repetitive nature. Computer is best suited for these such techniques. It will save a lot of their valuable time. The storage facility which the computers provides is of immense help to the researcher.

COMPUTER IN THE RESEARCH PROCESS

Research process consists of series of actions or steps necessary to effectively carry out research and the desired sequencing of these steps.

The following order concerning various steps provides a useful procedural guideline regarding the research process:

(1) formulating the research problem;

(2) extensive literature survey;

(3) developing the hypothesis;

(4) preparing the research design;

(5) determining sample design;

(6) collecting the data;

(7) execution of the project;

(8) analysis of data;

(9) hypothesis testing;

(10) generalizations and interpretation, and

(11) preparation of the report or presentation of the results, i.e., formal write-up of conclusions reached.

There are five major phases of the research process. They are:

1. Conceptual phase
2. Design and planning phase
3. Data collection phase
4. Data Analysis phase and

5. Research Publication phase

1. Role of Computer in Conceptual Phase : The conceptual phase consists of formulation of research problem, extensive literature survey, theoretical frame work and developing the hypothesis. Use of computers in extensive literature review: computers help for searching the literatures (for review of literature) and bibliographic reference stored in the electronic databases. It helps in finding the relevant existing research papers so that researcher can find out the gap from the existing literature. Bibliographic references can also be stored through World Wide Web. In the latest computers, references can be written automatically in different styles like APA, MLA etc. This saves lot of time of researcher. He needs not to visit libraries and wastes his time.

It can thus be used for storing relevant published articles to the retrieved whenever needed. This has the advantage over searching the literatures in the form of books, journals and other newsletters at the libraries which consume considerable amount of time and effort.

2. Role of Computers in Design and Planning Phase : This phase consists of research design preparation and determining sample design. Design and planning phase also consists of population, research variables, sampling plan, reviewing research plan and pilot study. Role of Computers for Sample Size Calculation: Several software's are available to calculate the sample size required for a proposed study. The standard deviation of the data from the pilot study is required for the sample size calculation.

Computer can be used for, deciding population sample, questionnaire designing and data collection. These are different internet sites which help to design questionnaire. Several softwares can be used to calculate the sample size. It makes pilot study of the research possible. In pilot study, sample size calculation, standard deviation are required. Computer helps in doing all these activities.

3. Role of Computers in Data collection phase : This Empirical phase consists of collecting and preparing the data for analysis. In research studies, the preparation and inputting data is the most labor-intensive and time consuming aspect of the work. Typically the data will be initially recorded on a questionnaire or record for suitable for its acceptance by the computer.

To do this the researcher in conjunction with the statistician and the programmer, will convert the data into Microsoft word file or excel spreadsheet or any statistical software data file. These data can be directly opened with statistical software's for analysis.

Data collection and Storage : The data obtained from the subjects are stored in computes are word files or excel spread sheets or any statistical software data file. This has the advantage of making necessary corrections or editing the whole layout of the tables if needed, which is impossible or time consuming incase of writing in papers. Thus, computers help in data entry, data editing, data management including follow up actions etc. computers also allow for greater flexibility in recording the data while they are collected as well as greater ease during the analysis of these data. Examples of editors are WordPad, SPSS data editor, word processors, others like ultra edit etc.

Data exposition : Most researchers are anxious about seeing the data: what they look like; how they are distributed etc. you can also examine different dimension of variables or plot them in various charts using a statistical application.

4. Role of Computers in Data Analysis : This phase consist of the analysis of data, hypothesis testing and generalizations and interpretation. Data analysis phase mainly consist of statistical analysis of the data and interpretation of results. Many software's are now available to perform the mathematical part of the research process i.e. the calculations using various statistical methods. Softwares like SPSS and spreadsheets are widely used. They can be like calculating the sample size for a proposed study, hypothesis testing and calculating the power of the study. Familiarity with any one package will suffice to carry out the most intricate statistical analysis. Computers are useful not only for statistical analysis, but also to monitor the accuracy and completeness of the data as they are collected. These software's also display the results in graphical chart or graph form.

Data analysis and interpretation can be done with the help of computers. For data analysis, softwares are available. These softwares help in using the techniques for analysis like average, percentage and correlation etc. These softwares are SPSS, STATA, Sysat etc. These can also be used for checking the reliability of data, establishing and testing hypothesis etc. Computers are used in interpretation also. They can check the accuracy and authenticity of data. It helps is drafting tables by which a researcher can interpret the results easily. These tables give a clear proof of the interpretation made by researcher.

5. Role of Computer in Research Publication : This phase consists of preparation of the report or presentation of the results, i.e., formal write-up of conclusions reached. This is the research publication phase. The research article, research paper, research thesis or research dissertation is typed in word processing software and converted to portable data format (PDF) and stored and/or published in the World Wide Web. Online sites are available through which we can convert our word file into any format like html, pdf etc.

Various online applications are also available for this purpose. Even we can prepare our document using online word processing software and can store/edit/access it from anywhere using internet.

ROLE OF COMPUTERS IN SCIENTIFIC RESEARCH

There are various computer applications used in scientific research. Some of the most important applications used in scientific research are data storage, data analysis, scientific simulations, instrumentation control and knowledge sharing.

Data Storage Experimentation is the basis of scientific research. Every experiment in any of the natural sciences generates a lot of data that needs to be stored and analyzed to derive important conclusions, to validate or disprove hypotheses. Computers attached with experimental apparatuses, directly record data as it's generated and subject it to analysis through specially designed software. Data storage is possible in SPSS data file, lotus, etc.

References and Computer

After completing the word document, a researcher need to give source of the literature studied and discussed in references. Computers help in preparing references. References can be written in different styles like APA/MLA etc. All the details of authors, journals, publication volume, books can be filled in the options reference given in computer and it automatically change the information into the required style. Some softwares like Medley are also used to manage the references. A researcher needs not to worry about remembering all the articles from where literature in taken, it can be easily managed with the help of "Medley".

11

Documentation And Compiling Bibliography

INTRODUCTION

While writing research report, we are likely to use the information which is not yet own information. The information which is developed through secondary sources must be footnoted. It should also be listed in bibliography. It is advisable to acknowledge the referred material. For acknowledging the source, a standard reference system such as APA,MLA etc. should be selected.

Bibliography which is generally appended to the research report, is a list of books and other documents related to the research work. It should contain all the work which the researcher has consulted. The bibliography should be arranged alphabetically and according to some standard format. A bibliography, however typically includes resources in addition to those cited in the text and may include annoted description of the items listed.

Preparing footnotes : Footnotes are single spaces and indented five spaces with footnotes typed slightly above the line. Footnotes are of two types:

1. Contents notes and
2. Reference notes

Contents notes contains explanatory material. Reference notes serves as documentation of sources or as means of cross references.

Footnotes serve many purposes :

1. To acknowledge indebtedness : This acknowledgement is necessary when an exact quotation is used or when a passage of another writer is paraphrased. Common facts of general knowledge require no citation.

2. To clarify the ideas or information presented in the text : The footnotes used for this purpose are called contents footnotes. They are use to clarify thoughts or concepts presented in the text without complicating the presentation. These notes may include explanatory material, technical details, etc.

3. To established the validity of evidence : All important statements of facts must be supported by evidence of their validity. Reference is given in footnotes to the source of such evidence.

4. To refer the reader to further sources of information on the subject under discussion.

5. To give the original version of the material that has been translated in the text.

6. To provide cross references to various parts of the thesis.

Footnotes are single spaced, with double spacing between two consecutive citations. Footnotes are numbered consecutively within each chapter or throughout the entire report, if they are few in numbers.

Contents of footnotes

The footnotes citation should consists of : author, title of publication, place of publication, publisher's name, year of publication, page numbers etc. Page number to be preceded by "p" if single or "pp" if two or more pages.

Examples:

1. Singh, Gurdev. Information sources, services and systems, Delhi: PHI,2015,p.120.
2. Singh,Gurdev. Academic library systems and services, Delhi: Ess Ess, 2016, pp.34-67.

Use of 'ibid'

Consecutive reference is also form the same work, then simple us the Latin abbreviation' ibid' (meaning in the same work) and write the page numbers.

Example:

Singh, Gurdev. Information sources, services and systems, Delhi: PHI, 2015, p.120.

Ibid., pp.140.

Use of 'Op.cit.'

If the same work is cited after one or more citations from other publications, then write the author's name , abbreviation 'op.cit., and the page numbers.

Example: Singh, op. cit., p. 201.

Use of 'loc.cit'

When a second but non consecutive reference is made to the exact source(i.e. the same work and page) previously cited, 'loc.cit.', (' the place cited') is substituted for 'op.cit.', the auothor's name is given to identify the work, but page number are not mentioned , because they are unnecessary.

Example: Singh, loc.cit.

Typing instructions for footnotes

1. No space intervenes between the words , or he mark of punctuation, and the superscript that follows it.
2. No mark of punctuation is used after the superscript numeral, either in the text or in the footnotes.
3. Footnotes may be numbered 1, 2, 3, ... In each chapter.
4. All footnotes for citation on a page are listed at the bottom of the page.
5. At the bottom of the page, draw a dividing line below the last line of textual material (one and half inch from below)
6. When one or two footnotes appear at the bottom of a page, a double space is left between them.
7. For the sake of balanced appearance of a typed page, two or more consecutively numbered short footnotes are put on one line e.g. Singh, op.cit., p.30[12] Ibid.
8. A footnote to a table or chart is placed one double space below it, without a dividing line.

Annotated Bibliography

In this bibliography, each entry is followed by a one sentence or one small paragraph description of the content of the work cited.

Typing instructions for Bibliography/List of references

1. The heading BIBLIOGRAPY/REFERENCES is placed an inch space below the top of the paper. It is centered between the margin.
2. The first entry is placed a double space below the title. If, however there is a category heading, the heading is placed a triple space below the title, and the first entry is placed a double space below the category heading.

1. AMERCAN PSYCHOLOGICAL ASSOCIATION STYLE (APA)

Capitalization, Abbreviation, and Punctuation

The APA guidelines specify using sentence-style capitalization for the titles of books or articles, so you should capitalize only the first word of a title and subtitle. The exceptions to this rule would be periodical titles and proper names in a title which should still be capitalized. The periodical title is run in title case, and is followed by the volume number which, with the title, is also italicized.

If there is more than one author, use an ampersand (&) before the name of the last author. If there are more than six authors, list only the first one and use *et al.* for the rest.

Place the date of publication in parentheses immediately after the name of the author. Place a period after the closing parenthesis. Do not italicize, underline, or put quotes around the titles of shorter works within longer works.

Format Examples

Books by single Author

Format

Author Last Name, Author First Name or editor(s) (Year of Publication). Title of book: Capitalize first word of subtitle. Location(place of publication): Publisher name of the publisher)

Examples :

One author, in print

1. Singh,Gurdev (2013).Information sources, services and Information systems. New Delhi :PHI Learning.
2. Bandura, A. J. (1977). Social learning theory. Englewood Cliffs, NJ: Prentice Hall.

Kidder, T. (1981). *The soul of a new machine.* Boston, MA: Little, Brown & Company.

Works by multiple authors (two or three authors)

Two authors, in print

When a work has two authors, always cite both names every time the reference occurs in the text. In parenthetical material join the names with an ampersand (&).

1. Cone, J. D., & Foster, S. L. (1993). Dissertations and theses from start to finish: Psychology and related fields. Washington, DC: American Psychological Association.
2. Frank, R. H., & Bernanke, B. (2007). *Principles of macro-economics* (3rd ed.). Boston, MA: McGraw-Hill/Irwin.
3. Nicol, A. M., &Pexman, P. M. (1999). *Presenting your findings: A practical guide for creating tables.* Washington, DC: American Psychological Association.
4. Searles, B., & Last, M. (1979). *A reader's guide to science fiction.* New York: Facts on File, Inc.

Note

- When a work has three, four, or five authors, cite all authors the first time the reference occurs.
- If a book has more than six authors, follow the same rule for journals and abbreviate remaining authors as "et al."
- When a title is broken by a colon, capitalize the first letter of the following.
- In the narrative text, join the names with the word "and." as Leiter and Maslach (1998).

In all subsequent citations per paragraph, include only the surname of the first author followed by "et al." (Latin for "and others") and the year of publication.

Kahneman et al. (1991) foundword.

No Author or editor, in print

1. Merriam-Webster's collegiate dictionary (11th ed.). (2003). Springfield, MA: Merriam Webster.

In case of Edited book

Pereira, M. E., & Fairbanks, L. A. (Eds.). (1993). Juvenile primates: Life history, development, and behavior. New York: Oxford University Press.

- If only one editor, use (Ed.).

Book translated from original

Laplace, P. S. (1951). A philosophical essay on probabilities (F. W. Truscott & F. L. Emory, Trans). New York: Dover. (Original work published 1814).

Note

- For a book with the combination of one author and editor as well, list the editor in parentheses after the title, as a translator is treated.

No author given: Works with no author

When a work has no author, use the first two or three words of the work's title (omitting any initial articles) as your text reference, capitalizing each word. Place the title in quotation marks if it refers to an article, chapter of a book, or Web page. Italicize the title if it refers to a book, periodical, brochure, or report on climate change ("Climate and Weather," 1997)

Guide to Agricultural Meteorological Practices (1981)

Anonymous authors should be listed as such followed by a comma and the date.

on climate change (Anonymous, 2008)

Merriam-Webster's collegiate dictionary (10th ed.). (1993). Springfield, MA: Merriam-Webster.

Note

- When citing books in APA style, first you will need to write the names of each author. Write the last name of each author, followed a comma, followed by the first initial of the first name and then a period after this initial. If there is more than one author, separate the last two authors with a comma and an ampersand. For example, "Wilson, A., Chan, A. L., & Lawson, S."Publication Year
- For citing books in APA format, write only the year of copyright in parenthesis followed by a period, such as, "(2009)." If the book was republished, write the original date of publication and the new date in the text citation, separated by a slash symbol. For example, "(1961/2001)." If you do not see a date of publication listed, put the letters "n.d." in parenthesis followed by a period.
- Write the full title of the book, including the subtitle if there is one. Capitalize only the first word of the title, the first word of the subtitle and any proper names in the title. Otherwise, the rest of the title should be lowercase. If there is a subtitle, separate them with a colon. If the book is a volume that is part of a series, include the series title as a subtitle. The entire title must be in italics and end with a period.

Edition

- APA also has specific rules for numbered editions. In these instances, use the abbreviation for the order of the number that applies, then add "ed" in parentheses For example, "(2nd ed.)." For a revised edition, use the abbreviations "Rev. ed." in parentheses. Insert the edition information between the book title and its following period, without underlining. For example, "Book title (2nd ed.)."Publication Location".

- If the book was published in one of the following cities, simply list the city, followed by a colon: Baltimore, Boston, Chicago, Los Angeles, New York, Philadelphia, San Francisco, Amsterdam, Jerusalem, London, Milan, Moscow, Paris, Rome, Stockholm, Tokyo, Vienna. If the book was published in a different city in the United States, include the city and state abbreviation, separated by a comma. For example, "Royal Oak, MI." If the book was published in a different city outside the United States, include the city and country, separated by a comma. For example, "Toronto, Canada."

ENCYCLOPEDIA & DICTIONARY

Format

Author's last name, first initial. (Date). Title of Article. *Title of Encyclopedia* (Volume, pages). City of publication: Publishing company.

Examples

1. Bergmann, P. G. (1993). Relativity. In *The new encyclopedia britannica* (Vol. 26, pp. 501-508). Chicago: Encyclopedia Britannica.
2. Pettingill, O. S., Jr. (1980). Falcon and Falconry. *World book encyclopedia.* (pp. 150-155). Chicago: World Book.
3. Tobias, R. (1991). Thurber, James. *Encyclopedia Americana.* (p. 600). New York: Scholastic Library Publishing.

Dictionary

Merriam-Webster's collegiate dictionary (10th ed.). (1993). Springfield, MA: Merriam-Webster.

PERIODICALS

Articles in journals, magazines, and newspapers

References to periodical articles must include the following elements: author(s), date of publication, article title, journal title, volume number, issue number (if applicable), and page numbers.

Note

- Give the periodical title in full, in uppercase and lowercase letters.
- Give the volume number of journals, magazines and newsletters.
- Do not use "Vol." before the number. If, and only if, each issue of a journal begins on page 1, give the issue number in parentheses immediately after the volume number and not italicized.
- Give the date shown after the year, month day.
- If there is no volume number, include the month or season, for example (2001, August). includes a volume number, italicize it and then give the page range (in regular type) without "pp." If the periodical does not use volume numbers, as in newspapers, use *p.* or *pp.* for page numbers.
- Unlike other periodicals, p. or pp. precedes page numbers for a newspaper reference in APA style.
- If the article is in press, place "in press" instead of the year in parentheses.
- This format is used for up to and including six authors. When there are seven or more, abbreviate the seventh and additional authors as "et al."
- Spell out the full name of a group author (e.g., National Institute of Mental Health).

Format

Author Last Name, Author First Name (Year of

Publication). Title of article: Capitalize first word of subtitle. Title of Periodical, volume number (issue number), page-page.

Example

1. Bekerian, D. A. (1993). In search of the typical eyewitness. American Psychologist, 48, 574-576.
2. Singh,Gurdev (2013).Information seeking needs of Political Science teachers of colleges of University of Delhi : A case study. Library Herald,51, 1,66-78.

Magazine and Newspaper Articles

Format

Author's last name, first initial. (Publication date). Article title. *Periodical title, volume number(issue number if available)*,inclusive,pages.

Note : Do not enclose the title in quotation marks. Put a period after the title.

Magazine article

Kluger, J. (2008, January 28). Why we love. *Time, 171*(4), 54-60.

1. Henry, W. A., III. (1990, April 9). Making the grade in today's schools. *Time, 135*, 28-31.
2. Kalette, D. (1986, July 21). California town counts town to big quake. *USA Today, 9*, p. A1.
3. Kanfer, S. (1986, July 21). Heard any good books lately? *Time, 113*, 71-72.Trillin, C. (1993, February 15). Culture shopping. *New Yorker*, pp. 48-51.

Newspaper article, no author, in print

As prices surge, Thailand pitches OPEC-style rice cartel. (2008, May 5). *The Wall Street Journal*, p. A9.

New drug appears to sharply cut risk of death from heart failure. (1993, July 15). The Washington Post, p. A12.

- Alphabetize works with no author by the first significant word in the title.
- In text, use a short title for the parenthetical citation: ("New Drug," 1993).
- Precede page number(s) for newspaper articles with p. (single) or pp.(multiple).

WEBSITE OR WEBPAGE

Format

Online periodicals

Author's name. (Date of publication). Title of article. *Title of Periodical*, volume number, Retrieved month day, year, from full URL

Online document: Page on a Website

Author Last Name, Author First Name Initial. (Year Published, Month Published). Title of article: Capitalize first word of subtitle. Website.com. Retrieved from http://www.yourlink.com

Author's name. (Date of publication). *Title of work*. Retrieved month day, year, from full URL

Note : When citing Internet sources, refer to the specific website document. If a document is undated, use "n.d." (for no date) immediately after the document title. Break a lengthy URL that goes to another line after a slash or before a period. Continually check your references to online documents. There is no period following a URL.

Note : If you cannot find some of this information, cite what is available.

Examples : Devitt, T. (2001, August 2). Lightning injures four at music festival. *The Why? Files*. Retrieved January 23, 2002, from http://whyfiles.org/137lightning/index.html.

Dove, R. (1998). Lady freedom among us. *The Electronic Text Center.* Retrieved June 19, 1998, from Alderman Library, University of Virginia website: http://etext.lib.virginia.edu/subjects/afam.html.

Note : If a document is contained within a large and complex website (such as that for a university or a government agency), identify the host organization and the relevant program or department before giving the URL for the document itself. Precede the URL with a colon.

Works by associations, corporations, government agencies, etc.

The names of groups that serve as authors (corporate authors) are usually written out each time they appear in a text reference.

(National Institute of Mental Health [NIMH], 2007)

When appropriate, the names of some corporate authors are spelled out in the first reference and abbreviated in all subsequent citations. The general rule for abbreviating in this manner is to supply enough information in the text citation for a reader to locate its source in the Reference List without difficulty.

(NIMH, 2007)

Specific parts of a source

To cite a specific part of a source (always necessary for quotations), include the page, chapter, etc. (with appropriate abbreviations) in the in-text citation.

(Stigter & Das, 1981, p. 96)

De Waal (1996) overstated the case when he asserted that "we seem to be reaching ... from the hands of philosophers" (p. 218).

If page numbers are not included in electronic sources (such as Web-based journals), provide the paragraph number preceded by the abbreviation "para." or the heading and following paragraph.

(Mönnich & Spiering, 2008, para. 9)

Journal article, one author, accessed online

Ku, G. (2008). Learning to de-escalate: The effects of regret in escalation of commitment. *Organizational Behavior and Human Decision Processes, 105*(2), 221-232. doi:10.1016/j.obhdp.2007.08.002

Journal article, two authors, accessed online

Sanchez, D., & King-Toler, E. (2007). Addressing disparities consultation and outreach strategies for university settings. *Consulting Psychology Journal: Practice and Research, 59*(4), 286-295. doi:10.1037/1065- 9293.59.4.286

Journal article, more than two authors, accessed online

Van Vugt, M., Hogan, R., & Kaiser, R. B. (2008). Leadership, followership, and evolution: Some lessons from the past. *American Psychologist, 63*(3), 182-196. doi:10.1037/0003-066X.63.3.182

Article from an Internet-only journal

Hirtle, P. B. (2008, July-August). Copyright renewal, copyright restoration, and the difficulty of determining copyright status. *D-Lib Magazine, 14*(7/8). doi:10.1045/july2008-hirtle

Journal article from a subscription database (no DOI)

Colvin, G. (2008, July 21). Information worth billions. *Fortune, 158*(2), 73-79. Retrieved from Business Source Complete, EBSCO. Retrieved from: *http://search.ebscohost.com*

Group or corporate author

American Psychiatric Association. (1994). Diagnostic and statistical manual of mental disorders (4th ed.). Washington, DC: Author.

- When author and publisher are identical, use the word "author" as name of publisher.

Edited book

Gibbs, J. T., & Huang, L. N. (Eds.). (2001). *Children of color: Psychological interventions with culturally diverse youth.* San Francisco, CA: Jossey-Bass.

Multi-volume edited work

Koch, S. (Ed.). (1959-1963). Psychology: A study of science (Vols. 1-6). New York: McGraw Hill.

Bjork, R. A. (1989). Retrieval inhibition as an adaptive mechanism in human memory. In H. L. Roediger III & F. I. M. Craik (Eds.), Varieties of memory & consciousness (pp. 309-330). Hillsdale, NJ: Erlbaum.

The author at the beginning is the author of the chapter/article, not the book.

Group or corporate author

American Psychiatric Association. (1994). Diagnostic and statistical manual of mental disorders (4th ed.). Washington, DC: Author.

Note

- When author and publisher are identical, use the word "author" as name of publisher.

Multi-volume edited work

Koch, S. (Ed.). (1959-1963). Psychology: A study of science (Vols. 1-6). New York: McGraw-Hill.

Article or chapter in an edited book

Bjork, R. A. (1989). Retrieval inhibition as an adaptive mechanism in human memory. In H. L. Roediger III & F. I. M. Craik (Eds.), Varieties of memory & consciousness (pp. 309-330). Hillsdale, NJ: Erlbaum.

The author at the beginning is the author of the chapter/article, not the book.

Corporate author, author as publisher, accessed online

Australian Bureau of Statistics. (2000). *Tasmanian year book 2000* (No. 1301.6). Canberra, Australian Capital Territory: Author. Retrieved from *http://www.ausstats.abs.gov.au/ausstats/subscriber.nsf/0/CA2568710006989...$F*

Essays or chapters in edited books

References to an essay or chapter in an edited book must include the following elements: essay or chapter authors, date of publication, essay or chapter title, book editor(s), book title, essay or chapter page numbers, place of publication, and the name of the publisher.

One author

Labajo, J. (2003). Body and voice: The construction of gender in flamenco. In T. Magrini (Ed.), *Music and gender: perspectives from the Mediterranean* (pp. 67-86). Chicago, IL: University of Chicago Press.

Two editors

Hammond, K. R., & Adelman, L. (1986). Science, values, and human judgment. In H. R. Arkes & K. R. Hammond (Eds.), *Judgement and decision making: An interdisciplinary reader* (pp. 127-143). Cambridge, England: Cambridge University Press.

Encyclopedias or dictionaries and entries in an encyclopedia

References for encyclopedias must include the following elements: author(s) or editor(s), date of publication, title, place of publication, and the name of the publisher. For sources accessed online, include the retrieval date as the entry may be edited over time.

Encyclopedia set or dictionary

Sadie, S., & Tyrrell, J. (Eds.). (2002). *The new Grove dictionary of music and musicians* (2nd ed., Vols. 1-29). New York, NY: Grove.

Encyclopedia article

Kinni, T. B. (2004). Disney, Walt (1901-1966): Founder of the Walt Disney Company. In *Encyclopedia of Leadership* (Vol. 1, pp. 345-349). Thousand Oaks, CA: Sage Publications.

Research reports and papers

References to a report must include the following elements: author(s), date of publication, title, place of publication, and name of publisher. If the issuing organization assigned a number (e.g., report number, contract number, or monograph number) to the report, give that number in parentheses immediately after the title. If it was accessed online, include the URL. Dissertations

References for dissertations should include the following elements: author, date of publication, title, and institution (if you accessed the manuscript copy from the university collections). If there is a UMI number or a database accession number, include it at the end of the citation.

DISSERTATIONS AND THESES

Doctoral dissertation abstracted in DAI and obtained from UMI: Bower, D. L. (1993). Employee assistant programs supervisory referrals: Characteristics of referring and non referring supervisors. Dissertation Abstracts International, 54(01), 534B. (UMI No. 9315947).

1. For a master's thesis abstracted in Masters Abstracts International and obtained from UMI, use the format shown here.
2. Prior to Volume 24, the title of Masters Abstracts International was Masters Abstracts, and prior to Volume 30, the title of Dissertation Abstracts International was Dissertation Abstracts.

Dissertation, accessed online

Young, R. F. (2007). *Crossing boundaries in urban ecology: Pathways to sustainable cities*(Doctoral dissertation). Available from ProQuest Dissertations & Theses database. (UMI No. 327681)

Unpublished doctoral dissertation

Wilfley, D. E. (1989). Interpersonal analyses of bulimia: Normal-weight and obese. Unpublished doctoral dissertation, University of Missouri, Columbia.

- For a master's thesis abstracted in Masters Abstracts International and obtained from the university, use the format shown here.

CONFERENCE PROCEEDINGS

Unpublished paper presented at a meeting:

Lanktree, C., &Briere, J. (1991, January). Early data on the Trauma Symptom Checklist for Children (TSC-C). Paper presented at the meeting of the American Professional Society on the Abuse of Children, San Diego, CA.

Government report, accessed online

U.S. Department of Health and Human Services. (2005). *Medicaid drug price comparisons: Average manufacturer price to published prices* (OIG publication No. OEI-05-05- 00240). Washington, DC: Author. Retrieved from *http://www.oig.hhs.gov/oei/reports/oei-05-05-00240.pdf*

Technical and/or research reports, accessed online

Deming, D., &Dynarski, S. (2008). *The lengthening of childhood* (NBER Working Paper 14124). Cambridge, MA: National Bureau of Economic Research. Retrieved July 21, 2008, from *http://www.nber.org/papers/w14124*

Audio-visual media

References to audio-visual media must include the following elements: name and function of the primary contributors (e.g., producer, director), date, title, the medium in brackets, location or place of production, and name of the distributor. If the medium is indicated as part of the retrieval ID, brackets are not needed.

Videocassette/DVD

Achbar, M. (Director/Producer), Abbott, J. (Director), Bakan, J. (Writer), & Simpson, B. (Producer) (2004). *The corporation* [DVD]. Canada: Big Picture Media Corporation

Audio recording

NhatHanh,T.(Speaker).(1998). Mindful living: a collection of teachings on love, mindfulness, and meditation [Cassette Recording]. Boulder, CO: Sounds True Audio.

Motion picture

Gilbert, B. (Producer), & Higgins, C. (Screenwriter/ Director). (1980). *Nine to five* [Motion Picture]. United States: Twentieth Century Fox.

Entire Website

When citing an entire Web site (and not a specific document on that site), no Reference List entry is required if the address for the site is cited in the text of your paper. Witchcraft In Europe and America is a site that presents the full text of many essential works in the literature of witchcraft and demonology (*http://www.witchcraft.psmedia.com/*).

ELECTRONIC SOURCES

Format for Citing Electronic Sources

The variety of materials available on the Web, and the variety of ways in which it is structured and presented, can present challenges for creating useable and useful references. Authors should observe the following two guidelines when citing Internet sources:

- Direct readers as closely as possible to the information being cited – whenever possible, reference specific documents rather than home or menu pages.
- Provide addresses that work.

At the minimum, a reference of an Internet source should provide a document title or description, a date (either the date of publication or update or the date of retrieval), and an address (in Internet terms, a uniform resource locator, or URL). Whenever possible, identify the authors of a document as well.

- You might want to check the following webpage if you need further assistance with citing electronic sources: http://www.apastyle.org/elecref.html.

Below are some examples of citations that you might use in writing your research paper:

Internet articles based on a print source

VandenBos, G., Knapp, S., & Doe, J. (2001). Role of reference elements in the selection of resources by psychology undergraduates [Electronic version]. Journal of Bibliographic Research, 5, 117-123.

- If you have reason to believe that the online version differs from the text (e.g., the format differs or page numbers are not indicated) or that it includes additional data or commentaries, you will need to add the date you retrieved the document and the URL. For example:

VandenBos, G., Knapp, S., & Doe, J. (2001). Role of reference elements in the selection of resources by psychology undergraduates [Electronic version]. Journal of Bibliographic Research, 5, 117-123. Retrieved October 13, 2001, from http://jbr.org/articles.html.

Fredrickson, B. L. (2000, March 7). Cultivating positive emotions to optimize health and well-being. Prevention & Treatment, 3, Article 0001a. Retrieved November 20, 2000, from http://journals.apa.org/prevention/volume3/pre0030001a.html.

Daily newspaper article, electronic version available by search

Hilts, P. J. (1999, February 16). In forecasting their emotions, most people flunk out. New York Times. Retrieved November 21, 2000, from http://nytimes.com.

Message posted to an electronic mailing list: Hammond, T. (2000, November 20). YAHC: Handle Parameters, DOI Genres, etc. Message posted to RefLinks electronic mailing list, archived at http://www.doi.org/mail-archive/ref-link/msg00088.html.

- Provide the name of the mailing list and the address for the archived version of the message.

Electronic copy of a journal article retrieved from database

Borman, W. C., Hanson, M. A., Oppler, S. H., Pulakos, E. D., & White, L. A. (1993). Role of early supervisory experience in supervisor performance. Journal of Applied Psychology, 78, 443-449. Retrieved October 23, 2000, from PsycINFO database.

- If retrieving an abstract from a database, include "Abstract retrieved" after citation information.

Nonperiodical document on the Internet

University of California, San Francisco, Institute for Health and Aging. (1996, November). Chronic care in America: A 21st century challenge. Retrieved September

9, 2000, from the Robert Wood Johnson Foundation Web site *http://www.rwjf.org/library/chrcare/*.

2. MLA (Modern Language Association) Style Citations

MLA Style Citations, 7th ed.

This guide provides basic guidelines and examples for citing sources using the MLA Handbook for Writers of Research Papers, 7th ed. (2009).

Format Examples :

Books : References to an entire book should include the following elements:

- author(s) or editor(s)
- the complete title
- edition, if indicated
- place of publication
- the shortened name of the publisher
- date of publication
- medium of publication

Basic Format

Lastname, Firstname. *Title of Book*. Place of Publication: Publisher, Year of Publication. Medium of Publication.

Examples:

One Author

Format : Author Last, First. Title. Location of Publisher: Publisher, Year of Publication. Print.

Sample Citation

Book

1. Singh, Gurdev. Information sources, services and systems. Delhi: PHI Learning, 2013. Print.
2. Singh, Gurdev. Introduction to computers for library professionals. New Delhi : Ess Ess, 2007.

Another work, same author:

- Information sources, services and systems. Delhi : PHI Learning,2013.Print.

In case of editor :

Hall, Donald, ed. *The Oxford Book of American Literacy Anecdotes.* New York: Oxford UP, 1981.

Two Authors :

Format : Author Last, First, and First Last. Title. Location of Publisher: Publisher, Year of Pub. Print.

Sample Citation:

1. Mahapatra, Rabindra K. and Krushna C. Panda. Information Science and journalism: A symbiosys. Jaipur : Rawat Publications,2004.Print.

Multiple Authors :

Three Authors

Format : Author Last, First, Author First Last, and Author First Last. Title. Location of Publisher: Publisher, Year of Pub. Print.

Sample Citation:

1. Abel, Andrew B., Ben S. Bernanke and Dean Croushore. Macroeconomics. New Delhi: Pearson,2011.Print.
2. Patten, Michael A., Guy McCaskie, and Philip Unitt. Birds of the Salton Sea: Status, Biogeography, and Ecology. Berkeley: U of California P, 2003. Print.

In case of Edition is given

3. Lowi, Theodore, Benjamin Ginsberg, and Steve Jackson. *Analyzing American Government: American Government, Freedom and Power.* 3rd ed. New York: Norton, 1994. Print.

More than three Authors

If a source has more than three authors, only the first author should be listed, with the Latin phrase "et al." (meaning "and others") following their name.

Examples

1. Dhawan,S M. ,et al. Shaping the future of special libraries beyond boundaries: SLA-Asia chapter(ICo ASL 2008).New Delhi :Ane Books,2009.Print.
2. Gilman, Sander, et al. *Hysteria beyond Freud.* Berkeley: U of California P, 1993. Print.

Corporate author

Examples

Herbert F. Johnson Museum of Art. *A Guide to the Herbert F. Johnson Museum of Art,*Cornell University. Ithaca: Cornell U, 1973. Print.

Multivolume work

Morison, Samuel Eliot, Henry Steele Commager, and William E. Leuchtenburg. *The Growth of the American Republic.* 2 vols. New York: Oxford UP, 1980. Print.

No author or editor

Peterson's Annual Guides to Graduate Study. 33rd ed. Princeton, NJ: Peterson's, 1999. Print.

Chapter in Book

Format

Author last, First. "Title of chapter/article. Title of book. Ed. First Last. Location of Publisher: Publisher,year of Publication. Inclusive page numbers .Print.

Editor (anthology or collection of essays)

Hill, Charles A, and Marguerite Helmers, eds. *Defining Visual Rhetorics.* Mahwah, NJ: Lawrence Erlbaum Associates, 2004. Print.

Essay or Chapter in Edited Books or Anthologies

References to an essay or chapter in an edited book or compilation must include the following elements:

- essay or chapter author(s)
- essay or chapter title
- book title
- book editor(s) or compilers
- place of publication
- the shortened name of the publisher
- date of publication
- inclusive page numbers of the cited piece
- medium of publication

Article in a book

Ahmedi, FauziaErfan. "Welcoming Courtyards: Hospitality, Spirituality, and Gender." *Feminism and Hospitality: Gender in the Host/Guest Relationship.* Ed. Maurice Hamington. Lanham: Lexington Books, 2010. 109-24. Print.

Reprinted article

Hunt, Tim. "The Misreading of Kerouac." *Review of Contemporary Fiction* 3.2 (1983): 29-33. Rpt. in *Contemporary Literary Criticism.* Ed. Carl Riley. Vol. 61. Detroit: Gale, 1990. 308-10. Print.

Electronic Book

Format

Author Last, First. Title. Location of Publisher: Publisher, Year of Pub. Electronic Publisher. Web. Date of Access.

Sample Citation

Welch, Kathleen E. Electric Rhetoric: Classical Rhetoric, Oralism, and a New Literacy.

Cambridge: MIT, 1999. Net Library. Web. 21 Oct. 2004. Chapter in a Book

Format

Author Last, First. "Title of Chapter/Article." Title of Book. Ed. First Last.

Location of Publisher: Publisher, Year of Publication. Inclusive page numbers. Print.

Sample Citation

Wells, Ida B. "Lynch Law in All Its Phases." With Pen and Voice: A Critical Anthology of Nineteenth-Century African-American Women. Ed. Shirley Wilson Logan. Carbondale: Southern Illinois UP, 1995. 80-99. Print.

ARTICLE IN JOURNALS,MAGAZINES AND NEWSPAPERS

Journals/periodicals

References to periodical articles must include the following elements:

- author(s)
- article title
- publication title (journal, magazine, etc.)
- volume number
- publication date (abbreviate months, if used)
- the inclusive page numbers
- medium of publication

Issue numbers should be stated as decimals to a given volume number. In the example below, the number

Journal Article (Print)

Format

Author Last, First. "Title." (of article) Journal Name. Volume Number. Issue Number (Year of Pub): inclusive page numbers. Print.

If the issue number is not available, add the month or season of publication in parentheses with the year. See samples under "Journal Article: Multiple Authors.

Sample Citation

1. Singh,Gurdev."Use of college libraries by faculty members of University of Delhi." Library Herald 40.4 (2002):263-71. Print. (40.4 reads as Volume 40, issue 4).
2. Haraway, Donna J. "A Game of Cat's Cradle: Science Studies, Feminist Theory, Cultural Studies." Configurations 2.1 (1994): 59-71. Print

Journal Article with Two Authors

Format

Author Last, First, and Author First Last. "Title." Journal Name Volume Number. Issue Number (Year of Pub): inclusive page numbers. Print.

Sample Citation

1. Singh,Gurdev, and Taruna Arora. "Information seeking needs of political Science teachers of colleges of University of Delhi : a case study." Library Herald 51.1 (2013):66-78.Print.
2. Gautreau, Ronald, and Jeffrey M. Cohen. "Birth and Death of a Black Hole." American Journal of Physics 65 (May 1997): 444-6. Print.

Three Authors

Pridmore, William, Mitchell Chamlin, and Adam Trahan. "A Test of Competing Hypotheses About Homicide Following Terrorist Attacks: An Interrupted Time Series Analysis of September 11 and Oklahoma City." Journal of Quantitative Criminology 24(Dec. 2008): 381-96. Print.

Multiple Authors : More than three authors

Format

Author Last, First, and Author First Last. "Title." Journal Name Volume Number. Issue Number (Year of Pub): inclusive page numbers. Print.

Note : If a source has more than three authors, only the first author should be listed, with the Latin phrase "et al." (meaning "and others") following their name.

Journal Article: Published Only Online

Format

Author Last, First. "Title." Journal Name Volume Number. Issue Number (Year of Pub): inclusive page numbers. Web. Day Month Year of Access.

[Note: If an article online is not paginated, include the abbreviation "n. pag." instead.]

Sample Citation

Jobe, Karen D. "Women and the Language of Hackerdom: The Gendered Nature of Hacker Jargon." Kairos 5.2 (2000): n. pag. Web. 23 Mar. 2005.

Journal Article: from a Full-Text Database

Format

Author Last, First. "Title." Journal Name Volume Number. Issue Number (Year of Pub): inclusive page numbers. Database Name. Web. Day Month Year of Access.

Sample Entry

Vargas, Jose Antonio. "The Face of Facebook." *New Yorker* 86.28 (2010): 54-63. *Academic Search Premier.* Web. 25 Jan. 2011.

Sample Citation: Article in an online periodical

If pagination is unavailable or is not continuous, use n. pag. in place of the page numbers.

1. Chaplin, Heather. "Epidemic of Extravagance." *Salon* 19 Feb. 1999: n. pag. Web. 12 July 1999.
2. Ferrell, Robert H. "Truman's Place in History." Reviews in American History 18.1 (1990): 1-9. JSTOR. Web. 3 Feb. 2005.Magazines.

Newspaper article

When citing newspapers, it is important to specify the edition used (e.g. late ed.) because different editions of a newspaper may contain different material.

Example : Mahapatra, Dhananjay."More babus may face coal probe" The Time of India 9 July 2013 : 1.Print.

Newspaper article, no author

1. "Africa Day Celebrated in Havana." *Granma International* 31 May 2009, English ed.: 16. Print.

Newspaper article, one author, discontinuous pages

Bajaj, Vikas. "The Double-Edged Rupee." *New York Times* 27 Oct. 2010: B1+. Print.

RFERENCE BOOKS

Encyclopedias, Dictionaries, and Common Reference Books
Encyclopedia

Format

Author's last name, first name. "Title of Article." *Title of Encyclopedia.* Date.

Note: If the dictionary or encyclopedia arranges articles alphabetically, you may omit volume and page numbers.

Sample citations

1. Mercuri, Becky. "Cookies." *The Oxford Encyclopedia of Food and Drink in America*. Ed. Andrew F. Smith. Vol. 1. 2004. Print.
2. Smith, Hobart. "Horned Lizard." Encyclopedia Americana. 2004 ed. Print.
3. Tobias, Richard. "Thurber, James." *Encyclopedia Americana*. 1991 ed.

Articles or entries from reference books

If the article or entry is signed, place the author's name first; if it is unsigned, give the title first. For well-known reference works, it is not necessary to include full publication information. Include only the title of the reference source, edition, and date of publication.

Dictionary

Sample Citation: Dictionary entry

1. "Hospitality." Def. 1a. *Webster's Third New World Dictionary*. 1993. Print.
2. "Azimuthal Equidistant Projection." *Merriam-Webster's Collegiate Dictionary*. 10th ed. 1993.

Online Dictionary

3. "Kingdom." Oxford English Dictionary. 2nd ed. Web. 25 Aug.2007.Specialized.

Note on editions : For texts published without an edition number, include the year only. See sample. Note on reference works online: Include the word "Web" followed by the date of access to indicate the use of an electronic version of a common reference book.

Sample Citations for Common Reference Books Online:

1. Smith, Hobart. "Horned Lizard." Encyclopedia Americana. 2004 ed. Web. 4 Mar. 2008.

Citing Materials from Online Sources

Citations for online sources, like those for print sources, should provide information that both identifies a source and allows that source to be located and retrieved again. All citations should include the medium of publication (Web) and the date the content was accessed. If the source is difficult to locate or your instructor requires a URL, list the complete address within angle brackets after the date. In many cases, it is also necessary to identify the Web site or database that has made the material available online.

Because there are currently few standards that govern the organization and presentation of online publications, the information that is available to fulfill these objectives can vary widely from resource to resource. In general, references to online works require more information than references to print sources.

See sections 5.6.1-4 in the **MLA Handbook** for more complete information on creating citations for online sources.

Web page or website

This example includes the optional URL. All other examples below use the shorter citation format.

Format

Author's last name, first name (if available). "Title of work within a project or database." *Title of site, project, or database.* Editor (if available). Electronic publication information (Date of publication or of the latest update, and name of any sponsoring institution or organization). Date of access and <full URL>.

Note : If you cannot find some of this information, cite what is available.

Examples : Cornell University Library. "Introduction to Research." *Cornell University Library.* Cornell

University, 2009.Web. 19 June 2009 <http://www.library.cornell.edu/resrch/intro>.

Personal Web site

If a work is untitled, you may use a genre label such as Home page, Introduction, etc.

Rule, Greg. Home page. Web. 16 Nov. 2008.

Devitt, Terry. "Lightning injures four at music festival." *The Why? Files.* 2 Aug. 2001. 23 Jan. 2002 <http://whyfiles.org/137lightning/index.html>.

Dove, Rita. "Lady Freedom among Us." *The Electronic Text Center.* Ed. David Seaman. 1998. Alderman Lib., U of Virginia. 19 June 1998 <http://etext.lib.virginia.edu/subjects/afam.html>.

Lancashire, Ian. Homepage. 28 Mar. 2002. 15 May 2002 <http://www.chass.utoronto.ca:8080/~ian/>.

Online book with print information

Frost, Robert. *North of Boston.* 2nd ed. New York: Henry Holt and Co., 1915. *Google Books.* Web. 30 June 2009.

GOVERNMENT DOCUMENTS

References to government documents vary in their required elements. In general, if you do not know the writer of the document, cite the government agency that issued the document as author.

Format

Government name. Name of agency. Title of Publication. Location of Publisher: Publisher, Year of Publication. Print.

Note: Government documents vary and result in special problems for bibliographers. Consult pages 174-177 in the handbook or your librarian for assistance.

Sample Citation

United States. Dept. of the Treasury. National Security Information. Washington D.C.:GPO, 1990. Print.

State document

New York State. Commission on Capital Punishment. *Report of the Commission to Investigate and Report the Most Humane and Practical Method of Carrying Into Effect the Sentence of Death in Capital Cases.* Albany: Troy, 1888. Print.

International document

United Nations. General Assembly. *Convention on the Elimination of All Forms of Discrimination Against Women.* New York: United Nations, 1979. Print.

AUDIO VISUAL

Film or video recording

Annie Hall. Dir. Woody Allen. 1977. Videocassette. MGM/UA Home Video, 1991.

Sound recording

Counting Crows. *August and Everything After.* DGC, 1993. CD.

Sound recording, specific song

Counting Crows. "Mr. Jones." *August and Everything After.* DGC, 1993. CD.

CD-ROM

Citations should include the medium of the electronic publication (CD-ROM), the name of the vendor that made the material available on CD-ROM, and publications dates for the version used, if relevant.

"Marriage." *Encyclopedia Judaica.* CD-ROM. Vers. 1.0. Jerusalem: Judaica Multimedia, 1997.

Bibliography

1. Ackoff, Russell L.Scientific methods. New York: John Wiley, 1962.
2. Allen, T. Harrell. New methods in social science research. New York: Praeger Publishers, 1978.
3. Baden, David. User oriented evaluation of information systems and services. Hant: Gower,1990.
4. Baiey, Kenneth D. Methods of social research. New York,1978.
5. Bentley,T.J.Report writing in business. 1st ed.Delhi: Viva Books,2004.
6. Berdie, Douglas R and Anderson, John,F. Questionnaires : design and use. Metuchen, N.J.: The Scarecrow Press, 1974.
7. Best,John W. and Kahn James V. Research in education..5 ed. New Delhi: Prentice Hall of India,1986.
8. Bhattacharyya, Dipak Kumar. Research methodology. 2nd ed. Delhi: Excel Books, 2010.
9. Boot, John C.J. and Cox Edwin B. Statistical analysis for managerial decisions.2nd ed. New Delhi: McGraw Hill , 1979.
10. Bowley,A.L. Elements of Statistics. 6th ed. London: King and Staples,1937.

11. Brock, Susan L. Writing business proposals and report. Delhi: Viva Books, 2004.

12. Busha, Charles S and Stephen H Harter. Research methods in Librarianship: techniques and interpretation. New York: Academic Press,1988.

13. Cameron, Sheila. Business research methods. Delhi: Excel Books, 2011.

14. Chance William A. Statistical methods for decision making. Bombay: D. B. Taraporevala, 1975.

15. Chawvala, Deepak. Research methodology. Delhi: VikasPub. House, 2011.

16. Cochran, William G. Sampling techniques.3rd ed. Delhi: Wiley Eastern, 2011.

17. Cooper, Bruce M. Writing technical reports. London: Penguin Books, 1981.

18. Croxton, Frederic E. and Cowden, Dudley, Applied general statistics. 2nd ed. New Delhi: Prentice Hall of India, 1966.

19. David, F.N. A first course in statistics. 2nd ed. London : Griffin, 1971.

20. Deming W Edwards. Sample design in business research. New York: John Wiley, 1960.

21. Edward, Allen L. Statistical methods. 2nd ed. New York: Holt, Rinchart and Winston, 1967.

22. Emory, C.William. Business research methods. Illinois: Richar D Erwin,1976.

23. Feller, W. An introduction to probability theory and its applications. 3rd ed.vol 1. New York: John Wiley, 1966.

24. Festinger,Leon and Katz, Danials, Eds. Research methods in behavioral sciences. New Delhi: Amerind Pub.,1976 (forth Indian reprint).

25. Fiebleman, J.K.Scientific methods. Nitherlands : Martinus Nijhoff, 1972.

26. Fox, D.J.Research process in education. New York: Halt, Rinehart and Winston, 1969.
27. Freeman P.Prnciplas of scientific research. 2nd ed. New York: Pergamon Press, 1960.
28. Gatner, Elliot, S.M. and Cordasco, Francesco. Research and report writing. New York: Barmes and Noble, 1956.
29. Ghosh, B.N. Scientific methods and social research. New Delhi: Stearling Pub., 1982.
30. Ghosh, B.N.Scientific method and social research 2nd ed.Delhi: Sterling, 1984.
31. Gibbsons, J.D. Non parametric statistical inference. Tokyo: McGraw Hill Kogakusha,1971.
32. Glock,CharlesY. Survey research in social sciences. New York: Russel Sage Foundation,1967.
33. Godfrey, Arthur. Quantitative methods for managers. London: Edward Arnold, 1977.
34. Good,Carter Victor & Douglus Edger Scates. Methods of research: educational, psychological, sociological. Applenton-century-craft,1954.
35. Gopal M.H. An introduction to research procedure in social sciences. Bombay: Asia Pub. House,1964.
36. Gorden,Raymond L. Interviewing: strategy, techniques and tectics. Homewood, Ill. : Dorsey Pres,1975.
37. Gupta, S.L. and Hitesh Gupta. Research methodology. Delhi: International Book House, 2011.
38. Gupta, S.P. and Archana Agarwal. Statistical methods. New Delhi: Sultan Chand ,2010.
39. Gupta,Santosh.Research methodology and statistical techniques. Delhi: Deep and Deep,2001.
40. Iyer, Venkata. Writing readable business report. Delhi: Stearling,1988.

41. Johnson, Rodney, D. and Siskin, Bernerd R. Quantitative techniques for business decisions. New Delhi: Prentice Hall of India, 1977.

42. Karson, Marvin J. Multivariate statistical methods. Ames, Lowa: The Lova State University Press, 1982.

43. Kerlinger, Fred N. Foundations of behavioral research. 2nd ed. New York: Holt, Reinhart, and Winston, 1973.

44. Kothari, C.R. Research methodology, methods and techniques. 2nded. Delhi : New Age International, 2007.

45. Kothari,CR.Quantitative techniques 2nd ed. New Delhi: Vikas Pub. House, 1984.

46. Krishnaswami, O.R. Methodology of research in social sciences. Delhi: Himalaya Pub.House, 2013.

47. Kumar,Krishan.Research methods in Library and information Science. Delhi: Har-Anand Publications, 1992.

48. Kumar, Ranjit. Research methodology. Delhi: Sage Publications, 2011.

49. Kvale, Steinar. Interviews: an introduction to qualitative research interviewing. California: Sage Publication, 1996.

50. Kwatra,P.S. Library user studies: A manual for librarians and information scientists.Bombay: Jaico Pub.House, 1992.

51. Leedy, Paul D and Jeanne Ellis Ormrod. Practical research: planning and design, 11 ed. New York: Pearson Education, 2016.

52. Levin, Richar I. Statistics for management. New Delhi: Prentice Hall of India, 1979.

53. Line, Maurice, B. Library surveys. 2nd ed. London: Clive Bingley, 1982.

54. Loveday, Robert. Statistics; a second course in

statistics. 2nd ed. Cambridge; Cambridge University Press, 1977.

55. Maxwell, Albert E. Analyzing qualitative data. New York: John Wiley and Sons, 1961.
56. Rampal, M.K. Project report writing (organizing and writing a project report in an appropriate style).New Delhi: Galgotia Pub., 2001.
57. Rao, Aditham Bhujanga. Research methodology for management and social Sciences. Delhi: Excel Books, 2009.
58. Rao,C.R. and Mitra,S.K. and Mathai ,A ed. Formulas and tables for statistical work. Calcutta; Statistical Publishing Society, 1968.
59. Ravichandra Rao, I.K. Quantitative methods for library and information science. New Delhi: Wiley Eastern, 1983.
60. Radhakrishnan, D. Quantitative technique and data processing. Delhi: Kitab Mahal, 1988.
61. Riordan, Daniel G. Technical report writing today.8th ed. New Delhi: Biztantra, 2004.
62. Runeson, Goran. Writing research reports. Delhi: Anmol, 2006.
63. Sancheti, D.C. Quantitative methods. Delhi: Sultan Chand, 2006.
64. Sarangi,Prasant. Research methodology .Delhi: Taxman's Publications, 2010.
65. Saravanavel,P.Research and report writing.1st ed. Bareiley: V.K. Pub. House, 1993.
66. Sarvanavel,P.Research methodology. Delhi: Kitab Mahal, 2013.
67. Sharma Lokesh. Dictionary of terms in research methods. Delhi: The Readers Paradise, 2015.
68. Sharma, R.C. Business correspondence and report writing. Delhi: Tata McGraw Hill, 2004.

69. Sharma, Sandhir and Gautam Bansal. Research methodology. New Delhi: Novatech Scientific and Informatics,2009.

70. Sharma,Sandhir.Research methodology. New Delhi: Novatech Scientific and Informatics,2009.

71. Simpson,George and Kafks, Fritz.Basic statistics: A textbook for the first course .Calcutta: Oxford and IBH,,1965.

72. Simpson,I.S.Basic statistics for librarians. London: Clive Bingley,1975.

73. Simpson,IS. Basic statistics for librarians.3rd ed. London: Library Association, 1988.

74. Sproull,Natalie L. Handbook of research methods: A guide for practitioners and students in social sciences. Metuchen, N.J.: Scarecrow Press,1988.

75. Srivastava, U. K. Quantitative techniques. Delhi: Wiley Eastern, 1985.

76. Thompson, S.K. and G.A. Seber. Adaptive Sampling. New York : John Wiley and Sons, 1996.

77. Tirpathi, P.C.A textbook of research methodology, in management and social sciences. Delhi: Sultan Chand, 2014

78. Tuckman, Bruce, W. Conducting educational research. California: Harcourt Brace Jovanovich, 1998.

79. Verma, A.P. Quantitative techniques. Delhi; Asian Books, 2011.

80. Verma, R. K. Research methodology. Delhi: Common wealth Publications, 1992.

Glossary of the Terms Used

Bar Chart : Qualitative data is usually represented in the form of a bar chart. A bar chart is a graph that consists of numbers of bars of equal width arrange vertically or horizontally. The length of the bars varies with the magnitude of the data collected over a period of time and space.

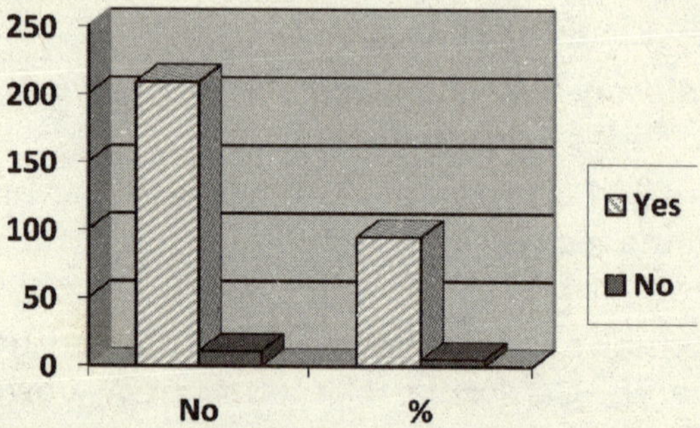

Case : The data in a file that refers to one individual or one unit.

Census : A survey based on the complete enumeration of a population.

Character : One of a set of symbols that can be represented in a computer. It can be letter, number, punctuation mark etc.

Chi square test : A measure of how well a theoretical probability distribution fits a set of data.

Citation Analysis : Citation analysis is a counting

techniques which are used in the evaluation of scientific activities for the last few years. The main objectives of citation analysis are to evaluate and to interpret citations received by authors, journals etc. It is very useful for making ranking of journals.

Class Interval : The range of values covered by a class when coding or grouping a quantitative variable. For any one class, it is given by difference between its upper and lower boundaries.

Class limit : The upper and lower limit of the class.

Clustered Sampling : In clustered sampling, the population is, as in stratified sampling, divided into groups. These groups become the sampling units.

Coefficient : A multiplying factor. For example in the equation $2x^2 + 3x = 0$.

Where x is variable, the coefficient of x^2 is 2 and the coefficient of x is 3.

Coefficient of Correlation : It is usually denoted by r, is often called Pearson's Product Moment correlation. The correlation coefficient measures the extent to which the data conform to a linear relation of the type

$$y = a + bx.$$

Cofficient of Variation : The coefficient of variation is :

$$= 100 \times \frac{\sigma}{\text{Mean}} = 100 - \frac{\sigma}{\overline{\overline{X}}}$$

Correlation : The term denotes the relationship between two or more quantitative variables. It is sometimes loosely used to denote statistical association even when the variables are qualitative.

Correlation coefficient : A measure of the linear relationship between two quantitative variables also known as the person product moment coefficient of correlation. It is denoted by the letter r and its value range from -1 to +1, where 0 indicates the absence of any linear relationship, and -1 and +1 indicates a perfect negative and perfect positive relationship.

Critical value : The dividing values between the acceptance region and the rejection region.

Cumulative distribution function : A synonym for the distribution function.

Data : Data is the information which is collected in a systematic way, organized and recorded in such a way that it can be interpreted correctly. Data is raw, but when it is interpreted and processed, it become information.

Data file : A file in a paper or electronic format that contains all the data collected in a research or used in a statistical analysis.

Dependent variable : In statistical analysis, it is the variable which we try to explain as a function of other variables called the independent variables. One of the objective of a statistical analysis is to predict the values of the dependent variable in terms of the value of the independent variable.

Descriptive statistics : Any treatment of data which aim at summarizing it and presenting it in a way that that facilitates its interpretation. Descriptive statistics does not involve generalizations. It includes measures of central tendency, measures of variation, etc. and graphical representations, as well as measures of skewness and kurtosis.

Deviation from the mean : The amount by which an individual observation differs from the mean, thus, the deviation of the ith observation xi from the mean-x is given by xi – x. An important property of deviations from the mean is that, for any set of data, their sum is always equal to zero.

Dispersion : The extent to which the data values are spread out, or vary from each other. Measures of dispersion could also be called measures of variation.

The standard deviation (SD) is a measures of dispersion.

Distribution : A list of the observed values of a variable together with the frequencies of occurrence. It could also describe an abstract, theoretical pattern of values such as normal distribution.

Estimate : The proposed value for a parameter, computed on the basis of a known sample statistic. It is usually formulated as an interval estimate, that is, a whole range of likely values for the parameter and it is accompanied by a confidence level, that is probability that the interval estimate does includes the parameter.

Expected frequency : A cell frequency calculated on the basis of some appropriate assumptions in the analysis of the distribution of the data related to a given variable. For example, for a contingency table, the expected frequency of a cell is the count we would have in the cell if the entries in the various cells were distributed with the same proportion as they are in the marginal total.

Frequency : The number of items, or cases, falling (or expected to fall) into a category or classification.

Frequency curve : We get a frequency curve by plotting for each class of its midpoint s against its frequency and joining the point s plotted by a smooth curve.

Frequency distribution : A classification of data showing the number of occurrences of each class interval or category of a variable.

Geometric Mean : Geometric mean is the Nth root of the products of N items. If there are two items, we take the square root, if three cube root, and so on.

Graph : A drawing that shows the relationship between numbers or quantities.

Graphical presentation : The main objective of graphical presentation of data is to summaries clearly the facts and inferences drawn from the data. The data can easily be understood and interpreted. It can be used as a mean of identifying changes in library services. A graph in addition to the title should also have the scale and headings or x-axis and frequencies on the y-axis.

Histogram : A histogram represents the class frequencies in a frequency distribution with vertical bars. Each bar represents a class interval whose area is proportional to the class frequency in that interval. Class intervals are plotted along the x-axis and frequencies are plotted along the y-axis. Histogram present frequency distribution by bars of two dimensions.

Hypothesis : A statement like "E(X)=μ" is called a hypothesis. A hypothesis that is being tested is called the null hypothesis. Methods of making inferences are usually based on statistical tests of hypothesis.

Hypothesis testing : A procedure that allow us to test whether a given hypothesis is likely to be true or false. If the results are 'too far' from the values proposed in the hypothesis, the hypothesis is rejected, with a certain probability of error. Otherwise , it is accepted (again with the probability of error).

Independent variable : In statistical analysis it is the variable which we try to explain as a function of other variables called the independent variable.

Kurtosis : A numerical measures of the degree to which a distribution is flat or peaked.

Level of significance : In a significance test, the probability of rejecting a null hypothesis which is true is reality, It is the probability of commenting a type 1 error.

Logarithm : A number expressed as the exponent of another number. An my number x can be written in the form of $x= z^y$

where y is than the logarithm to the base of x.

Mean : The mean of n number is their sum divided

by n. technically it is called the arithmetic mean but the term average is also used in everyday language. A mean is a value that results when sum of all the items in the series is divided by the number of items in a sample or a population. The mean is the one of measures of central tendency is the sum of all items divided by their total number. It is a representative or expected value for a set of numbers.

Mean Deviation : A measure of the spread or dispersion of a sample of population. Deviation of individual observations from a reference point, usually the arithmetic mean, are calculated.

Measures of Central tendency : A common way to describe a large set of data is to find a single number that represents what is average or typical value of that set of data. Such a value is known as a measure of central tendency.

Measures of Dispersion : In addition to the measures of the central tendency statisticians also study the measures of variation present in the data.

Median : A median is the value of the variable which divide the area under the frequency curve into two equal parts. The value of middle entry (if the number of entries is odd) or the mean of the values of the two middle entries (if the number of entries are even) and the data is arranged in increasing order. The middle number of a set of numbers arranged in order.

Mode : The value which occurs with the highest frequency. A distribution can have more than one mode, or no mode at all when no two values are alike. Mode is the value of a variable for which the frequency is maximum. The number that occurs most frequently in a set of numbers. For example: the mode of (5, 6, 2, 1, 2,) is 2.

Negative correlation : Two quantitative variables are said to be negatively correlated when individuals(or units) scoring high on one variable tend to score low on the other variable. In this case the correlation coefficient is negative.

Normal Curve : The graph of normal distribution ; it has the shape of a vertical cross section of a bell.

Normal distribution : A distribution which can be represented by a normal curve. When _ = 0 and _ =1 , it is referred to as standard normal distribution.

Null hypothesis : A hypothesis H_0 which is to be tested against an alternative hypothesis H_1.It is denoted by H_0.The hypothesis that we are willing to accept if do not accept the null hypothesis is called the alternative hypothesis and is denoted by H_1.

Observed frequency : The actual number of data values falling into a class of a distribution or into a cell of a contingency table.

Open class : A class at the lower or upper end of a frequency distribution having no stated lower or upper limit. For instance class such as less than Rs. 200 or Rs. 50,000 or more are open classes.

Pie chart : A pie chart consists of circle sub divided into sectors whose sizes are proportional to the quantities or percentage they represents. A pie chart is one of the most common diagram used for the presentation of a set of data. Each partition of the data is as a portion of a pie.

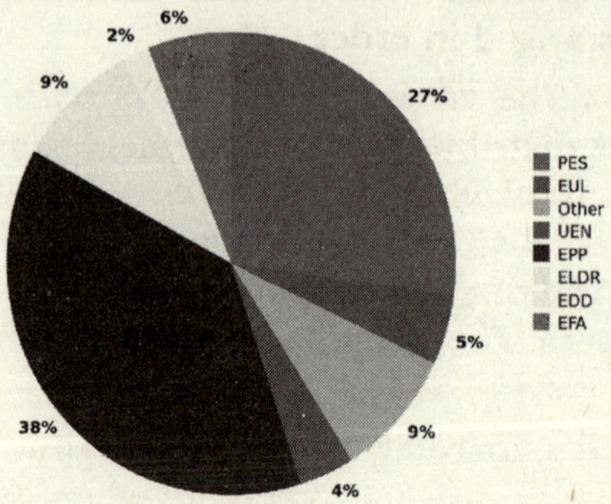

Population : The set of all units under study. Some authors refer to the set of all units as the universe.

Population size : The number of elements in a finite population. It is generally denoted by the letter N.

Positive correlation : Two variables are said to be positively correlated, when individuals scoring high on one variable tend to score high on the other. In this case, the correlation coefficient is positive.

Primary data : Statistical data which are published by the same organization by which they are collected.

Probability sample : A sample obtained by a method in which every element of a finite population has a known (not necessary equal) chance of being included in the same.

Quantitative methods : Quantitative methods are procedures and techniques used to analyses data numerically, they include a study of the valid method used for collecting data, as well as a discussion of the limits of validity of any given procedure, and of the ways the results are to be interpreted.

Questionnaire : A list of questions given to a subject in a survey.

Quota sampling : A type of judgment sampling, in which the interviewer has to sect by any means interviewees with certain characteristics in set proportions. There is no attempt to randomize the selection of subjects within each group.

Random numbers : Published table of random numbers consists of pages on which the digit 0, 1, 2, 3, ... 9 occur with the same probability as if they had been generated completely at random a large number of successive times.

Random sample : Referrers to sample which is selected by a method of random selection.

Range : It is a simple measures of dispersion. It is

defined as the difference between the highest and the lowest values of a variable observed in an experiment or a set of data.

Raw Data : The data from a survey or experiment in their original form i.e. before being modified or analyzed in any way. Raw data are, however, often assumed to be edited and coded.

Regression line : A graphical presentation of the trend of a relationship between two variables.

Representative sample : A sample which displays the same characteristics as the population from which it came and that are relevant to a given study, and in similar proportion.

Sample design : The number of observations (or units) in a sample. It is usually denoted by the letter n.

Sample size : Is the size of the population how much population to be included. Sampling theory help us in arriving at good estimates of a sample size.

Sampling : It is very difficult to conduct a survey on a large population. In such a case we try to make an estimate of the characteristics of the whole population through the of a sample drawn from it. The part of the population selected for investigation is called sample. The method is called sampling. The selection of a representative subset from a whole population. This is called statistical inference.

Sampling distribution : The distribution of a statistic, that is, the set of values of the statistic on all possible samples of a given size.

Sampling Frame : The list of all units from which the sample is to be chosen.

Scaling : Scaling is the process of measuring, that is, the set of values of the statistic on all possible samples of a given size.

Scatter Diagram : A graphical representation of data from a bi variate distribution (x, y).

Secondary Data : Statistical data which is published by an individual or an organization other than the one that collected the data.

Simple Random Sampling : A simple random sample is drawn unit by unit. The unit is the population are serially numbered from 1 to N, where N is the population size.

Size of the population : The number of elements in a finite population .It is generally denoted by the letter N.

Skewness : A measure of the degree of asymmetry of a distribution. If the frequency curve has a long tail to the right (left) and the short one to the left (right), it is called skewed to the right (left) or positively (negatively) skewed.

Standard deviation (SD) : The standard deviation of a distribution is the square root of the variance. It is denoted by σ (sigma).

Statistics : A quantity calculated for a sample.

Stratified Sampling : In stratified sampling, we try to increase the efficiency of sampling by dividing a heterogeneous population.

Survey design : A detailed description of the procedures that will be followed in conducting a survey, including the methods used for collecting he data.

Symmetrical distribution : A distribution is systematical if value that are equally distant from the mean have identical frequencies. The curve representing it is divided into two mirror images around its centre.

Systematic error : A non-random error which introduces a bias into all the observations; such errors are generally the result of poor design of the observation method.

Systematic sample : A systematic sampling is selected by including every i^{th} item from the population. The first unit to be chosen in the list is generally chosen at random among the first i units.

Tabular Presentation : Data are often presented in tabular form. A table is the systematic organization of statistical data in columns and rows. Rows are horizontal arrangement and columns are vertical arrangements. The table usually simplifies the presentation and facilitates the comparison of two or more data sets. A table consists of title, stub, caption and the body.

Test of Hypothesis or hypothesis testing : A procedure for deciding whether to accept or reject a hypothesis.

Test of significance : A statistical procedure used for deciding whether an observed difference in one or several samples is due to chance, or whether it is significant, that is, it is likely to reflect a real difference at the level of the whole population.

Treatment : A treatment is a condition whose effects are to be studied in an experiment. It is applied to an experimental group but not to the control group.

Type I error and Type II error : Refers to those errors which occur when, respectively, a true null hypothesis has been rejected and a false null hypothesis has been accepted. In hypothesis testing the error results from the rejection of a null hypothesis when it is true in reality. (type 1 error) and in hypothesis testing, the error resulting from accepting the null hypothesis when it is false in reality (type II error).

Unit : A reference value of a quantity used to express other values of the same quantity.

Validity : The extent to which a test measure what it claim to measure.

Variable : A changing quantity, usually denoted by

a letter in algebraic equation, that might have any one a range of possible value.

Variance: The variance of a distribution is denoted by σ^2 (sigma square) A number of the dispersion of a statistical sample. In a sample of n observations x_1, x_2, x_3, ... xn with a sample mean x, the sample varience is $s^2 = (xi - x)^2 + (xi - x)^2 + (x^2 - x)^2 \ldots\ldots (x_n - x)^2/n - 1$.

Weighted mean : The average of a set of numbers obtained by multiplying each numbers y a weight expressing its relative importance. The sum of the weight should add up to 1. Refers to a result produced by a technique design to give recognition to the importance of certain factors when compiling the average of a group of values. In general the weighed mean :

$$\frac{w_1x_1 + w_2x_2 + w_3x_3 + \ldots\ldots w_nx_n}{w_1 + w_2 + \ldots\ldots + w_n}$$

Index

A

Abstract, 294
Accidental Sampling, 86-87
  Advantages of-, 87
  Disadvantages of-, 87
  Usefulness of-, 87
Action research,7,13
Analysis of Data, 174
  Need of-,175
Analytical research, 14
APA Style, 321-338
Applied research, 5,9,10
Arithmetic Mean, 204-207
  Calculation of-, 207
  Limitations of-, 210-211
  Merits of-, 210

B

Bar Chart, 194, 301-302
  Features of-, 195
  Types of-, 196
Basic research, 5, 7,9-10
Bowley,s Method, 232

C

Calculation of Sample Size, 93
Canonical Analysis, 202
Case Study Method, 169
  Advantages of-, 170-171
  Limitations of-, 171-172
  Procedure of-, 172-173
  Scope of-, 170
  Sequence of-, 173
Census, 44-46
Central Tendency, 203
  Need of-, 203-204
Chi-square Test, 266-273
  Cautions in Using-, 273
  Characteristics of-, 272-273
  Meaning of-, 267-268
  Steps of-, 270-271
Characteristics of good sample, 51-52
Citation Analysis Method, 167-168
  Demerits of-, 169
  Merits of-, 168-169
  Usefulness of-, 168
Classification of Data, 179-184
  Requirement of-, 180
  Meaning of-, 179-180
  Methods of-, 180,183-184
Cluster Sampling, 77-78
  Advantages of-, 80-81

Disadvantages of-, 81
What is?-, 77
Coding, 178
Coefficient of Correlation, 236-241
Calculation of-, 238-241
Compiling Bibliography, 317-349
Computer Applications in Research, 308-316
Computerized Tabulation, 191
In Research Process, 312-316
Need of-308-311
Conceptual research, 13
Controlled Observation, 164
Correlation Analysis, 234-241

D

Data, 97
Importance of-, 98
Degree of Precision, 92
Demographic Data, 97
Descriptive Analysis, 201-202
Descriptive research, 6
Diagnostic research, 6

E

Empirical research, 13
Exploratory research, 5,13

F

Factor Analysis, 202
Footnotes, 317-319

G

Graphic Presentation, 192
Guidelines for sample selection, 52

H

Histogram, 197
Parts of-, 198
Steps of-, 199
Use of-, 198
Historical research, 14
Horizontal Bar Chart, 196
Hypothesis, 30,248
Approaches to-, 257-259
Definitions of-249-251
Formulation of-, 256
Importance of-, 255-256
Nature of-, 251
Need of-, 255
Procedure for-, 261-262
Sources of-, 252
Steps in-, 262-265
Testing of-, 30-31,256-257
Types of-, 253-254

I

Identification of Cluster Sampling, 81
Independent research, 40
Indirect Method, 167
Inferential Analysis, 202
Interpretation of Data, 274-278
Meaning of-, 274-275
Need of-, 276-277
Precaution in-, 277-278
Technique of-, 277
Interview Method, 146-157
Advantages of-, 149-150
Disadvantages of-, 150
Importance of-, 148-149
Objectives of-, 148
Problems of-, 155-156
Types of-, 151-152

J

Judgment Sampling, 90
  Advantages of-, 91
  Applications of-, 91
  Disadvantages of-, 91

K

Karl Pearson's Method, 232-233, 236-37

L

Longitudinal Survey, 56
Lottery Drum Method, 69-70

M

Mail Survey Method, 116-117
  Advantages of-, 118
  Disadvantages of-, 118
  Procedure, 116-117
Measurability, 92
Measures of Dispersion, 221-223
Median, 214-217
  Advantages of-, 216-217
  Disadvantages of-, 217
Methods of Collecting Primary Data, 102
Methods of Collecting Secondary Data, 173
MLA Style, 338-349
Mode, 217-221
  Advantages of-, 218
  Calculation of-, 218-220
  Disadvantages of-, 218
  Use of-, 220-221
Multiphase Sampling, 85
  Usage of -, 86
Multiple Classification, 181-182
Multiple Discriminant Analysis, 202
Multiple Regression Analysis, 201-202
Multistage Sampling, 79-80,83
  Advantages of-, 84-85
  Disadvantages of-, 85
  Stages of-, 83-84
  Usage of-, 84

N

Negatively Skewed Distribution, 230
Non Participant Observation, 163
Non Probability Sampling, 64-65
  merits of-, 65
Non Probability Sampling Methods, 86-93
Null Hypothesis, 259-261

O

Observation Methods, 158-167
  Advantages of-, 164
  Characteristics of-, 160
  Disadvantages of-, 165-166
  Types of-, 160-161
One Way Tabulation, 187-188
Organizational Data, 98

P

Participant Observation, 162
  Demerits of-, 163
Pearson's Coefficient of Skewness, 233-234
Periodic Survey, 55
Personnel Interview, 146-148
Pictogram, 196, 302
Pie Chart, 193,302
  Features of-, 193
  When to Use, 194

Pilot Study, 144-145
Popular Report, 282-283
Population, 44
Positively Skewed Distribution, 230
Post Stratification, 82-83
  Advantages of-, 83
  Disadvantages of-, 83
Presentation of Data, 299-303
Primary Data, 98
Primary Sources, 99
Probability Sampling, 63,66
  Characteristics of-, 64
Processing of Data, 175
  Steps in Processing, 176-178
Purposive Sampling see judgement sampling

Q

Qualities of good research, 22-23
Quantitative research, 10
Questions Sequence, 108
Questionnaire, 109
  Advantages of-, 122
  Construction of-, 112-114
  Design of-, 111
  Disadvantages of-, 123-124
  Features of-, 109
  need of-, 145
  Pretesting of-, 114, 145-146
  Procedure, 145-146
  Specimens of, 117,124-144
  Types of-, 120-121
Questionnaire Method, 105
Quota Sampling, 88-90
  Advantages of-, 89
  Application of-, 88
  Disadvantages of-, 89-90

R

Range, 221-223
  Advantages of-, 222
  Disadvantages f-, 222
Regression Analysis, 241-247
  Calculation of-, 245-247
Regression Equation, 242-245
Research, 2
  Objectives of- , 4
  Characteristics of- ,4
  Significance of-, 14-18
  Stages of-, 18-22
  Types of- 4
Research methods, 18
Research Design, 33
  Aspects of-, 37
  Features of-, 37
  meaning of-, 33-34
  need of-,36-37
  Steps in-,38-40
  Typesof-,41-42
Research methodology, 18
Research problem, 24, 31-32
  Areas of-, 26-27
  Components of-, 25
  Function of-, 280
  Steps involve in-, 28-30
  Types of-, 280-283
  What is-, 25-26
Research Report Writing, 278
  Characteristics of-, 279
  Guidelines of-, 294-295
  Parts of-, 285-289
  Precaution of-, 303-305
  Presentation of-, 299-303
  Purpose of-, 278-279
  Qualities of, 296

Significance of-, 279
Size of-, 279
Steps in-, 283-285
What is-, 278
Revolutionary researches, 10
Rules for Construction of Table, 190-191

S

Sample selection, 52-57
Sampling, 43
Advantages of-, 48-49
Disadvantages of-, 49
Meaning of-, 43-44
Need of-, 46-47
Objectives of-, 47-4
Principles of-, 50-51
Process of-, 58-63
Types of-, 63-66
Sampling Methods/techniques, 63-66
Sampling/non Sampling Errors, 94-96
Schedule Method, 106-108
Scientific Research, 2
Secondary Data, 98
Advantages of-, 100
Disadvantages of-, 101
Purpose of-, 101
Use of-, 100
Secondary Sources, 99
Features of-, 99-100
Simple Classification, 181
Simple Random Sampling, 66-67
Advantages of-, 68-69
Disadvantages of-,69
features of-, 68
Methods of-, 70-72
Procedure of-, 67-68
Single Stage Sampling, 78
Skewness, 227-234
Characteristics of-, 231
Measures of-, 231-232
Methods of-,232-234
Properties of-, 229-230
Tests of-, 231
What is? - 227-229
Sources of Data, 99
Standard Deviation, 223-227
Advantages of-, 226-227
Calculation f225-226
Disadvantages of-, 227
Steps for Calculating, 223
Stratified Random Sampling, 74-77
Advantages of-, 75-76
Disadvantages of-, 76
Need of-, 74
Process of-, 76-77
Structure Direct, 120
Structure Indirect, 120
Unstructured Direct, 120-121
Unstructured, Indirect, 121
Statistical Analysis, 200
Purpose of-, 200-201
Types of-, 201-202
Statistical Estimation, 202
Structured Direct Interview, 151
Advantages of-, 151
Disadvantages of-, 151
Structured Observation, 161
Survey Method, 104
Survey Question, 105
Systematic Sampling, 70-72
Advantages of-, 72
Disadvantages of-, 73-74

Limitations of-, 73

T

Table of Contents, 294
Tabulation of Data, 179,185-191
Meaning of-, 185
Presentation of-, 185-186
Tabular Presentation, 186,301
Components of-, 189-190
Technical Report, 281-282
Telephone Interviewing, 156-157
Disadvantages of-, 157
Uses of-, 156-157
Territorial Data, 98
Test the Survey, 105
Testing Hypothesis, 202
Textual Presentation, 186,300-301
Three Way Table, 187,189
Total Error, 95-96
Two Stage Sampling, 78-79
Two Way Table, 187-188
Type 1 and Type 2 error, 261
Types of Graphs, 301-303
Types of Statistical Average, 204
Types of Statistical Measures, 203
Types of Tabulation, 187-189
Typing the Report, 302-303

U

Uncontrolled Observation, 164
Advantages of-, 152
Limitations of-, 152
Process of-, 152-154
Unstructured Observation, 162
Use of ibid, 319
Use of Op.cit, 319
Use of loc.cit, 319

V

Vertical Bar Chart, 196
Variance, 222-223
Advantages of-, 222
Disadvantages f-, 222

W

Weighted Arithmetic Mean, 211-213

Z

Z-test